NEW GENDER MAINSTREAMING SERIES ON GENDER ISSUES

Mainstreaming Informal Employment and Gender in Poverty Reduction

A Handbook for Policy-makers and Other Stakeholders

Martha Alter Chen
Joann Vanek
Marilyn Carr

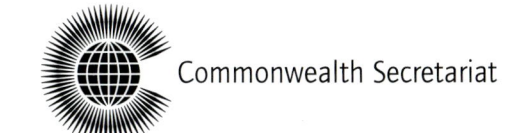

Commonwealth Secretariat

IDRC * CRDI

WIEGO

Gender Section
Social Transformation
Programmes Division
Commonwealth Secretariat
Marlborough House, Pall Mall,
London SW1Y 5HX
Tel: +44 (0)20 7747 6284
Fax: +44 (0)20 7930 1647
E-mail: gad@commonwealth.int
www.thecommonwealth.org/gender

© The Commonwealth Secretariat, 2004

The views expressed in the document are those of the authors and do not necessarily reflect the official position or policy of the Commonwealth Secretariat, the International Development Research Centre or any other agency or government identified.

Layout design: Wayzgoose
Cover design: Pen and Ink
Printed and bound by The Charlesworth Group, Wakefield, UK
Published by the Commonwealth Secretariat

Co-published by the Commonwealth Secretariat and the International Development Research Centre

Wherever possible, the Commonwealth Secretariat uses paper sourced from sustainable forests or from sources that minimise a destructive impact on the environment.

International Development Research Centre
PO Box 8500, Ottawa, ON
Canada K1G 3H9
ISBN: 1-55250-173-6
This book may be browsed online:
www.idrc.ca/pub@idrc.ca

Copies of this publication can be ordered direct from:
The Publications Manager
Communication and Public Affairs Division
Commonwealth Secretariat
Marlborough House
Pall Mall, London SW1Y 5HX
United Kingdom
Tel: +44 (0)20 7747 6342
Fax: +44 (0)20 7839 9081
E-mail:
r.jones-parry@commonwealth.int

ISBN: 0-85092-797-8

Price: £12.99

Gender Management System Series

Gender Management System Handbook
Using Gender Sensitive Indicators: A Reference Manual for Governments and Other Stakeholders
Gender Mainstreaming in Agriculture and Rural Development: A Reference Manual for Governments and Other Stakeholders
Gender Mainstreaming in Development Planning: A Reference Manual for Governments and Other Stakeholders
Gender Mainstreaming in Education: A Reference Manual for Governments and Other Stakeholders
Gender Mainstreaming in Finance: A Reference Manual for Governments and Other Stakeholders
Gender Mainstreaming in Information and Communications: A Reference Manual for Governments and Other Stakeholders
Gender Mainstreaming in Legal and Constitutional Affairs: A Reference Manual for Governments and Other Stakeholders
Gender Mainstreaming in the Public Service: A Reference Manual for Governments and Other Stakeholders
Gender Mainstreaming in Science and Technology: A Reference Manual for Governments and Other Stakeholders
Gender Mainstreaming in Trade and Industry: A Reference Manual for Governments and Other Stakeholders

A Quick Guide to the Gender Management System
A Quick Guide to Using Gender Sensitive Indicators
A Quick Guide to Gender Mainstreaming in Development Planning
A Quick Guide to Gender Mainstreaming in Education
A Quick Guide to Gender Mainstreaming in Finance
A Quick Guide to Gender Mainstreaming in the Public Service
A Quick Guide to Gender Mainstreaming in Trade and Industry
A Quick Guide to Gender Mainstreaming in Information and Communications

New Gender Mainstreaming Series on Development Issues

Gender Mainstreaming in HIV/AIDS: Taking a Multisectoral Approach
Gender Mainstreaming in the Health Sector: Experiences in Commonwealth Countries
Promoting an Integrated Approach to Combating Gender-Based Violence
Gender Mainstreaming in Poverty Eradication and the Millennium Development Goals
Gender Mainstreaming in the Multilateral Trading System
Engendering Budgets: A Practitioner's Guide to Understanding and Implementing Gender-Responsive Budgets
Integrated Approaches to Eliminating Gender-Based Violence

The GMS Toolkit: An Integrated Resource for Implementing the Gender Management System Series

About the Authors

Martha Alter Chen is a Lecturer in Public Policy at the Kennedy School of Government and Co-ordinator of the global research policy network Women in Informal Employment: Globalizing and Organizing (WIEGO). An experienced development practitioner and scholar with a doctorate in South Asian Regional Studies from the University of Pennsylvania, her areas of specialisation are gender and poverty alleviation, with a focus on issues of employment and livelihoods. Before joining Harvard University in 1987, Dr. Chen lived for 15 years in Bangladesh, where she worked with BRAC, one of the world's largest NGOs, and in India, where she served as field representative of Oxfam America for India and Bangladesh. She is the author of numerous books including, most recently, *Women and Men in the Informal Economy: A Statistical Picture* (co-authored with Joann Vanek) and *Perpetual Mourning: Widowhood in Rural India*.

Joann Vanek, a gender/social statistician, is the Director of the Statistics Programme of WIEGO. She retired from the United Nations Statistics Division after 20 years of work. At the United Nations, she developed the programme on gender statistics and co-ordinated the production of three issues of the UN global statistical report on women, *The World's Women: Trends and Statistics*. Her most recent publication, co-authored with Martha Chen, is *Women and Men in the Informal Economy: A Statistical Picture*, a book prepared for the International Labour Conference.

Marilyn Carr is a Research Associate, Institute of Development Studies, University of Sussex and Director, WIEGO Global Markets Programme. Formerly, she served as Senior Economic Adviser at the United Nations Development Fund for Women (UNIFEM), as well as a research fellow at the Radcliffe Institute of Advanced Studies; a senior research fellow at the International Development Research Centre (IDRC), Ottawa; and a visiting fellow at the International Institute for Environment and Development (IIED) in London. Prior to working with UNIFEM, she was Senior Economist with the Intermediate Technology Development Group (ITDG) in London, and worked on gender and technology throughout Africa with the Economic Commission for Africa in Addis Ababa.

Publication Team

Project Co-ordinator: Sarojini Ganju Thakur
GMS Series Co-ordinator: Rawwida Baksh
Editor: Tina Johnson
Production: Rupert Jones-Parry
Production Assistant: Marais Canali

Contents

Abbreviations	vii
Foreword	ix
Executive Summary	xiii
1. Employment: The 'Missing Link' in the Poverty Debates	1
The Globalisation–Growth–Poverty Debate	1
The growth–poverty debate	1
The globalisation–poverty debate	4
Terms of the Debate	5
What is poverty?	5
What is globalisation?	6
The 'Missing Link' in the Debate	9
Conclusion	12
2. Informal Employment, Gender and Poverty	14
The Informal Economy	14
The informal workforce	14
Discovery of the informal sector	15
Debates about the informal sector	16
Rethinking the informal economy	19
Women and Men in the Informal Economy	25
Developing countries	26
Developed countries	28
The Links Between Informal Employment, Poverty and Gender	29
Informal employment and household poverty	31
Earnings in the informal economy	33
Poor women and the informal economy	37
Gender Segmentation of the Informal Economy	39
The framework	39
Empirical findings	41
Hidden Costs of Informal Employment	45
Underemployment	45
Seasonality of work	47

Multiple activities	47
Occupational health hazards	48
The Global Horticulture Value Chain: An Illustrative Case Study	50
Employment in the horticulture sector	51
Horticulture workers and income poverty	53
Gender Segmentation of the Informal Economy and Poverty	54

3. The Changing World of Work: Linking Economic Reforms–Gender–Poverty — 58

Economic Reforms and Poverty	61
Economic reforms	61
Conceptual frameworks	64
Types of evidence and analysis	75
Trade and Employment	80
Quantity of employment	81
Terms and conditions of employment	86
Illustrative cases	93
The Changing Nature of Work	101
The place of work	101
Employment status	104
The production system	107
Conclusion	112

4. Decent Work for Informal Workers: Promising Strategies and Examples — 117

Goal 1: Promoting Opportunities	118
Promoting employment-oriented growth	118
Promoting a supportive environment	121
Increasing market access and competitiveness	127
Improving skills and technologies	136
Goal 2: Securing Rights	139
Securing rights of informal wage workers	139
Securing rights of the self-employed	150
Goal 3: Promoting Protection	152
Promoting protection against common contingencies	152
Promoting protection for migrant workers	156
Goal 4: Promoting Voice	157
Organising informal workers	157
Promoting collective bargaining	165
Building international alliances	167

Supporting Strategy – Collecting Statistics on the   170
  Informal Economy
  Conclusion   171

5. Informal Employment and Gender: A Strategic   172
  Policy Approach
  Policy Perspective   173
    Alternative policy perspectives   173
    Informed and comprehensive policy perspective   174
  Policy Goals   176
    Specific goals   176
    Overarching goals   176
  Substantive Policy Areas   177
    Macroeconomic policies   179
    Regulatory environment   186
    Labour policies   189
    Social protection policies   192
    Labour statistics   194
    Other policy areas   196
  Key Actors   198
  Policy Process   202

References   205

Appendices   223
1 ILO Convention on Home Work, 1996   223
2 Recommendations to Extend National Labour   229
   Legislation to Informal Women Workers in India
3 Draft Umbrella Legislation on Informal Sector   233
   Workers, India
4 Bellagio Declaration of Street Vendors, 1995   246

Boxes, Tables and Figures

Boxes
1 Thumbnail History of the Growth-Poverty Debate   3
2 Three Waves of Economic Globalisation   7
3 Informal Employment and Poverty   12
4 Three Dominant Schools of Thought on the Informal   17
   Sector
5 Continuum of Employment Relationships: 51
   Horticultural Sector (Chile and South Africa)

6	Key Points Raised in Gender Analysis	69
7	Integrating Informal Labour Market and Gender Analyses	74
8	Using Value Chain Analysis to Trace Profits and Benefits	79
9	India: An Example of Growth without Increased Employment	82
10	Job Loss Due to Inexpensive Imports	84
11	NAFTA'S Impact on the Female Workforce in Mexico	85
12	Joining Global Markets on Unfavourable Terms	91
13	The Precarious Position of Homeworkers	95
14	Examples of Migrants' Vulnerability to Exploitation	100
15	Who Employs the Homeworker?	106
16	Buyer-driven Value Chains: A Classic Example	110
17	Value Chains and Non-timber Forest Products	111
18	Two Support Programmes Offered by the Durban/eThekwini Municipality	128
19	Fair Trade Organisations	131
20	Effectiveness of Codes of Conduct and Ethical Trade Initiatives	143
21	Welfare Funds for *Bidi* Workers in India	145
22	Extending National, State or Provincial Legislation to Informal Workers: Further Examples	149
23	Examples of Social Protection Systems	155
24	The Self-Employed Women's Association (SEWA) of India	159
25	Domestic Workers' Unions	162
26	International Alliance of Street Trader and Hawker Organisations	168
27	Building the Network of Organisations of Informal Workers	170
28	Addressing Informality, Reducing Poverty	175
29	A Framework for Assessing Policy Biases Affecting Informal Enterprises and Informal Workers (Women and Men)	180
30	Fiscal Policies and the Informal Economy	183
31	Government Budgets and the Informal Economy	186
32	Review of National Labour Legislation in India	191

Tables

1	Old and New Views of the Informal Economy	20
2	Wage and Self-employment in Non-agricultural Informal Employment, by Sex (1994/2000)	28
3	Average Monthly Income of and Wages Paid by Micro-entrepreneurs (as multiples of legal minimum wage)	36
4	Percentage Distribution of Informal Sector Employment by Employment Status and Sex, Tunisia 1997	41
5	Daily Net Earnings from Common Informal Occupations, Ahmedabad City, India (2000) (in Indian rupees)	43
6	Monthly Mean Earnings by Employment Status in Bangladesh and Tanzania, 2001 (in US$)	45
7	Estimates of Employment in Horticulture Retailing Value Chain in Chile and South Africa and Share of Temporary and Female Employment	52
8	Levels of Mutually-reinforcing Constraints on Female Micro-enterprises	90
9	Characteristics of the Self-employed, Homeworkers and Employees	105

Figures

1	Definition and Segmentation of the Informal Economy	24
2	The Gender Segmentation of the Informal Economy	40
3	Overview of Global Value Chain for South African and Chilean Deciduous Fruit	50
4	Trade Policy and Poverty: Pathways of Impact	65

Abbreviations

ATO	alternative trading organisation
CAW	Committee for Asian Women
CCMA	Commission for Conciliation, Mediation and Arbitration, South Africa
DFID	Department for International Development, UK
EFTA	European Fair Trade Association
EPZ	export processing zone
ETI	Ethical Trading Initiative, UK
EU	European Union
FDI	foreign direct investment
FLO	Fairtrade Labelling Organisation
FNV	National Federation of Unions, the Netherlands
FUNDE	Fundación Nacional para el Desarrollo, El Salvador
GAWU	General Agricultural Workers' Union, Ghana
GDP	gross domestic product
GTUC	Ghana Trade Union Congress
ICLS	International Conference of Labour Statisticians
ICTs	information and communications technologies
IFAT	International Federation for Alternative Trade
IFWEA	International Federation of Workers' Education Associations
IIED	International Institute for Environment and Development
ILC	International Labour Conference
ILO	International Labour Organization
IMF	International Monetary Fund
MDGs	Millennium Development Goals
MSEs	micro and small enterprises
NAFTA	North American Free Trade Agreement
NALEDI	National Labour and Economic Development Institute, South Africa
NASVI	National Alliance of Street Vendors of India
NEWS	Network of World Shops
NGO	non-governmental organisation
NOTU	National Organisation of Trade Unions, Uganda
NTAE	non-traditional agricultural export
NTFP	non-timber forest product
OECD	Organisation for Economic Co-operation and Development
PRS	poverty reduction strategy

PRSP	poverty reduction strategy paper
RESPECT	Rights, Equality, Solidarity, Power, Europe Corporation Today
RLS	ratcheting labour standards
SEWA	Self Employed Women's Association, India
SEWU	Self Employed Women's Union, South Africa
SIBTTA	Sindicato Dos Trabalhadores da Industria Bordadoros, Tapecarias, Texteis e Artensanato, Madeira
SMEs	small and medium-sized enterprises
TCFUA	Textile, Clothing and Footwear Union of Australia
TNC	transnational corporation
TRIPS	trade related intellectual property rights
TUC	Trade Union Congress, Ghana
UNCTAD	United Nations Conference on Trade and Development
UNDAW	United Nations Division for the Advancement of Women
UNDP	United Nations Development Programme
UNICEF	United Nations Children's Fund
UNIFEM	United Nations Development Fund for Women
UPEU	Uganda Public Employees Union
WIEGO	Women in the Informal Economy: Globalizing and Organizing
WTO	World Trade Organization

Foreword

The primary purpose of *Mainstreaming Informal Employment and Gender in Poverty Reduction: a Handbook for Policy-makers and Other Stakeholders* is to integrate a concern for employment, specifically the gendered dimension of informal employment, into poverty reduction strategies, including the Millennium Development Goals (MDGs) and the Poverty Reduction Strategy Papers (PRSPs) of specific countries. The Handbook is also intended to familiarise busy policy-makers and other stakeholders with the historical debate on the informal economy and with competing theoretical perspectives on the relationship of globalisation, growth and poverty.

The authors argue that hopes for poverty reduction largely hinge on the creation of more employment opportunities, particularly those accompanied by rights, protection and voice. Yet most governments – and the global community – have not adequately recognised this. Employment creation is not one of the eight Millennium Development Goals, and employment is neither a target nor an indicator under the first major goal of eradicating extreme poverty and hunger. However, this major goal cannot be achieved without promoting decent work opportunities for the poor, especially women. The authors illustrate why – and how – addressing the specific constraints and opportunities facing the working poor, especially women, in the informal economy is the central key strategy to poverty reduction. In brief, this is because the working poor are concentrated in the informal economy, earnings and benefits are lower on average in the informal economy than in the formal economy and there is a marked gender gap in earnings and benefits within the informal economy.

As far as possible, the Handbook draws on data and examples from Commonwealth countries. These are supplemented by data and examples from other countries. We hope that additional Commonwealth countries will be encouraged to collect data on the informal economy and to formulate appropriate policy responses to it.

The publication of this book has been made possible due to the contributions of many individuals and groups. We would like to thank the International Development Research Centre (IDRC), and Randy Spence, in particular, for their support for this initiative.

We would like to acknowledge the hard work and valuable expertise of the authors of the Handbook, Martha Alter Chen, Joann Vanek and Marilyn Carr, and the numerous individuals and organisations who have been willing to share information and experience with them. This includes the global research policy network Women in Informal Employment: Globalizing and Organizing (WIEGO), to which the authors belong and whose collective knowledge and experience has contributed to this Handbook. We would like to thank Jacques Charmes for the personal compilations of official national statistics included in Chapter 2, and Chris Bonner, Dan Gallin, Nancy Hafkin, Lou Haysom, Pat Horn, Renana Jhabvala, Rakawin Lee, Frances Lund, Caroline Skinner, Shalini Sinha and Daonoi Srikajon for providing some of the best practice examples included in Chapter 4. In addition, the authors would like to acknowledge Ralf Hussmanns, Lin Lim and Anne Trebilcock of the International Labour Organization (ILO) for their efforts to promote a concern for 'decent work and the informal economy' both within and outside the ILO and for their encouragement to the authors on this and earlier publications.

Our special thanks are due to Tina Johnson, who edited the book, and to Sarojini Ganju Thakur who co-ordinated the project. In addition we would like to acknowledge the contributions of Rawwida Baksh and Rupert Jones-Parry of the Commonwealth Secretariat and Marais Canali and Suzanne Van Hook of the WIEGO Secretariat in the production of the book. Finally, a special debt is also owed to outside readers who took time out of their busy schedules to provide critical feedback on early drafts of the Handbook: Debbie Budlender, Sarah Gammage, Caren Grown, James Heintz, Ralf Hussmanns, Renana Jhabvala and Frances Lund.

This Handbook is part of the Commonwealth Secretariat series on gender mainstreaming in critical development issues. It forms part of the continuing focus of the series on exploring the path to achieving the universally accepted goals of gender equality and poverty reduction, and complements other publications in the same series – *Gender Mainstreaming in Poverty*

Eradication and the Millennium Development Goals and *Gender Mainstreaming in the Multilateral Trading System*.

We hope that this book will enhance our understanding of the critical linkages between gender equality, informal employment and poverty reduction, and contribute to our efforts to eradicate poverty in the world.

Nancy Spence
Director
Social Transformation Programmes Division
Commonwealth Secretariat
July 2004

Executive Summary

The lack of sufficient economic opportunities for the working age population is a major contemporary problem. The International Labour Organization estimates that there are 550 million working poor and that these numbers may double before 2015 (the target year in the Millennium Development Declaration for halving extreme poverty) (ILO, 2004a). The United Nations estimates that over 80 per cent of the population in the least developed countries live on less than $2 per day and that about half of the people living in poverty are of working age (UNCTAD, 2000).

Employment – or, more precisely, decent work – is an essential pathway to poverty reduction. The ILO defines 'decent work' as employment opportunities accompanied by rights, protection and voice (ILO, 2002a).[1] Yet employment does not receive sufficient attention in poverty reduction strategies or even in the global debates on the links between globalisation, growth and poverty. Little consideration is given to the poverty outcomes of different types of work or, conversely, to how improvements in employment opportunities might lead to poverty reduction. In the process, two key global facts tend to be overlooked: (1) that the vast majority of the poor work; and (2) that the vast majority of the working poor, especially women, are engaged in the informal economy. As a result, the economic contributions of the working poor as a force for poverty reduction, as well as the impact of gender inequalities within the realm of work, are also overlooked.

This Handbook focuses on the links between being informally employed, being a woman or a man and being poor, and on the changing nature of informal employment. Based on a review of available evidence, it presents a strategic framework for how best to promote decent work for the poor and, in so doing, to reduce poverty. It also includes practical examples of ways of assisting working poor women and men to minimise the constraints and maximise the opportunities arising from trade liberalisation and growth.

Although the concept of the informal sector or informal economy has been debated since its 'discovery' in Africa in the early 1970s, it has continued to be used by many policy-makers, labour advocates and researchers because the reality it seeks to capture – the large share of the global workforce that is not covered by labour legislation or social protection – continues to be important and has been expanding over time. At present, there is renewed interest in the informal economy. This stems from the fact that informal work arrangements have not only persisted and expanded but have also emerged in new guises and in unexpected places, leaving the majority of the global workforce outside the world of full-time, stable and protected employment. Most observers now accept that informal employment is a feature of modern capitalist development, not just a residual feature of traditional economies.

Chapter 1 traces the history of the debates within the international development community on the relationship between globalisation, growth and poverty, focusing on recent shifts in the terms of the debate. It highlights the relative lack of focus on employment in these debates and makes the case that a focus on work and the working poor is a 'missing link' in the debates.

Over the past two decades, belief in the 'trickle-down' benefits of market-led growth has been tempered by a growing recognition of the systemic disadvantages of the poor and the need for broad-based labour-intensive patterns of economic growth as well as a complementary set of policies to manage growth and redistribute national income. Despite this shift in thinking, orthodox policy prescriptions continue to favour free markets over state interventions. This makes it difficult for developing countries to do what is needed to ensure that growth is equitable and reduces poverty. Moreover, although the quantity of employment generated by growth has received some attention, the quality of the work generated tends to be overlooked. Yet poverty is related more to the *nature* of employment than to the *absolute rate* of employment. In countries where there is no unemployment compensation and few safety nets, the poor have little choice but to work – no matter how low or irregular their earnings.

While the vast majority of the poor work, few are able to work their way out of poverty. This is because poor people working in the informal economy face lower incomes, greater financial risks, lower standards of human development and greater social exclusion compared to better-off workers, especially those who work in the formal economy. Yet these disadvantages of the working poor have not been adequately addressed in poverty reduction strategies. This Handbook makes the case for a coherent focus on employment – and related market relationships – to bridge the persistent divide between growth and redistribution, to refocus attention on discrimination in markets and, thereby, to design strategies that will more effectively reduce poverty.

Chapter 2 provides the rationale for paying greater attention to the informal economy, and particularly to women workers within it. This is done by providing the most recent available data on the size and composition of the informal economy and on the links between working in the informal economy, being a woman or man and being poor. These data reveal the following key facts:

Size

- Informal employment comprises one half to three quarters of non-agricultural employment in developing countries.

- Self-employment, part-time and temporary work comprise 30 per cent of overall employment in 15 European countries and 25 per cent of total employment in the United States. Although not all self-employed persons or part-time and temporary workers are informally employed, the majority receive few (if any) employment-based benefits or protection.

- Estimates of informal employment increase significantly when agriculture is included – rising, for example, from 83 to 93 per cent of total employment in India and 55 to 62 per cent in Mexico.

Composition

- Self-employment represents nearly one-third of all non-agricultural employment worldwide and comprises a greater share of informal employment (outside agriculture) than wage employment in all developing regions.

- Informal wage employment represents 30 to 40 per cent of informal employment (outside of agriculture) in developing regions.

- Informal employment is generally a larger source of employment for women than for men in the developing world.

- Women are particularly over-represented in low-paid informal or non-standard wage employment. Although fewer women than men are in the labour force, women represent 80 per cent or more of industrial outworkers/homeworkers in many developing countries and 60 per cent or more of part-time workers in all Organisation for Economic Co-operation and Development (OECD) countries reporting data.

To better capture this growing and changing phenomenon, an expanded definition of the informal economy has recently been introduced that includes both *self-employment in informal enterprises* (small unregistered enterprises) and *wage employment in informal jobs* (without secure contracts, worker benefits or social protection). Despite its diversity, the informal economy can thus be classified by *employment status* into two major groups (although some informal workers[2] – notably homeworkers – do not fit neatly into one or other of these categories):

- ***self-employed:*** including employers, own-account workers and unpaid family workers;

- ***informal wage workers:*** including employees of informal enterprises; casual workers without a fixed employer; domestic workers; and those temporary, part-time and contract workers who do not receive employment-based benefits or protection.

Chapter 2 also provides a conceptual framework – what it calls the gender segmentation of the informal economy – for analysing the linkages between working in the informal economy, being a woman or a man and being poor. There is an *overlap* between working in the informal economy and being poor. The poor are more likely than the non-poor to rely on the informal economy for their livelihoods; average wages or earnings are lower in the informal economy than in the formal economy; and a higher percentage of people working in the informal economy, relative to the formal economy, are poor. However, there is no simple relationship between working in the informal economy and being poor or working in the formal economy and escaping poverty. The relationship with informal employment appears only when informal workers are classified by employment status (i.e. employer, own account worker, wage worker or industrial outworker/homeworker). As a general rule, average earnings or wages decrease as one moves down the employment status ladder: from being a micro-entrepreneur who hires others to working on one's own account to working as a wage worker to being an industrial outworker. However, in some sectors or countries, informal wage workers earn more on average than own account workers.

There is a *significant overlap* between being a woman, working in the informal economy and being poor. Available evidence suggests that, in most regions, women are more likely than men to work in the informal economy; women in poor households are more likely to work in the informal economy than men in poor households or women in non-poor households; and the average wages or earnings of women in the informal economy are lower than those of men in the informal economy. But, again, there is no simple relationship between being a woman, working in the informal economy and being poor. It depends on what women do and under what conditions. One of the important reasons why women in the informal economy are likely to be poorer than men is because they are less likely to be micro-entrepreneurs who hire others (who often enjoy relatively high earnings) and more likely to be homeworkers (who typically earn extremely low piece rates). Also, even within specific categories of informal employment, women are likely to earn less than men. Chapter 2 illustrates the gender segmentation of the informal economy with a case study of employment in the export-oriented horticulture sector in Chile and South Africa.

The impact that changes in the global economy are having on the informal economy and on women and men within it is detailed in Chapter 3, which is divided into three major sections. The first section compares three different approaches – that of neo-classical economics, gender analysis and informal labour market analysis – to tracing the impact of economic trends on poverty and gender relations, identifying particular processes that have specific consequences for the informal workforce, both women and men.

The second section provides a review of available evidence – primarily case studies – on the likely impact of economic reforms on employment, including whether they create or destroy economic opportunities and the quality of opportunities created. There are three common ways through which the working poor, especially women, are inserted into the global workforce:

1. Creation of new jobs – but without rights and benefits;

2. Opening up of new markets – but with unequal access and competitiveness;

3. Increased risk and uncertainty – but without adequate protection.

Each of these indicates that, while new economic opportunities are being created, the terms and conditions of employment generated often mean the working poor may not be able to take advantage of them or may not benefit fully from their involvement. The first two scenarios relate to the *nature* and the *quality of economic opportunities* associated with economic reforms. The third relates to *generalised effects* commonly associated with economic reforms, seen from the perspective of the working poor in the informal economy.

What is also clear is that the world of work itself is changing because of these economic processes. The third section of Chapter 3 details three key dimensions of the changing nature of work in today's world – place of work, employment status and production system – and the consequences of these for the working poor, especially women.

The majority of the global workforce now works in so-called 'non-standard' places of work, employment relationships and production systems. Some of these arrangements may have benefits for the workers involved, such as more flexible work hours, but they may also be associated with specific costs and risks, such as lack of benefits or long-term security. Effective poverty reduction requires maximising the benefits and minimising the costs associated with the employment opportunities available to the poor. As such, it needs to be based on an understanding of the costs and benefits associated with different work arrangements.

Building on this analysis, Chapter 4 presents a set of strategies and promising examples that respond to the opportunities and risks associated with trade liberalisation and the changing nature of work. These do not aim to be comprehensive, but rather to further our understanding of the ways in which different key actors – international agencies, governments, private corporations, trade unions and organisations of informal workers, non-governmental organisations (NGOs) and civil society – can assist the working poor in the informal economy to minimise the negative effects and maximise the opportunities associated with macroeconomic trends and policies. The four pillars of the ILO's Decent Work agenda – opportunities, rights, protection and voice – are used to organise the strategies and examples in a meaningful way.

It is important to note that most of these initiatives require advocacy and/or monitoring by civil society – notably by organisations of informal workers – to ensure that they are properly designed and implemented. In sum, these examples suggest a *key pathway to poverty reduction and gender equity*: namely, by supporting informal enterprises, improving informal jobs, providing protection to informal workers and recognising organisations of informal workers.

Finally, Chapter 5 outlines a strategic policy approach to the gender segmentation of the informal economy that is informed by an understanding of the economic contributions of the informal economy and premised on the notion that (a) *all* policies – both economic and social – affect the informal economy; and (b) policies have differential effects on the formal and informal economy and on women and men within the informal economy. The strategic policy approach calls for informed and comprehensive policies as well as the concerted action of different key players. Most critically, it underscores the need to build, strengthen and recognise the organisations of informal workers – and to promote their representative 'voice' in institutions that determine policies and other 'rules of the (economic) game' that affect their work lives.

The overarching policy goals of such a policy approach should be to:

- ***promote opportunities*:** for both self-employed and informal wage workers through a mix of service provision (microfinance, skills training, improved technologies and other business development services) as well as policy interventions;

- **secure rights:** of informal wage workers through extending the scope of existing legislation, promoting collective bargaining agreements and/or enforcing labour standards; and of the self-employed through enabling equal access to credit and other resources and through equitable policies for formal and informal enterprises;

- **protect informal workers:** through providing insurance coverage for illness, maternity, property, disability, old age and death through extending existing schemes and/or developing alternative schemes; and

- ***build and recognise the 'voice' of informal workers:*** through the organisation of informal workers and their representation in relevant policy-making institutions.

Each of these goals needs to be translated into context-specific goals depending on which category of the informal workforce is being targeted, under what conditions and in which economic sector. They also need to take into account the different needs and circumstances of women and men within each category.

The policy process should be:

- based on an informed understanding of the *economic* importance of informal workers. This requires improved official statistics on the size, composition and contribution of the informal economy;

- aimed at *mainstreaming* the concerns of the informal workforce in those institutions that deal with economic planning and development;

- *gender sensitive*, taking into account the roles and responsibilities of women and men in the informal economy. Compared to men workers, women workers tend to earn less and to be less likely to have social protection or be organised. As a result, they have the greatest need for supportive policies;

- *context-specific*, based on the reality of different categories of informal workers in specific locales and industries and recognising and supporting both the self-employed and paid workers in the informal economy; and

- *participatory and inclusive*, allowing policies to be developed through consultation with informal workers. In order to have voice, those who work in the informal economy must be organised and their efforts to organise into trade unions and co-operatives must be encouraged and supported.

Key messages

A key message of this Handbook is that the renewed interest in the informal economy needs to be translated into a greater emphasis on employment in poverty reduction strategies and in economic planning. More specifically, poverty reduction strategies need to be premised on the following two related facts: (1) decent employment is an essential pathway to poverty reduction; and (2) informal employment is less likely than formal employment to be decent work. As the Director General of the ILO argued in his 2002 report on 'Decent Work and the Informal Economy', those in informal employment suffer greater decent work deficits than those in formal employment (ILO, 2002a).

Since the early1990s, the international community has increasingly reoriented its development approach to focus on poverty reduction. Reflecting this concern, the Bretton Woods institutions agreed in 1999 that national poverty reduction strategy papers, developed through participatory processes, should provide the basis for concessional lending by the World Bank and International Monetary Fund (IMF) and for debt relief to the heavily-indebted poor countries.[3] In 2000, at the Millennium Summit, the member countries of the United Nations agreed to attack severe poverty worldwide and halve the proportion of the global population that survives on less than $1 a day by the year 2015. Following the Summit, the various UN agencies collectively identified eight Millennium Development Goals and a set of 18 targets (and some 40 relevant indicators) to measure their progress.

These two initiatives – PRSPs and MDGs – are meant to reinforce each other. However, neither pays sufficient attention to employment as a key pathway to poverty reduction. For example, employment creation is not one of the eight MDGs, and employment is neither a target nor an indicator under the first major goal of eradicating extreme poverty and hunger. Yet this major goal cannot be achieved without promoting decent work opportunities for the poor, especially women. Admittedly, youth employment is a priority target under Goal 8 (Develop a Global Partnership for Development) and women's share of non-agricultural wage employment is one of the main indicators specified under Goal 3 (Promote Gender Equality and Empower Women). But the gender employment indicator, as currently formulated, is not an adequate indicator of women's equality and empowerment. As the evidence provided in this Handbook will illustrate, an increase in women's wage employment (both non-agricultural and agricultural) is likely to be associated with an increase in flexible or informal employment arrangements: that is, in employment without rights, protection or voice. This criticism was also made by the Millennium Project Task Force on Education and Gender Equality. This group has recommended that an indicator on informal employment either be substituted for the indicator on wage employment or be added (United Nations Millennium Project, 2004). Efforts are now being made to develop the appropriate indicator.

There is a clear need to better integrate the ILO's Decent Work agenda – with a special focus on the informal workforce and women – into current poverty reduction initiatives. However, within the international development discourse, there is a dominant school of thought that argues that the demand for labour should be left to the market and that social protection is affordable only for the formally employed. For those holding this view, labour and employment issues are not relevant to poverty reduction strategies. Overcoming such misconceptions will require continued research and advocacy (ILO, 2002c).[4] This Handbook seeks to help in this effort by focusing on the linkages between informal employment, gender and poverty.

In sum, renewed attention needs to be paid to employment in economic planning, including in the PRSPs for heavily-indebted countries and the MDGs for the world at large. More specifically, poverty reduction strategies need to address the 'decent work deficits' in the informal economy as well as gender differentials within it. This Handbook makes the case for a focus on informal employment – especially women informal workers – in poverty reduction strategies, and then suggests ways in which the opportunities, rights, protection and voice of the informal workforce, especially women, can be enhanced.

The unique perspective of the Handbook is that it seeks to:

- put employment, specifically the gender segmentation of employment in the informal economy, at the centre – to provide a 'missing link' – of development discourse, policies and practices regarding poverty reduction;
- investigate how different groups of the working poor in the informal economy – especially women – are integrated into the economies of their own countries and into the global economy;
- investigate the quantity and quality of work – for women and men – created by different patterns of economic growth and global integration; and
- identify appropriate policies, regulations and practices to manage and govern the employment arrangements of the working poor in the informal economy.

Notes

1 Under the directorship of Juan Somavia, the ILO formulated and adopted the four pillars of Decent Work as its strategic agenda: (a) employment opportunities; (b) respect for fundamental principles and rights at work; (c) social protection; and (d) social dialogue (ILO, 2001). We refer to these in the Handbook as opportunities, rights, protection and voice.
2 The term 'informal workers' is used in this Handbook in a broad, inclusive sense to include wage workers, small producers, service providers and traders.
3 Earlier that year, in June, at a meeting of the G8 in Cologne, Germany, the political leaders of democratic industrialised counties announced a joint initiative for debt relief and poverty reduction for heavily indebted poor countries (HIPC2). The origins of HIPC2 and the PRSP initiative lie substantially with civil society movements that forced the issue of debt reduction onto the international agenda in the late 1990s, culminating in Jubilee 2000.
4 In working closely with national partners in several countries on the development of their PRSPs, the ILO has recommended that employment-intensive growth be made an explicit objective (ILO, 2002c).

1. Employment: The 'Missing Link' in the Poverty Debate

Within the international development community, there has been a long-standing – and often heated – debate about the links between economic growth and poverty. During the 1990s, especially after the East Asian and other financial crises, the focus of this debate shifted to globalisation. Does – or can – globalisation work for the world's poor? This is the central question around which the debate now revolves (Rodrik, 1997). However, to fully understand the debate, it is important to draw a distinction between the globalisation of different markets (capital, goods, services and labour); between globalisation, growth and related policy prescriptions; and between income poverty and other dimensions of poverty. In Chapter 1 we provide a brief history of the globalisation-growth-poverty debate, highlighting these distinctions, and argue that employment – specifically the gender dimensions of informal employment – remains a 'missing link' in the debate.

Employment – specifically the gender dimensions of informal employment – remains a 'missing link' in the [globalisation-growth-poverty] debate.

The Globalisation-Growth-Poverty Debate

The growth-poverty debate

In North America and Europe, the two decades after World War II have been characterised as the 'golden age' of full employment. During the 1950s and 1960s, governments in most developed countries sought not only to provide social welfare to their citizens but also to lead industrial development, expand aggregate demand and create jobs. Because of the successful experience in North America and Europe, there was widespread belief among international development specialists in the 'trickle-down benefits' of growth, including the assumption that industrial development would create enough jobs to absorb surplus labour in developing countries (Lewis, 1954).

However, things began to change in the 1970s. In the developed North, production became more flexible and specialised, and belief in both the welfare-providing and economic-regulating functions of governments began to erode. In the developing South, there was growing recognition that economic growth does not automatically translate into jobs or other benefits for the poor. In response to persistent widespread unemployment, the International Labour Organization (ILO) mounted a series of large, multi-disciplinary 'employment missions' to various developing countries (ILO, 1972). By the mid-1970s, in response to persistent widespread poverty, an influential team of observers (within the World Bank) called for a complementary set of policies to manage growth and redistribute national income (Chenery et al, 1974).

Despite the fact that 'trickle down' economics had been discredited, orthodox policy prescriptions continued to favour free markets. By 1980, in North America and much of Europe, a different economic system was in place: one that emphasised the supremacy of market forces, questioned the welfare-providing function of the state and eschewed government regulation of labour, product or capital markets (Singh, 1998). To conform to this new economic system, developing countries were encouraged to restructure their economies by curbing inflation, stabilising their currency, privatising their public industries and deregulating markets. However, when the short-term costs of adjustment were recognised, another influential team of observers (this time from the United Nations) called for 'adjustment with a human face' (Cornea et al, 1987).

During the 1990s, despite the recognition of the costs of economic adjustment, the shift in favour of free markets over state interventions only intensified. In regard to employment, those who prescribe free market policies believe that demand for labour should be left to the market and that social protection is only affordable – through some mix of employer and individual contributions – for those who are formally employed. For free market advocates, labour or employment standards are not relevant to poverty reduction (ILO, 2002c).

Since 1990, however, there has been renewed concern about poverty in the international development community. More emphasis has been placed on job-led growth and rural livelihoods (World Bank, 1990) and a new focus on human development has been introduced (UNDP, 1990). Underlying the call for job-led or labour-intensive growth was the recognition that growth *per se* was not producing enough jobs to absorb people of working age. And underlying the call for human development was the recognition that economic growth at the national level (measured in terms of GDP per capita) does not necessarily translate into human development at the individual level (measured in terms of education, health and longevity). More recently, the Millennium Development Goals and the Poverty Reduction Strategy (PRS) initiative reflect the renewed commitment of the international community to poverty reduction.

In brief, over the past three decades, belief in 'trickle-down' economics has been tempered by a growing recognition of: (a) the systemic disadvantages of the poor; and (b) the need to supplement growth with a broader set of economic policies to manage it and social policies to redistribute it (see Box 1). Yet, over the same period, there has been a broader transformation in the economic policy environment, away from state interventions to free-market policies.

The Millennium Development Goals and the Poverty Reduction Strategy initiative reflect the renewed commitment of the international community to poverty reduction.

Box 1 Thumbnail History of the Growth–Poverty Debate

1950–60s: Growth through import-substituting industrialisation (Lewis, 1954).

1970s: Growth through import-substituting industrialisation, agricultural production, micro-enterprise development and redistribution (ILO, 1972; Chenery et al, 1974).

1980s: Export-oriented growth through structural adjustment with a human face (Cornea et al, 1987).

1990s: Labour-intensive growth with human development and security (World Bank, 1990; UNDP, 1990).

2000: Broad-based economic growth with opportunities, rights, protection and a voice for the poor (World Bank, 2000; ILO, 2002a; ILO, 2003; United Nations Millennium Development Declaration, 2000).

The globalisation–poverty debate

The best-known protagonists in the current globalisation debate are the pro-globalisation policy-makers and the anti-globalisation protestors. Those who are pro-globalisation tend to subscribe to three related assumptions: (1) that liberalisation, privatisation and stabilisation policies lead to economic growth; (2) that opening up an economy to trade and foreign direct investment (FDI) leads to economic growth; and (3) that economic growth leads to poverty reduction. Those who are anti-globalisation tend to take the opposite stance on each of these assumptions. They argue that economic growth and global integration tend to erode the incomes or livelihoods of the poor, while at the same time increasing the costs of public goods and services and thus increasing rather than reducing poverty.

Why do these two groups disagree so fundamentally? Much of the disagreement is a result of different approaches to assessing poverty, economic policies and the links between the two (Kanbur, 2001).

Those who are pro-globalisation tend to look at the incidence of poverty at the national or global level, to consider the medium- and long-term impact of economic policies and to subscribe to the standard economic model of perfectly competitive market structures.

Those who are anti-globalisation tend to look at the poverty levels of specific groups of people at the local level, to consider the short-term consequences (on the poor) and the long-term consequences (on the environment) of economic policies and to see markets as riddled with market power exercised by big corporations over small enterprises and by employers over employees.[1]

These rather stylised positions represent, of course, two extremes of a spectrum of perspectives. In real life, the debate tends to be less polarised and more nuanced. Many of the so-called critics of globalisation are not anti-globalisation *per se* but against the associated 'rules of the game' prescribed by powerful players – the International Monetary Fund (IMF) and the World Trade Organization (WTO) – including the lack of accountability of these institutions and the undermining of labour and environmental standards.[2] Many people feel that globalisation "has developed in an ethical vacuum based on a 'winner-take-all' mentality ... [and] conceived for the strong – leaving the rest at a serious disadvantage" (Somavia, 2004). There is also a middle group of observers who seek to help the poor address the costs and seize the opportunities associated with macroeconomic trends and policies.

Tobacco pickers, India
MARTHA CHEN

Terms of the Debate

What is poverty?

As part of the broader debate on globalisation–growth–poverty, there has been a related debate on how to conceptualise and measure poverty. Some parties to this debate focus on the various dimensions of poverty that are not captured in the standard measures of what is now called 'income poverty', while others focus on how to improve the standard income-expenditure measures of income poverty. Today, there are several broad approaches to conceptualising and measuring poverty, including:

- ***income and basic needs:*** that focuses on the income, expenditures and basic needs of the poor;
- ***human development:*** that focuses on the health, education, longevity and other human capabilities of the poor; and

The Decent Work agenda of the ILO offers a critical missing dimension to the debate on poverty: one that unites the international drive to eradicate poverty with the fundamental right to work in freedom.

- *social inclusion:* that focuses on the political participation, social dialogue and 'voice' of the poor.

From the perspective of the poor, each of these dimensions of poverty is of critical importance. But none of these focuses on employment *per se*; even the income poverty school pays surprisingly little attention to the *sources* of income. However, the work arrangements of the poor represent a key pathway to their well-being, capabilities, dignity and freedom.

The Decent Work agenda of the ILO offers a critical missing dimension to the debate on poverty: one that unites the international drive to eradicate poverty with the fundamental right to work in freedom. Each of the four pillars of the agenda offers tools to help reduce poverty, as follows:

- **Opportunities:** promotion of investments and policy support to job creation, entrepreneurship and sustainable livelihoods, and the requisite skills development.

- **Rights:** promotion of legal recognition and mobilisation of effective demand to secure the right to work and associated rights at work.

- **Protection:** extension of existing social security measures to cover the informal workforce and development of alternative measures to insure them against illness, disability, loss of employment opportunities and old age.

- **Voice:** promotion of the representation and effective participation of the working poor in collective bargaining, conflict resolution and rule-setting bodies.

What is globalisation?

In the broadest sense, globalisation refers to the international flows of ideas and culture, or people, as well as goods, services and capital – to global integration in the social, political and economic spheres. As used in this Handbook, globalisation refers to economic globalisation: to international flows of capital, goods, services and labour. The current wave of globalisation, dating back to 1980, represents the third major wave of globalisation over the past 150 years (see Box 2).

Box 2 Three Waves of Economic Globalisation

Economic globalisation occurs through some mix of trade, migration and capital flows. Over the past 150 years, there have been three waves of globalisation. Each of these waves has had distinctive features, as follows:

First wave of globalisation: 1870–1914

Triggered by falling transport costs (resulting from the switch from sail to steamships) and reductions in tariff barriers (pioneered by an Anglo-French agreement), the resulting patterns of trade mainly involved the exchange of primary commodities (from Argentina, Australia, New Zealand and the United States as well as some developing countries) for manufactured goods (from Europe and North America). But migration – from Europe to the Americas and within Asia – was probably more important than either trade or capital flows (Lindert and Williamson, 2001b). Nearly 10 per cent of the world's population is estimated to have migrated during the first wave of globalisation.

Second wave of globalisation: 1945–1980

After a period of nationalism, during which substantial trade barriers were erected, governments in the North began to co-operate to reduce these barriers, particularly to the trade of manufactured goods. But the barriers facing developing countries were not reduced, except for those primary commodities that did not compete with agriculture in the developed countries. In response, most developing countries erected barriers against developed countries and each other. The resultant globalisation was very lopsided: developing countries still faced severe barriers to trade in manufactured goods and agriculture; and the international movements of capital and labour were not restored.

Third wave of globalisation: 1980-present

The current wave of globalisation, which began about 1980, is distinctive from the others. First, and most spectacularly, a large group of developing countries have

> **Box 2** (continued)
>
> broken into global markets, not only for primary commodities but also for manufactured goods and services. At the same time, however, other developing countries have become increasingly marginalised. Second, the movements of capital and labour, which were negligible during the second wave of globalisation, have again become substantial. However, unlike during the first wave when migration was actively encouraged, international migrants face considerable legal barriers to migration.
>
> Source: World Bank, 2000

As noted earlier, popular discourse on globalisation tends to blur the distinction between economic restructuring and economic integration, and between trade liberalisation and other dimensions of economic integration. It is important to distinguish between:

- *economic restructuring*, including *privatisation* of public enterprises and the public sector, *deregulation* of different markets (for goods, services, capital and labour) and *stabilisation of currency*; and

- *economic integration*, including liberalisation of *capital* markets, of *markets for goods and services* (i.e. 'trade liberalisation') and of *labour markets*.

To illustrate, it was liberalisation of short-term capital accounts that triggered the Asian and other financial crises, not trade liberalisation or economic integration writ large (Bhagwati, 2004). It is also important to distinguish between trade liberalisation, growth and the policy prescriptions associated with them. It is now widely recognised that developing countries that complied with the orthodox policy prescriptions in opening up their economy have fared less well than developing countries that pursued their own domestic development strategy while opening up their economy (notably, China and India) (Rodrik, 1997; Stiglitz, 2003b).

In this Handbook, we try to draw these distinctions wherever relevant. But in real life it is hard to know which economic process is driving what; and in analysing data it is difficult to isolate the impact of a single economic reform or a single type of economic integration. This is because none of these economic processes operates in isolation.

The 'Missing Link' in the Debate

Although the quantity of employment generated by growth has received some attention, in terms largely of aggregate employment rates, the quality of the work generated tends to be overlooked. Yet poverty is related as much to the *nature* of employment as to the *absolute level* of employment. In developing countries where there is no unemployment compensation and few safety nets, the rate of poverty is far higher than the rate of unemployment. Most of the poor continue to work, no matter how low or irregular their earnings. A major gap in the debate on globalisation-growth-poverty is the absence of any systematic analysis of the role of employment in the working of these linkages. To illustrate this point, consider the perspectives of the different parties to the debate.

Most pro-globalisation proponents subscribe to standard neo-classical assumptions regarding labour and development:

- that labour is just another factor (like capital, land or any other good);
- that labour markets behave just like other markets; and
- that inflexible labour markets – specifically, wage rigidity – have adverse effects.

Based on these assumptions, their ready prescription for developing countries with chronic unemployment or underemployment is to abolish minimum wages, lower wages, eliminate job protection and privatise social security. Further, they tend to emphasise greater efficiency in economic policy and to overlook the risks, vulnerabilities and volatility associated with economic reforms and globalisation. More fundamentally still, they tend to de-link issues of efficiency and distribution, putting the primary focus of economic policies (including labour market legislation) on efficiency and handling issues of distribution through general legislation aimed at redistribution.

> *Poverty is related as much to the* nature *of employment as to the* absolute level *of employment. ... Most of the poor continue to work, no matter how low or irregular their earnings.*

> *The quantity and quality of work generated are, we contend, the key determinants of the poverty and equity outcomes of different patterns of economic growth or global integration.*

Clearly, some anti-globalisation critics have voiced concerns about labour standards. But their concern has focused largely on formal workers or workers in export processing zones (EPZs) and on international labour standards in the context of global trade agreements, to the relative neglect of informal workers, domestic labour legislation and country-specific economic reforms.

Various groups within the international development community have expanded the scope of their work to encompass a concern for work and livelihoods:

- **Human rights community:** has begun to specify what is meant by economic rights and how to claim or enforce workers' rights.

- **Women's movement:** has promoted the notion that women's unpaid housework and care activities should be seen as part of the economy and has investigated the implications for women of being integrated into labour markets (see Chapter 3 for more on gender analysis).

- **Environmental movement:** includes a focus on rural livelihoods with a natural resource base and on increasing and securing assets as well as intellectual property rights.

- **Micro-finance movement** and related **micro-enterprise development** initiatives: have provided financial and business development services to micro-enterprises.

- **Fair Trade movement:** has focused attention on fair labour standards for wage workers and fair competition for small-scale producers.

However, outside the international labour movement, which historically has focused on the formal workforce, none of the groups within the international development community has adopted a primary focus on employment issues.[3]

The quantity and quality of work generated are, we contend, the key determinants of the poverty and equity outcomes of different patterns of economic growth or global integration. This relative neglect of employment issues represents, therefore, a 'missing link' in poverty reduction strategies. In the context of trade liberalisation, this neglect seems particularly hard to explain. Under pressure from the rich countries, the barriers to international trade in goods, financial services and investment flows have been lowered to the advantage of capital over labour and of large firms over small or micro firms and, in most instances, to the disadvantage of wage workers and own account producers in the informal economy. Arguably, the need to provide this 'missing link' in development discourse and practice – to introduce an explicit focus on the working poor in the informal economy – has never been more acute than in the present context of rapid global integration.

Underlying the lack of a systematic focus on employment in development circles is another quite fundamental debate: on the relative roles of markets and the state:

- The *free-market school* focuses on growing the economy through a judicious mix of market forces and economic policies, placing greater emphasis on efficiency and deflation than on employment.

- The *government-mediated school* focuses on redistributing national income through social policies, placing greater emphasis on social indicators than on economic opportunities.

Neither school pays sufficient attention to discrimination in the market place or to how this contributes to poverty. Under the free-market – or neo-liberal – school of thought, the dominant concern of macroeconomic policies has shifted from an earlier commitment to expanding aggregate demand and promoting job opportunities – or 'full employment' à la Keynes – to the current priority of controlling inflation and promoting investments and efficiency. Under the neo-liberal policy approach, the mechanism for dealing with employment – or, more precisely, the problem of *unemployment* – is deregulation of labour markets by eliminating or weakening minimum wage mandates, health and safety standards and measures supporting unionisation. Overall, it is not clear what impact these measures have had on employment rates, especially in developing countries where the problem of *underemployment* is far more pronounced than the problem of unemployment. But it is clear that such measures are likely to increase the flexibility of labour markets and weaken the bargaining power of workers. See Chapter 3 for a further discussion of these issues.

Those who work in the informal economy are likely to have greater deficits in opportunities, rights, protection and voice ... than those who work in the formal economy .... And among the working poor in the informal economy, women are more likely than men to be worse off in all of these respects.

Conclusion

The vast majority of the poor work, but few are able to work their way out of poverty. This is because most of them are engaged in the informal economy, where they are likely to face lower incomes, greater financial risks, lower standards of human development and greater social exclusion compared to better-off workers, especially those who work in the formal economy. Box 3 presents a framework for thinking about the consequences of working in the informal economy.

Box 3 Informal Employment and Poverty

Income poverty: if one or more members of the household are formally employed, income flows into the household are typically higher (as average wages or earnings are higher in the formal economy than in the informal economy) and expenditure flows out of the household are typically lower (as formal workers have more secure work and greater access to social protection).

Human development gaps: those who work in the informal economy are less likely than formal workers to have access to social services and more likely to have low levels of health, education and longevity.

Social exclusion: those who work in the informal economy are more often excluded, than formal workers, from state, market and political institutions that determine the 'rules of the game' in these various spheres.

It is also the case that those who work in the informal economy are likely to have greater deficits in opportunities, rights, protection and voice – the four pillars of the Decent Work agenda – than those who work in the formal economy (ILO, 2002a). And among the working poor in the informal economy, women are more likely than men to be worse off in all of these respects.

The evidence suggests that the terms on which women and men engage in the labour market have a direct bearing on their level of income, human development and social inclusion, and on whether or not they enjoy decent work. Yet employment – much less the terms of employment – has not been adequately analysed or addressed in poverty reduction strategies. This Handbook makes the case for a coherent focus on employment – and related market relationships – to bridge the persistent divide between growth and redistribution, to refocus attention on discrimination in markets and, thereby, to design strategies that will more effectively reduce poverty.

The relationship between trade liberalisation, growth and poverty continues to be hotly debated, with some observers claiming that trade liberalisation contributes to both growth and poverty reduction and others that it adversely affects the poor. There is further debate on the differential impact on women and men among the poor. The linkages are, at best, ambiguous as the empirical evidence points in both directions. Inserting a focus on informal employment and its gender dimensions into the trade-growth-poverty debate should help identify the circumstances under which economic reforms, trade liberalisation and growth generate pro-poor outcomes. This point is discussed in more detail in Chapter 3. But first, in Chapter 2, we will review available data on the links between being informally employed, being a woman or man and being poor.

Notes

1 See Kanbur (2001) for a detailed analysis of the proponents and opponents of globalisation.
2 See Stiglitz (2003b) for a discussion of the policies or 'rules of the game' managing globalisation.
3 Two recent studies by the International Labour Office analyse the 'nexus' of economic growth, employment and poverty reduction and make the case that, for it to reduce poverty, economic growth has to be accompanied by employment growth with rising productivity (Khan, 2001; Islam, 2004). While one study addresses both self-employment and wage employment (Khan, 2001), neither study addresses informal wage employment.

2. Informal Employment, Gender and Poverty

The Informal Economy

The informal workforce

The most visible occupational groups in the informal economy are those who work on the streets or in the open air. City streets and village lanes in most developing countries – and in many developed countries – are lined with barbers, cobblers, garbage collectors and vendors of vegetables, fruit, meat, fish, snack-foods or a myriad of non-perishable items from used clothing to locks and keys or soaps and cosmetics to electronic goods. In many countries, head-loaders, cart pullers, bicycle peddlers, rickshaw pullers, bullock or horse cart drivers jostle to make their way down narrow village lanes or through the maze of cars, trucks, vans and buses on city streets. In rural areas, the vast majority of people earn their livelihoods working on farms, raising livestock, making handicrafts or collecting and processing minor forest products.

Somewhat less visible are the informal workers who work in factories or small workshops that repair bicycles and motorcycles; recycle scrap metal; make furniture and metal parts; tan leather and stitch shoes; weave, dye and print cloth; polish diamonds and other gems; make and embroider garments; sort and sell cloth, paper and metal waste; and more. The least visible informal workers, the majority of them women, sell or produce goods from their homes: stitching garments, weaving cloth, embroidering textile goods, making crafts, making shoes, processing food or assembling electronic and automobile parts.

The largest occupational categories within the informal economy, in most developing countries, include casual day labourers in agriculture and construction, small farmers, forest gatherers, street vendors, domestic workers, workers in EPZ factories or small unregistered workshops, and industrial outworkers who work from their homes (also called homeworkers). Other categories of informal employment that are common in both developed and developing countries include casual workers in restaurants and hotels; sub-contracted janitors, security guards and gardeners; and temporary office helpers or off-site data processors.

Conditions of work and the level of earnings differ markedly among those who scavenge on the streets for scrap metal or paper, those who produce garments on a sub–contract from their homes, those who sell goods on the streets and those who work as temporary data processors. And, even among home-based workers, there is a difference between those who work on their own account and those who work on a piece-rate basis for a contractor or a firm. In every country, the informal economy is highly segmented by location of work, sector of the economy and employment status and, in addition, by social group and gender.

Despite its diversity, the informal economy can be usefully categorised by employment status into two broad groups: (1) the self-employed who work in small unregistered enterprises; and (2) wage workers who work in insecure and unprotected jobs (although, as we will discuss in Chapter 3, some informal workers or producers – notably homeworkers – do not fit neatly into one or other of these categories). Also, most of those who work in the informal economy share one thing in common: the lack of economic security and legal protection.

Discovery of the informal sector

It was widely assumed during the 1950s and 1960s that, with the right mix of economic policies and resources, poor traditional economies could be transformed into dynamic modern economies. In the process, the traditional sector comprised of petty traders, small producers and a range of casual jobs would be absorbed into the modern capitalist – or formal – economy and thereby disappear.[1] This perspective was reinforced by the successful rebuilding of Europe and Japan after World War II and the expansion of mass production in Europe and North America. By the early 1970s, however, the optimism about the prospects for economic growth in developing countries began to give way to concerns about persistent widespread unemployment. Reflecting this concern, the ILO mounted a series of large, multi-disciplinary 'employment missions' to various developing countries. The first of these was to Kenya in 1972.

The Kenya employment mission, through its fieldwork and in its official report, recognised that the traditional sector had not just persisted but had expanded to include profitable and efficient enterprises as well as marginal activities (ILO, 1972). To highlight this fact, the mission chose to use the term 'informal sector' rather than 'traditional sector' for the range of small-scale and unregistered economic activities. This term had been coined the previous year by a British economist, Keith Hart, in his 1971 study of economic activities in urban Ghana (Hart, 1973).

Debates about the informal sector

Although both Hart and the Kenya mission team were very positive about the informal sector – noting its efficiency, creativity and resilience – the concept received a mixed review in development circles. Many observers subscribed to the notion that the informal sector was marginal or peripheral and not linked to the formal sector or to modern capitalist development. Some of them continued to believe that the informal sector in Ghana, Kenya and other developing countries would disappear once these countries achieved sufficient levels of economic growth or modern industrial development. Other observers argued that industrial development might take a different pattern in developing countries – including the expansion of informal economic activities – from the way in which it had in developed countries.

Over the years, these debates crystallised into three dominant schools of thought regarding what gives rise to the informal sector, its defining characteristics and its links to the formal sector or the formal regulatory environment: the dualist, structuralist and legalist schools of thought (see Box 4). While the dualist school is now considered rather outdated, both the structuralist and legalist perspectives are still evoked to explain different components of the informal economy. In particular, the legalist perspective is used to explain the behaviour of the entrepreneurial class among the informal workforce who seek to avoid the costs associated with formalising their enterprises; and the structuralist perspective is used to explain the subordinate relationship of sub-contracted firms and workers to the lead firms who sub-contract work to them.

Box 4 Three Dominant Schools of Thought on the Informal Sector

The *dualist* school, popularised by the ILO in the 1970s, subscribes to the notion that the informal sector is comprised of marginal activities – distinct from and not related to the formal sector – that provide income for the poor and a safety net in times of crisis (Hart, 1973; ILO, 1972; Sethuraman, 1976; Tokman, 1978). According to this school, the persistence of informal activities is due largely to the fact that not enough modern job opportunities have been created to absorb surplus labour, due to a slow rate of economic growth and/or to a faster rate of population growth.

The *structuralist* school, popularised by Caroline Moser and Alexandro Portes (among others) in the late 1970s and 1980s, subscribes to the notion that the informal sector should be seen as subordinated economic units (micro firms) and workers that serve to reduce input and labour costs and, thereby, increase the competitiveness of large capitalist firms. In the structuralist model, in marked contrast to the dualist model, different modes and forms of production are seen not only to co-exist but also to be inextricably connected and interdependent (Moser, 1978; Castells and Portes, 1989). According to this school, the nature of capitalist development (rather than a lack of growth) accounts for the persistence and growth of informal production relationships.

The *legalist* school, popularised by Hernando de Soto in the 1980s and 1990s, subscribes to the notion that the informal sector is comprised of 'plucky' micro-entrepreneurs who choose to operate informally in order to avoid the costs, time and effort of formal registration (de Soto, 1989). According to de Soto et al, micro-entrepreneurs will continue to produce informally so long as government procedures are cumbersome and costly. In this view, unreasonable government rules and regulations are stifling private enterprise.

Whereas globalisation generates new jobs and new markets, available evidence suggests that not all the jobs are 'good' jobs and that the most disadvantaged producers have not been able to seize new market opportunities.

During the 1980s, the focus of the informal sector debate expanded to include changes that were occurring in advanced capitalist economies. In both North America and Europe, production was increasingly being reorganised into small-scale, decentralised and more flexible economic units. Mass production was giving way to 'flexible specialisation' or, in some contexts, reverting to sweatshop production (Piore and Sabel, 1984). These new patterns of capitalist development were (and are still) associated with the informalisation of employment relations – standard jobs being turned into non-standard[2] or atypical jobs with hourly wages but few benefits, or into piece-rate jobs with no benefits – and with the sub-contracting of the production of goods and services to small-scale informal units and industrial outworkers/homeworkers. In the process, the informal economy becomes a permanent, albeit subordinate and dependent, feature of capitalist development (Portes et al, 1989).

Meanwhile, in the 1980s, the economic crisis in Latin America served to highlight another feature of the informal sector: that employment in the informal sector tends to grow during periods of economic crisis (Tokman, 1992). In the Asian economic crisis a decade or more later, millions of people who lost formal jobs in the former East Asian Tiger countries tried to find jobs or create work in the informal economy (Lee, 1998). Meanwhile, structural adjustment in Africa and economic transition in the former Soviet Union and in Central and Eastern Europe were also associated with an expansion of employment in the informal economy. Informal employment tends to expand during periods of economic adjustment or transition because:

- when private firms or public enterprises are downsized or closed, retrenched workers who do not find alternative formal jobs have to turn to the informal economy for work because they cannot afford to be unemployed; and

- in response to inflation or cutbacks in public services, households often need to supplement formal sector incomes with informal earnings.

During the 1990s, globalisation of the economy contributed to the informalisation of the workforce in many industries and countries (Standing, 1999). Whereas globalisation generates new jobs and new markets, available evidence suggests that not all the jobs are 'good' jobs and that the most disadvantaged producers have not been able to seize new market opportunities (see Chapter 3). This is because global competition tends to erode employment relations by encouraging formal firms to hire workers at low wages with few benefits or to sub-contract (or out-source) the production of goods and services (Rodrik, 1997). Global integration also reduces the competitiveness of many informal firms or self-employed producers vis-à-vis imported goods (in domestic markets) and vis-à-vis larger, more formal firms (in export markets).

Current thinking regarding the informal economy, as summarised below, suggests the need for an integrated approach that looks at which elements of the dualist, legalist and structuralist schools of thought are most appropriate to which segments and contexts of informal employment. Clearly, some poor households and individuals engage in survival activities that have – or seem to have – very few links to the formal economy and the formal regulatory environment (dualist school); some micro-entrepreneurs choose to avoid taxes and regulations (legalist school); while other units and workers are subordinated to larger firms (structuralist school).

Rethinking the informal economy

Although interest in the informal sector has waxed and waned since its 'discovery' in 1972, it has continued to prove useful as a concept to many policy-makers, activists and researchers concerned with labour issues. This is because the reality it seeks to capture – the large share of the global workforce that remains outside the world of full-time, stable and protected employment – is so significant. At present, there is renewed interest in the informal sector worldwide. This re-convergence of interest stems from the fact that the informal economy has not only grown worldwide but also emerged in new guises and unexpected places. For this reason, the renewed interest has been accompanied by significant rethinking of the concept. Some key differences between earlier and current thinking on the informal economy are presented in Table 1.

Although interest in the informal sector has waxed and waned since its 'discovery' in 1972, it has continued to prove useful as a concept to many policy-makers, activists and researchers concerned with labour issues. This is because the reality it seeks to capture – the large share of the global workforce that remains outside the world of full-time, stable and protected employment – is so significant.

Table 1: Old and New Views of the Informal Economy

The Old View	The New View
The informal sector is the traditional economy that will wither away and die with modern, industrial growth.	The informal economy is 'here to stay' and expanding with modern, industrial growth.
It is only marginally productive.	It is a major provider of employment, goods and services for lower-income groups. It contributes a significant share of GDP.
It exists separately from the formal economy.	It is linked to the formal economy – it produces for, trades with, distributes for and provides services to the formal economy.
It represents a reserve pool of surplus labour.	Much of the recent rise in informal employment is due to the decline in formal employment or to the informalisation of previously formal employment relationships.
It is comprised mostly of street traders and very small-scale producers.	It is made up of a wide range of informal occupations – both 'resilient old forms' such as casual day labour in construction and agriculture as well as 'emerging new ones' such as temporary and part-time jobs plus homework for high tech industries.
Most of those in the sector are entrepreneurs who run illegal and unregistered enterprises in order to avoid regulation and taxation.	It is made up of non-standard wage workers as well as entrepreneurs and self-employed persons producing legal goods and services, albeit through irregular or unregulated means. Most entrepreneurs and the self-employed are amenable to, and would welcome, efforts to reduce barriers to registration and related transaction costs and to increase benefits from regulation; and most non-standard wage workers would welcome more stable jobs and workers' rights.
Work in the informal economy is comprised mostly of survival activities and thus is not a subject for economic policy.	Informal enterprises include not only survival activities but also stable enterprises and dynamic growing businesses, and informal employment includes not only self-employment but also wage employment. All forms of informal employment are affected by most (if not all) economic policies.

New term and expanded definition

In recent years, a group of informed activists and researchers, including members of the Women in Informal Employment: Globalizing and Organizing (WIEGO) network,[3] have worked with the ILO to broaden the concept and definition of the 'informal sector' to incorporate certain types of informal employment that were not included in the earlier concept and definition (including the official international statistical definition). They want the whole of informality included, as it is manifested in industrialised, transition and developing economies and the real world dynamics in labour markets today, particularly the employment arrangements of the working poor. These observers want to extend the focus from *enterprises* that are not legally regulated to *employment relationships* that are not legally regulated or protected. In brief, their new definition of the 'informal economy' focuses on the nature of employment in addition to the characteristics of enterprises.

Under this new definition, the informal economy is seen as comprised of all forms of 'informal employment' – that is, employment without formal contracts (i.e. covered by labour

Vegetable vendor, Fiji Islands
FOOD AND AGRICULTURE ORGANIZATION/P. BEHLEN-DEXTER

> *The recent re-convergence of interest in the informal economy stems from the recognition that the informal economy is growing and is not a short-term but a permanent phenomenon.*

legislation), worker benefits or social protection – both inside and outside informal enterprises, including:

- Self-employment in informal enterprises: workers in small unregistered or unincorporated enterprises, including:
  – employers;
  – own account operators;
  – unpaid family workers.

- Wage employment in informal jobs: workers without formal contracts, worker benefits or social protection for formal or informal firms, for households or with no fixed employer, including:
  – employees of informal enterprises;
  – other informal wage workers such as casual or day labourers, domestic workers, unregistered or undeclared workers and temporary or part-time workers;[4]
  – industrial outworkers (also called homeworkers).

Key features of the informal economy

What follows is a discussion of key features of the informal economy broadly defined: (a) its significance and permanence; (b) the continuum of employment relations within it; and (c) its segmented structure. The discussion ends on the issue of its legality or illegality as there is a widespread misconception that the informal economy is somehow illegal or is the equivalent of the underground, or even criminal, economy.

(a) Significance and permanence: The recent re-convergence of interest in the informal economy stems from the recognition that the informal economy is growing and is not a short-term but a permanent phenomenon. Also, it is not just a traditional or residual phenomenon but a feature of modern capitalist development, associated with both growth and global integration. For this reason, the informal economy needs to be seen not as a marginal or peripheral sector but as a basic component – the base, if you will – of the total economy.

(b) Continuum of economic relations: Earlier, observers who subscribed to the *dualist* theory considered the informal and formal sectors to be two distinct economic sectors without direct links to one another The reality is, as always, far more complex. To begin with, production, distribution and employ-

ment relations tend to fall at some point on a continuum between pure 'formal' relations (i.e. regulated and protected) at one pole and pure 'informal' relations (i.e. unregulated and unprotected) at the other, with many categories in between. Depending on their circumstances, workers and units are known to move with varying ease and speed along the continuum and/or to operate simultaneously at different points on the continuum. Consider, for example, the self-employed garment maker who has to supplement what she makes on her own by stitching clothes under a sub-contract, or shift to working on a sub-contract for a garment firm or trader when her customers decide they prefer to buy ready-made garments rather than tailor-made ones. Or the public sector employee who has an informal job on the side.

Moreover, the formal and the informal ends of the economic continuum are often dynamically linked. For instance, many informal enterprises have production or distribution relations with formal enterprises, supplying inputs, finished goods or services either through direct transactions or sub-contracting arrangements. Also, many formal enterprises hire wage workers under informal employment relations. For example, many part-time workers, temporary workers and home-workers work for formal enterprises through contracting or sub-contracting arrangements.

(c) *Segmentation*: The informal economy consists of a wide range of informal enterprises and informal jobs. Yet there are meaningful ways to classify it. Figure 1 provides a graphic depiction of the universe of informal employment that also shows: (i) on the left, how the earlier definition of the 'informal sector' is a component part of the recently-expanded definition of the 'informal economy'; and (ii) on the right, the two broad components of the informal economy – self-employment and wage employment – and the various sub-components of each. Throughout the Handbook, we make the case that this segmented structure of the informal economy and the characteristics of work associated with it are key determinants of the poverty and gender outcomes of economic processes.

Figure 1: Definition and Segmentation of the Informal Economy

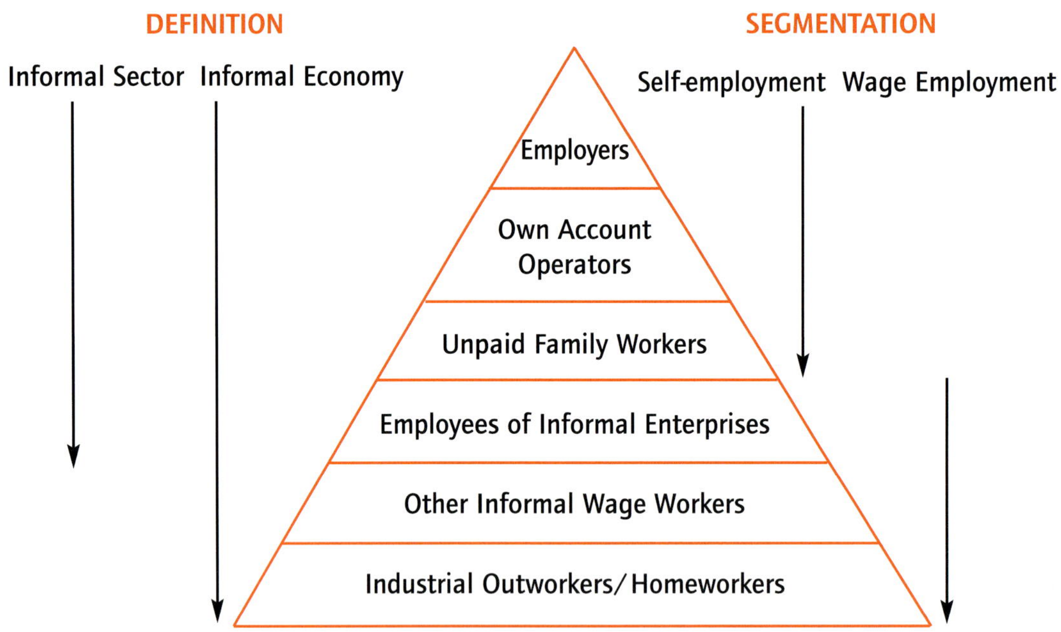
DEFINITION
Informal Sector
Informal Economy
SEGMENTATION
Self-employment
Wage Employment
Employers
Own Account Operators
Unpaid Family Workers
Employees of Informal Enterprises
Other Informal Wage Workers
Industrial Outworkers/Homeworkers

Legality or semi-legality

Previously, there was a widespread assumption that the informal sector was comprised of unregistered and unregulated enterprises whose owner operators chose to avoid registration and, thereby, taxation. While it is important to understand informal employment in relation to the legal framework in any given country, this is far from being the whole story.

- There is a distinction between illegal *processes or arrangements* and illegal *goods and services*. While production or employment arrangements in the informal economy are often semi-legal or illegal, most informal workers and enterprises produce and/or distribute legal goods and services. Admittedly, one part of the informal economy – the criminal economy – not only operates illegally but also deals in illegal goods and services. But it is only a small part of a larger whole that is, for the most part, not illegal or criminal.
- Many owner operators of informal enterprises operate semi-legally or illegally because the regulatory environment is

too punitive, too cumbersome or simply non-existent. Also, many activities in the informal economy do not generate enough output, employment or income to fall into existing tax brackets.

- Most owner operators would be willing to pay the costs of registration and pay taxes if they were to receive the incentives and benefits of formality (enjoyed by registered businesses).

- It is very important to note that, in the case of informal wage work, it is not the workers but their employers, whether in formal or informal firms, who are avoiding registration and taxation.

Most fundamentally, operating outside the statutory legal framework is seen to have more costs than benefits for most informal workers. Most self-employed and wage workers in the informal sector are deprived of secure work, workers' benefits, social protection and representation or voice. The self-employed have to take care of themselves and their enterprises as well as their employees (if they hire others) or unpaid contributing family members (if they run a family business). Moreover, they often face competitive disadvantage vis-à-vis larger formal firms in capital and product markets. Informal wage workers also have to take care of themselves as they receive few (if any) employer-sponsored benefits. In addition, both groups receive little (if any) legal protection through their work or from their governments. As a result of these and other factors, a higher percentage of people working in the informal economy, compared to those working in the formal economy, are poor.

Women and Men in the Informal Economy

Compiling statistics on the size, composition and contribution of the informal economy is hampered by the lack of sufficient data. While many countries have by now undertaken a survey on employment in the informal sector, very few countries undertake these on a regular basis. Furthermore, only two or three countries have collected the data that provide for measures of informal employment outside informal enterprises.[5] In addition, the available data are not comprehensive. Many countries

Most self-employed and wage workers in the informal sector are deprived of secure work, workers' benefits, social protection and representation or voice.

exclude agriculture from their measurement of the informal sector, and some measure only the urban informal sector. There are also a number of problems that limit the international comparability of data. However, in the absence of reliable data collected directly, various indirect methods to estimate the size and composition of the informal economy can be used. What follows is a summary of main findings from the most recent and most comprehensive set of estimates of the informal economy, including its gender dimensions, using indirect methods where necessary.[6]

Developing countries

Size of the informal economy

Informal employment comprises one half to three quarters of non-agricultural employment in developing countries: specifically, 48 per cent in North Africa; 51 per cent in Latin America; 65 per cent in Asia; and 72 per cent in sub-Saharan Africa. If South Africa is excluded, the share of informal employment in non-agricultural employment rises to 78 per cent in sub-Saharan Africa; and if comparable data were available for other countries in South Asia in addition to India, the regional average for Asia would likely be much higher.

Some countries include informal employment in agriculture in their estimates. This significantly increases the proportion of informal employment: from 83 per cent of *non-agricultural* employment to 93 per cent of *total* employment in India; from 55 to 62 per cent in Mexico; and from 28 to 34 per cent in South Africa.

Informal employment is generally a larger source of employment for women than for men in the developing world. Other than in North Africa, where 43 per cent of women workers are in informal employment, 60 per cent or more of women workers in the developing world are in informal employment (outside agriculture). In sub-Saharan Africa, 84 per cent of women non-agricultural workers are informally employed compared to 63 per cent of men; and in Latin America the figures are 58 per cent of women in comparison to 48 per cent of men. In Asia, the proportion is 65 per cent for both women and men.

Composition of the informal economy

As noted earlier, in the discussion of its segmented structure, informal employment is comprised of both self-employment in informal enterprises (i.e. small and/or unregistered) and wage employment in informal jobs (i.e. without secure contracts, worker benefits or social protection). In all developing regions, self-employment comprises a greater share of informal employment (outside of agriculture) than wage employment: specifically, self-employment represents 70 per cent of informal employment in sub-Saharan Africa, 62 per cent in North Africa, 60 per cent in Latin America and 59 per cent in Asia. If South Africa is excluded, since black-owned businesses were prohibited during the apartheid era and have only recently begun to be recognised and reported, the share of self-employment in informal employment increases to 81 per cent in sub-Saharan Africa.

Informal wage employment is also significant in the developing world, comprising 30 to 40 per cent of informal employment (outside of agriculture). Informal wage employment is comprised of employees of informal enterprises as well as various types of informal wage workers who work for formal enterprises, households or no fixed employer (see definition above).

In most countries for which data are available, women in informal employment are more likely to be in self-employment than in wage employment (see Table 2). In North Africa, Asia, three of the five sub-Saharan African countries and half of the Latin America countries, more women in informal employment (outside agriculture) are in self-employment than in wage employment. By contrast, informal wage employment is more important for women in Kenya, South Africa and four countries in South America – Brazil, Chile, Columbia and Costa Rica. In these countries more than half of women in informal employment are wage workers. Moreover, in all but one of these countries – South Africa – women are more likely to be informal wage workers than men.

In all developing regions, self-employment comprises a greater share of informal employment (outside of agriculture) than wage employment.

Table 2: Wage and Self-employment in Non-agricultural Informal Employment, by Sex (1994/2000)

Country/Region	Self-employment as a Percentage of Non-agricultural Informal Employment			Wage Employment as a Percentage of Non-agricultural Informal Employment		
	Total	Women	Men	Total	Women	Men
North Africa	62	72	60	38	28	40
Algeria	67	81	64	33	19	36
Egypt	50	67	47	50	33	53
Morocco	81	89	78	19	11	22
Tunisia	52	51	52	48	49	48
Sub-Saharan Africa	70	71	70	30	29	30
Benin	95	98	91	5	2	9
Chad	93	99	86	7	1	14
Guinea	95	98	94	5	2	6
Kenya	42	33	56	58	67	44
South Africa	25	27	23	75	73	77
Latin America	60	58	61	40	42	39
Bolivia	81	91	71	19	9	29
Brazil	41	32	50	59	68	50
Chile	52	39	64	48	61	36
Colombia	38	36	40	62	64	60
Costa Rica	55	49	59	45	51	41
Dominican Republic	74	63	80	26	37	20
El Salvador	65	71	57	35	29	43
Guatemala	60	65	55	40	35	45
Honduras	72	77	65	28	23	35
Mexico	54	53	54	46	47	46
Venezuela	69	66	70	31	34	30
Asia	59	63	55	41	37	45
India	52	57	51	48	43	49
Indonesia	63	70	59	37	30	41
Philippines	48	63	36	52	37	64
Syria	65	57	67	35	43	33
Thailand	66	68	64	34	32	36

Source: ILO (2002b) based on data prepared by Jacques Charmes from official national statistics

Developed countries

In developed countries, the terms 'informal sector' and 'informal economy' are not used in the collection and classification of labour statistics. The most common term is 'non-standard work', which refers to all work that is not regular, stable and protected. In the late 1990s, three categories of non-standard or atypical work – self-employment, part-time work and temporary work – comprised 30 per cent of overall employment in 15 European countries and 25 per cent of total employment in the United States. Although not all self-employed, part-time workers and temporary workers are informally employed, the majority receive few (if any) employment-based benefits or protection. In the United States, for instance, less than 20 per cent of regular part-time workers have employer-sponsored health insurance or pensions.

Self-employment comprised 12 per cent of total non-agricultural employment in developed countries. Part-time work represented about 14 per cent of total employment for the Organisation for Economic Co-operation and Development (OECD) countries as a whole and more than 20 per cent of total employment in eight of these countries. In the countries of the European Union (EU), temporary work comprised 11 per cent of total employment.

Although women's labour force participation rates are lower than men's, women comprise a significant share of non-standard employment. Women represented 60 per cent or more of part-time workers in all OECD countries reporting data. Their share of part-time work for specific countries was as high as 98 per cent in Sweden, 80 per cent in the United Kingdom and 68 per cent in both Japan and the United States. In many countries of the EU the majority of workers in temporary employment are women. In nine of the (then) 15 EU countries, women accounted for about half or more of temporary employment. And in OECD countries, women comprised one-third of self-employed workers in 1997 and this share of women appears to be growing.

The Links between Informal Employment, Poverty and Gender

As the Director General of the ILO, Juan Somavia, stated in his 2003 report to the International Labour Conference: "We know only too well that it is precisely the world of work that holds the key for solid, progressive and long-lasting eradication of poverty. It is though work that people can expand their

> *"Poverty elimination is impossible unless the economy generates opportunities for investment, entrepreneurship, job creation and sustainable livelihoods"*
> *– Juan Somavia*

choices to a better quality of life. It is through work that wealth is created, distributed and accumulated. It is through work that people find a dignified way out of poverty. … Poverty elimination is impossible unless the economy generates opportunities for investment, entrepreneurship, job creation and sustainable livelihoods" (ILO, 2003: 3 and 7).

Since a growing majority of the global workforce is engaged in informal employment, the informal economy will need to be a focus of efforts to alleviate poverty. To illustrate this point, a recent report by the Special Group on Targeting Ten Million Employment Opportunities per year over the Tenth Plan period in India emphasised the policy relevance of the informal economy in that country. The task force concluded that it is necessary to target the informal economy – what India calls the unorganised sector – in order to generate new jobs and to improve the vast majority of existing jobs (Government of India, 2001 as cited in Sastry, 2004). Essential to such planning is understanding the relationship between informal employment, poverty and gender.

Similarly, the Task Force on Gender Equality of the UN Millennium Project has given strategic priority to low-income women and efforts to make them economically more secure. Reflecting this priority, the Task Force has highlighted the need for improved data on informal employment and the gender wage gap as indicators for planning and programming in pursuit of the Millennium Development Goals (Millennium Project Task Force on Education and Gender Equality, 2004).[7]

Some of the key assumptions regarding the linkages between informality, gender and poverty may be summarised as follows:

- The poor are more likely to work in the informal than in the formal economy.

- More poor women than non-poor women work in the informal economy.

- Average earnings are lower in the informal than in the formal economy.

- Workers in the informal economy are more likely than workers in the formal economy to earn less than the minimum wage.

- There is a gender gap in wages/earnings in the informal economy with women earning less on average than men.

Unfortunately, data are not readily available to test these assumptions. A major problem is that the assumptions involve different types of data that in turn use different units of analysis. Specifically, labour force data are collected at the *individual* level while standard poverty measures are based on income and expenditure data for *households*. There are technical – though not insurmountable – problems in linking these two types of data. In addition, detailed data is required on informal employment. While increasing numbers of countries are collecting such data, this topic is not yet a well-established part of national programmes of data collection and tabulation. Official data from national surveys do not permit extensive comparisons of the labour force in terms of formal and informal employment, the status in employment of women and men workers in these categories or their wages or poverty status.

Only limited official data are thus now available on the linkages between working in the informal economy, being a man or woman and being poor. These will be reviewed along with findings from more qualitative research to lay out the complex issues that are involved. In addition, surprisingly few studies have investigated the questions about these linkages that are raised by the key assumptions noted above. For example, are those who work in the informal economy poorer than those who work in the formal economy? And are female informal workers poorer than male informal workers? Two of the studies reviewed here investigate such questions at the level of the household in terms of standard expenditure-based measures of poverty; the other studies looked either at wages and earnings (as a reasonable proxy for the poverty level of individuals) or at the quality of work (using different measures).

Informal employment and household poverty

Two recent labour force surveys – the 2002 Labour Force Survey in South Africa and the 1999–2000 National Sample Survey of India on employment and unemployment – provide unique data that begin to answer questions regarding the relationship between informal employment and poverty. Both surveys collected household expenditure data as well as data on employment, including informal employment; and both studies tried to link these variables in a meaningful way by classifying households by sources of income and by expenditure categories. They both found an overlap between depending on informal employment and being poor at the household level (NALEDI, 2003; Sastry 2004).[8]

The South Africa study looked at the relationship between monthly household expenditure categories and the nature of employment in households: that is, by presence in a household of a person or persons in permanent employment, in informal employment, in domestic work or unemployed (NALEDI, 2003). The higher the monthly expenditure category, the higher the percentage of households with persons in permanent employment. Moving down the expenditure categories, the percentage of households with persons in informal employment (including domestic services) increases. Not surprisingly, the lowest expenditure category had the highest percentage of households with an unemployed person or persons (using an expanded definition of unemployment). It should be noted that, given the legacy of apartheid and current restructuring of the agricultural and manufacturing sectors, unemployment rates are very high in South Africa (ibid).

The India study looked at the distribution of poor households across households classified by type of work *within the informal economy* (Sastry, 2004). In marked contrast to South Africa, unemployment in India is not high, and the vast majority of workers – 92 per cent – are in informal employment (using the expanded definition of informal employment). India has a more limited old-age pension and child support system than South Africa, so that the poor cannot afford not to work and have to pursue whatever economic opportunities they can to sustain themselves and their families. Households in which wage employment in informal enterprises is the main source of income are the least likely to be poor, while households that depend on casual labour as their primary source of income are the most likely to be poor.

Another study in India, also using data from the National Sample Survey (from two earlier surveys, in 1987/88 and 1993/94), found a similar relationship between poverty and the nature of employment – although this analysis did not distinguish between formal and informal employment. Dubey et al (2001) analysed the probability of urban households being poor according to their main source of income – classified as regular salary, self-employment and casual wage labour – and by the size of the city or town in which they were located. Their analysis shows that, for cities or towns of all sizes and both points in time, households with regular salaried employees have the lowest probability of being poor, while those that depend on casual day labour have the highest probability (with households that depend on self-employment falling roughly half-way in between).[9] All employment groups fared better in larger cities. And, between the two rounds of the survey, the probability of being poor declined for all groups.

Earnings in the informal economy

Additional insight on the links between informal employment and poverty can be seen by considering the wages or earnings of different categories of informal workers and by seeing how they compare to those in formal employment.

Earnings in formal and informal employment

A first comparison is the contrast between average wages or earnings in formal and informal employment, taken as a whole. An important source of data on these relationships are from a current set of comparative workforce development studies in five countries – Egypt, El Salvador, India, Russia and South Africa.[10] These studies were designed to look at workforce development needs in these countries. Following a common framework of questions, they all studied the links between macroeconomic processes and labour force development (though they varied in the measures used). Most importantly, for our purposes here, they also disaggregated the labour force by formal and informal employment, men and women. The three studies that were able to compare earnings data confirm that, on average, wages or earnings are higher in formal than in informal employment. The results are summarised below:

- **Egypt:** Average real wages of the formal and informal workforce, both sexes, were measured at two points in time (1988 and 1998). The results suggest a large gap between formal and informal real wages in both years and for both sexes, but a narrowing of the gap by the second point of time as formal real wages declined more rapidly than informal real wages. However, between the two points in time, female informal wages declined faster than female formal wages (El Mahdi and Amer, 2004).

- **El Salvador:** Earnings from formal employment in relation to the minimum wage were compared to those for informal employment for 2002. A relatively small share (14%) of the formal workforce earns below the minimum wage. Within the informal workforce, a higher share of rural workers (77%) than urban workers (49%) earn below the minimum wage (Lara, 2004). It should be noted that the minimum wage is set at a level that would not cover the cost of 'basic goods'.

- **South Africa:** The income of formal and informal sector workers for 2001 was compared. While the majority of formal workers earn above R1,000 per month, the majority of informal workers earn less than R1,000. The estimated minimum level of income needed for a family of five is set at R1,777 per month (NALEDI, 2003).

Similarly, a 1994 UNICEF survey in Haiti found that, outside of the capital city Port-au-Prince, a higher percentage of those who worked in the informal sector (79%) compared to those who worked in the formal sector (64%) were concentrated in the lowest third of income distribution (UNICEF, 1994).

Comparative earnings in the informal sector

A second comparison is the difference in average wages or earnings *within* the informal economy. As noted earlier, the informal economy is diverse and segmented. The different segments are associated with different earning potentials that would be concealed by the average for the informal economy as a whole. For example, a study of employment in the informal sector (small unregistered enterprises) in Tunisia found that the employers who hire others – the micro-entrepreneurs – are not poor. Indeed, the average income of micro-entrepreneurs was found to be four times as high as the legal minimum salary and 2.2 times the average salary in the formal sector (Table 3 below).

Although micro-entrepreneurs may have relatively high earnings in Tunisia – and elsewhere – most workers in informal employment do not fare so well. For example, the micro-entrepreneurs in Tunisia pay their employees on average roughly the legal minimum wage of 200 dinars per month. The Tunisian study also included information on earnings in jobs outside informal enterprises – notably for homeworkers. Homeworkers, who are paid by the piece, earn an average of 60 dinars per month, which is only 30 per cent of the minimum wage (Charmes and Lakehal, 2003).

More broadly, data from 14 countries compiled by Jacques Charmes show the disparities in earnings within informal employment. Table 3 compares data on the average monthly income of micro-entrepreneurs and the average monthly wage of employees of micro-enterprises, both expressed as multiples of the legal minimum wage level in those countries. In some cases, noted in brackets, Charmes compared average monthly income to average salaries in the formal economy. In every case, except Kenya, the average monthly income of micro-entrepreneurs is higher than the average monthly wages of the employees of micro-enterprises. Generally, the wages of employees tend to hover around the minimum wage – which in itself may be less than the minimum needed for survival.

Comparing the earnings of micro-entrepreneurs and own account operators

Another important comparison is between the average earnings of micro-entrepreneurs and of own account operators. Two countries in Table 3, Columbia and India, clearly distinguish between employers and own account operators. The lowest multiple of average monthly income to legal minimum wage (1.34) was for own account operators in India. In marked contrast, the average monthly income of employers in India was 5.4 times the legal minimum wage. A similar contrast can be seen in urban Columbia, where employers earn 4.2 times the legal minimum wage and own account operators earn only 1.6 times. In fact, in urban Columbia the employees of micro-enterprises earn nearly as much as own account operators: 1.5 times the legal minimum wage. In sum, in both Colombia and India, employers earn higher monthly average income than own account operators; and own account operators have only slightly higher average earnings than employees of informal enterprises.

Table 3: Average Monthly Income of and Wages Paid by Micro-entrepreneurs (as multiples of legal minimum wage)

Region/Country	Year	Income — Multiples of Legal Minimum Wage	Wages Paid[a] — Multiples of Legal Minimum Salary
North Africa			
Morocco	1997	1.7	1.0
Tunisia	1997	4.0 (2.2)	1.1
Sub-Saharan Africa			
Benin	1992	3.0	1.7
Street vendors		1.7	
Burkina Faso	1988	3.3	1.1
Chad	1995–96	1.6	0.6
Ethiopia (urban)	1996		
Gabon	1985	1.6	0.8
Kenya	1999	2.6	2.7
Mali	1996	5.8	0.9
Niger	1995	1.5	
Latin America			
Brazil (urban)	1997	(0.9)[b] (1.7)[c]	(0.4)
Colombia (urban)	1996	1.6[d] 4.2[e]	1.5
Mexico (urban)	1998		1.7
Asia			
India	1999–2000	1.34[d] 5.4[e] 1.8[f]	0.9 1.1 1.1
Indonesia	1998	3.0[g]	

Source: Prepared by Jacques Charmes, based on official national sources
Notes: Figures in brackets are multiples of average salary in the formal sector.
[a] apprentices and family workers excluded
[b] main activity
[c] main and secondary activities
[d] own-account operators
[e] employers of micro-enterprises (less than ten workers)
[f] own account and employers combined
[g] multiple of the average wage of production workers under supervisory level

Poor women and the informal economy

The inter-relationships of informal employment, poverty and gender are very complex and not well understood. This is perhaps not surprising as there is only limited understanding of the links between poverty and gender. It is often assumed that women make up the overwhelming majority of poor people in the world – and figures are frequently cited on the proportion of the world's poor who are women. However, such figures are not based on solid evidence. Analysis using survey data has not confirmed a large magnitude of difference in poverty between women and men. Moreover, research shows variation from country to country. For example, a comprehensive review of survey data for 14 developing countries undertaken by the International Food Policy Research Institute (IFPRI) found that, in general, there are more women than men in poor households and that, in many of the countries studied, female-headed households were poorer than male-headed households (United Nations, 1995:129). However, in a number of the countries, there was no clear pattern of greater poverty among women or female-headed households (ibid). Additional analysis by IFPRI of a subset of these countries also found 'weak' evidence that women as well as households headed by women are over-represented among the poor (Quisumbing et al, 2001). The 1999–2000 National Sample Survey data for India suggests that not all female-headed households suffer greater poverty than male-headed households (Sastry, 2004). Finally, a review of World Bank Poverty Assessments also found that female-headed households are worse off than male-headed households in some countries though not all (Lampietti and Stalker, 2000).

While quantitative evidence does not point to large differentials in poverty levels between women and men and women- and men-headed households, it does show that substantial numbers of women live in poverty and that differences in poverty levels between women and men vary across countries. These findings justify looking beyond the relative poverty levels of women and men to focus on how gender norms influence the economic and social processes leading to poverty and the escape routes out of it. This Handbook seeks to highlight the intersection of informal employment and gender as a key path-

While quantitative evidence does not point to large differentials in poverty levels between women and men and women- and men-headed households, it does show that substantial numbers of women live in poverty and that differences in poverty levels between women and men vary across countries.

way between macroeconomic trends or policies and poverty outcomes.

To that end, we have gathered as much data as is readily available on the links between informal employment, poverty and gender. Our basic starting proposition is that most women in poor households seek remunerative work. In developing countries that have no social protection or unemployment insurance, poor women have little choice in this regard. However, it is difficult to test this proposition. Data on economic activity that distinguish participation among poor and non-poor women are generally not available. Further, in spite of improvements in measurement, many countries still do not fully enumerate women's economic activity, particularly those in the informal economy. The effect is an underestimation of the economic activity of poor women (United Nations, 1991:85).

Data on the differential labour participation of poor and non-poor women have been compiled for a small number of countries using World Bank poverty assessment reports (Lampietti and Stalker, 2000). However, the results are not consistent. Data for several of the countries show that poor women are more likely to be employed than non-poor women. Yet for other countries – notably six out of nine countries in Latin America – poor women have lower labour force participation rates than non-poor women.

In a study of Peru, more poor women than non-poor women participate in the labour force, except in the 25–44 age group for which economic activity rates are slightly lower for poor women (Bravo, 2003). Further, women's income is a major component of income in poor households in Peru, so much so that if women did not contribute to household income, in 1999 an additional 17 per cent of all households would be below the poverty line and an additional 14 per cent of all households would be below the extreme poverty line (ibid).

The related proposition is that most working poor men and (more so) women are in the informal economy. While we do not have data to prove this proposition, we do know that the majority of *all* economically active women in most developing countries work in the informal economy. And we can safely assume that an even higher percentage of economically-active *poor* women are in the informal economy.

What are the other links between working in the informal economy, being a woman and being poor? To help answer this question, and to guide future research and policy analysis on these issues, we propose the following framework as a key tool for assessing the links between informal employment, poverty and gender.

Gender Segmentation of the Informal Economy[11]

The framework

Earlier in this chapter, we presented a figure that depicts the various segments of the informal economy, categorised by employment status. At the top of the figure is the most visible or best known segment – employers/micro-entrepreneurs; at the base is the least visible and least understood segment – homeworkers (see Figure 1). From available field studies and official data, two stylised global facts emerge about the segmented informal economy. The first is that, around the world, men tend to be over-represented in the top segment and women tend to be over-represented in the bottom segment. While the shares of men and women in the intermediate segments tend to vary across sectors and countries, women tend to be over-represented as unpaid family workers.

The second global fact is that, around the world, there are significant gaps in wages or earnings within the informal economy: on average, employers have the highest earnings; homeworkers have the lowest; and own account workers and wage workers earn somewhere in between, depending on the economic sector and country. The net result is a significant gender gap in earnings within the informal economy, with women earning less on average than men.

These twin global facts are depicted graphically in Figure 2. To the right, the figure depicts the gender segmentation of employment: women are over-represented in the lowest segment of the structure and under-represented in the top segment of the informal economy. To the left, the figure depicts the average earnings associated with the different employment status categories within the informal economy: average earnings tend to decline as one moves down the figure.

Around the world, there are significant gaps in wages or earnings within the informal economy: on average, employers have the highest earnings; homeworkers have the lowest; and own account workers and wage workers earn somewhere in between .... The net result is a significant gender gap ... with women earning less on average than men.

Figure 2: The Gender Segmentation of the Informal Economy

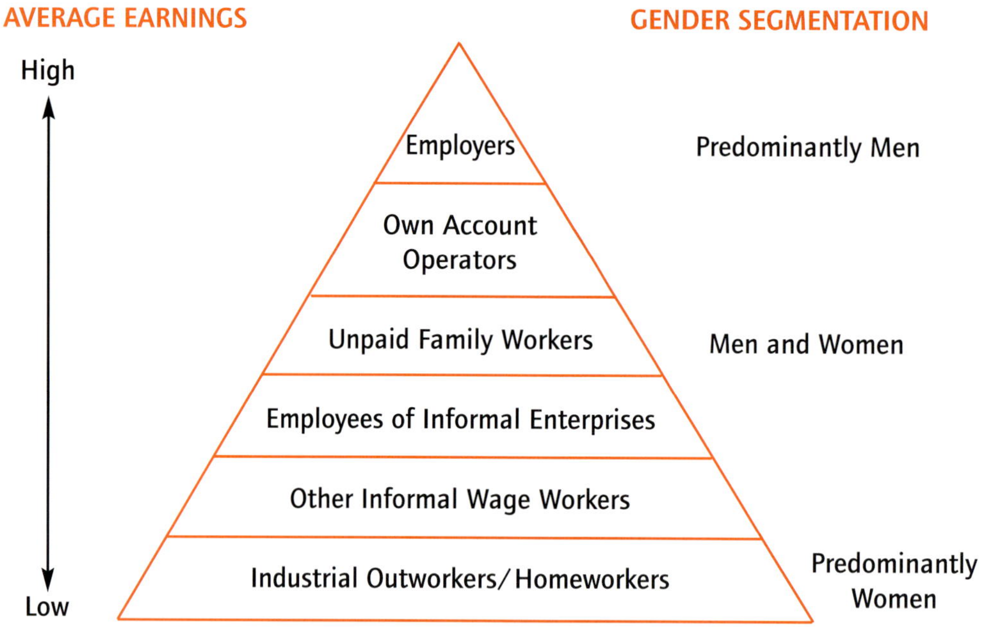
AVERAGE EARNINGS
GENDER SEGMENTATION
High
Low
Employers
Own Account Operators
Unpaid Family Workers
Employees of Informal Enterprises
Other Informal Wage Workers
Industrial Outworkers/ Homeworkers
Predominantly Men
Men and Women
Predominantly Women

An additional fact, not captured in Figure 2, is that there is further segmentation of employment within these broad status categories. Women tend to be employed in different types of activities, associated with different levels of earning, than men – with the result that they tend to earn less even within specific segments of the informal economy. Some of this difference can be explained by the fact that men tend to have better tools of the trade, operate from better work sites/spaces and have greater access to productive assets and financial capital. In addition, or as a result, men often produce or sell a higher volume or a different range of goods and services. For instance, among street vendors in some countries, men are more likely to sell non-perishable goods while women are more likely to sell perishable goods (such as fruits and vegetables). In addition, men are more likely to sell from push-carts or bicycles while women are more likely to sell from baskets on their heads or on the ground, or simply from a cloth spread on the ground. This is also because men are more likely to be heads of family businesses, while women are more likely to be unpaid contributing family members.

In the next section, we have compiled data from various

studies to provide a glimpse into how gender segmentation of the informal economy works. We acknowledge that the data are limited, but we hope that they will illustrate how fruitful this line of analysis can be and the need to do more such analyses.

Empirical findings
Gender segmentation of employment
While it is now widely recognised that the formal economy is segmented by gender, it is less widely recognised that this is also the case with the informal economy. However, a number of recent studies confirm the existence of gender segmentation within the informal economy. For instance, a recent study in Peru found that a far higher percentage of employed women (36%) than men (12%) are unpaid family workers, while a far lower percentage of women (14%) than men (35%) are wage workers (Bravo, 2003). Similarly, data from the 1998–99 Ghana Living Standards Survey show that 23 per cent of employed women are unpaid family workers in contrast to only 11 per cent of men. (Ghana Statistical Service, 2000).

Data for Tunisia in 1997 illustrate the gender segmentation of that component of the broader informal economy comprised of small, unregistered enterprises (Charmes and Lakehal, 2003). Many fewer women employed in the informal sector are employers (14%) compared to men (24%) (Table 4). Most women in the informal sector are employed in the lower strata in Figure 2 as unpaid family workers or employees (55%) while most men in the informal sector are in the upper strata as employers and own account workers (60%).

While it is now widely recognised that the formal economy is segmented by gender, it is less widely recognised that this is also the case with the informal economy.

Table 4: Percentage Distribution of Informal Sector Employment by Employment Status and Sex, Tunisia 1997

	Women	Men
Employers	14	24
Own account operators	27	36
Unpaid family workers	18	9
Employees	37	23
Other	4	8

Source: Prepared by Jacques Charmes from data of the National Statistical Institute (Tunisia)

MAINSTREAMING INFORMAL EMPLOYMENT AND GENDER IN POVERTY REDUCTION

Vegetable vendor, India
MARTHA CHEN

Recent field research in Ahmedabad City, India, illustrates both the gender segmentation of employment and the gender gap in earnings within the informal economy, including the fact that women often earn less than men even within specific trades or employment statuses (Table 5). In an admittedly small study sample, no women were salaried workers, employers who hire others or employees of micro-enterprises and no men were industrial outworkers/homeworkers. Salaried workers (all men) commanded the highest earnings followed by some forms of *male* own account activities and *male* wage employment in informal enterprises. Two categories of women workers – homeworkers and inexperienced vegetable vendors – earned the least. Among street vendors, no women sold perishable goods that are associated with higher earnings and women

Table 5: Daily Net Earnings from Common Informal Occupations, Ahmedabad City, India, 2000 (in Indian rupees)[a]

Occupation	Male	Female
Industrial outwork/ homework		
Bidi rolling	–	25–35
Own account vending		
Soap, garlic and onion vendors	40–85	
Vegetable and fruit vendors	80–100	25–30 (inexperienced) 60–100 (experienced)
Incense sticks, bag and sandal vendors	100–165	
Own account shops[b]	150	–
Own account tailoring	125–145	85
Own account embroidery	165	–
Own account tyre repair/sales	350	–
Wage work in micro-enterprises		
Powerloom workshops	40–45	–
Embroidery workshops	65–85	
Tailoring, metal value and screen Printing workshops	100–140	
Diamond polishing workshops	120–160	
Salaried Work for Formal Firms	125–210	–

Source: Chen and Snodgrass, 2001
Notes:
[a]The average exchange rate in 2000 was US$1 = Rs. 45.1
[b]Often small shops are run as family businesses, with the wife and/or children helping the household head run the shop. In some rare cases, the wife or a widow runs the shop with the help of her husband and/or son

vegetable vendors earned less on average than male vegetable vendors. And, among garment makers, no women ran small tailoring shops, which are associated with higher average earnings than home-based garment making.

Gender gap in earnings

Available evidence confirms that there are pervasive gender gaps in earnings/wages within the informal economy. One study of the urban informal economy in five countries in Central America found that "(o)ne of the strongest patterns in each of the data sets is a much larger difference between male and female earnings in the informal sector than in the formal sector" (Funkhouser, 1996: 1744). In Peru, within the urban informal economy, women earn 87 per cent of what men earn among employees of informal enterprises, 65 per cent among employers and 56 per cent among own account workers (Bravo, 2003). A 1994 UNICEF study in Haiti also found a gender gap in earnings among those who worked in the informal sector, with 87 per cent of women but only 69 per cent of men clustered in the lowest third of the income distribution (UNICEF, 1994).

In Egypt, national labour force data for 1998 show that female informal workers were consistently paid less than their male counterparts across all education levels (El-Mahdi and Amer, 2003). In South Africa, the 2000 Labour Force Survey found that female informal workers were also consistently paid less than their male counterparts, except in mining and in domestic work where they were paid roughly the same. Among informal workers, the lowest discrepancy between male and female workers was among transport workers followed closely by construction and manufacturing. But the average informal wages for men and women within these sectors mask the fact that in mining, the few women that are employed work primarily as nurses and administrative workers (not labourers); in transport, women are mainly in administration; and in construction, very few women are employed (Debbie Budlender, personal communication). This points to the need to look at different employment statuses within economic sectors – to look, that is, at segmentation in the informal economy (as above).

Recent comparative surveys in Bangladesh and in Tanzania provide some telling insights into the gender gaps in earnings.[12] In both countries, earnings are highest among employers, followed by own account workers and then wage workers, who earn the least (Table 6). With one exception, women earn less in each of these employment categories than men (the exception is that female employers in Tanzania earn more than male employers). The earning gap between women and men is considerably less in Tanzania than in Bangladesh. In Bangladesh, men own account workers earn more than three times the earnings of women own account workers, while male employers earn about four times more than female ones.[13]

As a result of this large earning gap in Bangladesh, a far

higher proportion (64%) of female own account workers than male own account workers (4%) are concentrated in the lowest income group (Dasgupta and Barbattini, 2003). This study also found that men in Bangladesh were far more likely than women to belong to the top income group – representing 93 per cent of this group. In Tanzania, where the gender gap is not so stark, men represented a far lower majority (55%) of the top income group.

Table 6: Monthly Mean Earnings by Employment Status in Bangladesh and Tanzania, 2001 (in US$)[a]

	Own Account Work			Wage Workers			Employer		
	Women	Men	Total	Women	Men	Total	Women	Men	Total
Bangladesh	18.81	61.35	49.56	61.69	71.44	69.65	27.29	114.84	98.70
(Number)	(355)	(925)	(1279)	(211)	(939)	(1151)	(292)	(1294)	(1586)
Tanzania	30.59	41.11	35.68	78.60	91.70	86.73	129.37	112.98	119.10
(Number)	(1349)	(1265)	(2614)	(196)	(320)	(516)	(88)	(148)	(236)

Source: Dasgupta and Barbattini, 2003 and additional calculations provided by authors
Note: [a]Data based on a question on net earnings in the previous month

Hidden Costs of Informal Employment

The precarious nature of informal employment has significant implications for hours worked and income earned and thus the economic well-being of these workers. Workers in informal employment tend to be underemployed, in that most of them either work fewer hours than desired or than normal, or work longer hours to attain a minimum wage. In addition, they face seasonal fluctuations in work and often need to take on multiple jobs.

Underemployment

A recent study in El Salvador found that underemployment characterised a large proportion of the labour force. By 2002 almost two in three workers involuntarily worked less than 40 hours per week, or worked more than 40 hours but earned less than minimum wage. Of these 86 per cent worked *overtime* (>40 hrs per week) but were paid below the minimum wage,

Workers in informal employment tend to be underemployed, in that most of them either work fewer hours than desired or than normal, or work longer hours to attain a minimum wage. In addition, they face seasonal fluctuations in work and often need to take on multiple jobs.

and 14 per cent involuntarily worked *undertime* (<40 hrs per week) (Lara, 2004:25–26). Further, 31 per cent of women were underemployed while 28 per cent of men were.

In Egypt, informal workers work over-time, but without extra compensation, to meet production demands and/or to earn sufficient wages, and they work longer hours on average than formal workers (El Mahdi and Amer, 2003:23).

A survey in 2000 of 611 workers in urban areas and 625 workers in rural areas of Gujarat state, India, suggests that, as might be expected, formal salaried workers enjoy the most days of work per year on average. Within the informal workforce, the self-employed enjoy more days of work per year on average than casual day labourers or homeworkers (Unni and Rani, 2002):

Casual workers = 254 days
Piece-rate workers = 259 days
Self-employed: agriculture = 338 days
Self-employed: non-agriculture = 321 days
Salaried = 354 days

However, these average figures disguise deep pockets of severe underemployment, defined in this study as less than 150 working days per year. Among each of these categories, a sub-set of workers had far fewer days of work per year.

Casual workers: 36.3 per cent worked an average of 137 days
Piece-rate workers: 24.7 per cent worked an average of 113 days
Self-employed: agriculture: 7.5 per cent worked an average of 134 days
Self-employed: non-agriculture: 9.8 per cent worked an average of 67 days
Salaried: 1.4 per cent worked an average of 37 days

What is striking is that severe underemployment appears to be both more pervasive and more intense among the self-employed engaged in non-agricultural activities than among the self-employed engaged in agriculture activities (which are widely recognised to be highly seasonal).

Seasonality of work

There is a seasonal dimension to many occupations in the informal economy, both urban and rural. In Ahmedabad City, India, for example, there are marked seasonal fluctuations in the supply and price of different varieties of fruits, vegetables and other fresh produce that street vendors purchase and sell. Also, the demand for fruits and vegetables rises in summer, falls during the monsoon and winter months and peaks during the major festivals and the wedding season. Similarly, the demand for garments typically falls in summer, rises in winter and peaks just before (and drops sharply after) the major annual festivals and the wedding season. During the monsoon season, the lack of sun and dry spells disrupts many occupations: outside construction work; screen printing, block printing and cloth dyeing; laundry services; pepper or spice drying; and incense stick rolling. Although few women who rolls *bidis* (hand-made cigarettes) suspend their work during the monsoon season, many complain that mildew grows on the leaves in which the tobacco is rolled (Chen and Snodgrass, 2001).

There are few measures and little data to capture the impact of these risks and dynamics on the income and well-being of the working poor. In the 2000 survey in Gujarat state, India, many informal workers reported that their work was irregular: 44 per cent of casual workers, 27 per cent of homeworkers, 12 per cent of self-employed in agriculture and 9 per cent of self-employed in non-agriculture. In marked contrast, less than 1 per cent of the formal salaried workers reported irregular work (Unni and Rani, 2002).

Multiple activities

To earn a living it is often necessary for workers in informal employment to have two or more jobs simultaneously or from season to season. Women, for example, are more often than men involved in secondary activities for the processing of agricultural and food products that they may sell in the market or use at home (Charmes and Unni, 2003).

Evidence suggests that the increase in informal employment has been accompanied by an increase in multiple job holding. For example, in Mali in 1989, 15 per cent of those

To earn a living it is often necessary for workers in informal employment to have two or more jobs simultaneously or from season to season.

working in the informal sector were engaged in secondary jobs; by 1996 the percentage had grown to 21 per cent. Similarly, in Burkina Faso in 1985, one quarter of the labour force were engaged in secondary activities; by 1995 the percentage had risen to one third (Charmes and Unni, 2003).

The survey in Gujarat state, India, found that a high percentage of the self-employed in agriculture and of casual day labourers work at multiple activities in a single day and across the year as follows:

> Casual workers: 26% (day) + 42% (year)
> Piece-rate workers: 6% (day) + 18% (year)
> Self-employed – agriculture: 40% (day) + 51% (year)
> Self-employed – non-agriculture: 15% (day) + 27% (year)
> Salaried workers: 20% (day) + 22% (year)

Whether multiple activities are a measure of labour market security or insecurity is a matter of debate or perspective. Those who study labour markets as aggregate abstractions tend to consider multiple activities as a measure of labour market security. Those who work with low-income workers tend to see multiple activities as a symptom of – a response to – labour market insecurity. From the perspective of the working poor in the informal economy, increasing work hours, taking on multiple activities and diversifying sources of income are seen as both protection from financial risk and a source of additional income or earnings. In other words, while the informal workforce often intensifies or diversifies their work out of necessity, they recognise the long-term benefits of doing so (Chen and Snodgrass, 2001).

Occupational health hazards

Workers in the informal economy are subject to a range of occupational health hazards. In India, the National Commission on Self-Employed Women and Women in the Informal Sector identified the following:

- the *posture of work* (*bidi* workers, home-based craft workers, cashew and coir workers, agriculture workers, fish processors);
- being in contact with *hazardous materials* (workers in match, fireworks, glass, slate pencil and ceramic factories);

- their *work environment* (lack of light, latrines, water, space, shelter);

- lifting *weights* (head loaders, mine and quarry workers, construction workers, hand cart pullers);

- *long hours* of work (piece-rate workers, vendors, hawkers);

- *repetitiveness of movements* (*agarbati* (incense-stick), *papad* (snack food) and *bidi* rollers, tie and dye, block printers, screen printers);

- *technology* (especially when new technology is introduced without training opportunities); and

- *mental health* (constant fear and tension of sexual assault, police, contractor, loss of jobs, eviction, indebtedness, semi-unemployment). (Shramshakti, 1988)

In brief, this analysis has highlighted certain qualitative dimensions of employment that are 'hidden costs' of working informally. Based on the evidence summarised above, as well as evidence that will be presented in Chapter 3, these ' hidden costs' include:

- high cost of doing business, including indirect taxes;
- great insecurity of work and incomes;
- high exposure to work-related risks;
- no health, disability, property, unemployment or life insurance;
- few (if any) worker rights and benefits, such as paid sick leave, overtime compensation or severance notice and pay;
- little (if any) employment-based social protection;
- limited (if any) access to formal sources of capital;
- high indebtedness to informal sources of capital;
- uncertain legal status; and
- lack of organisation.

MAINSTREAMING INFORMAL EMPLOYMENT AND GENDER IN POVERTY REDUCTION

The Global Horticulture Value Chain: An Illustrative Case Study[14]

How do all of these dimensions of work play themselves out in the work lives of actual women and men? To illustrate these complex realities, consider the case of horticulture workers in Chile and South Africa.[15] The export of horticulture produce – notably grapes, apples and pears – from both Chile and South Africa increased dramatically during the 1990s. In both countries, most fruit for export is produced on medium-size commercial farms, while relatively little is produced either on large-scale plantations or on small farms. Figure 3 outlines the fruit value chain from Chile and South Africa to the UK.

Figure 3: Overview of Global Value Chain for South African and Chilean Deciduous Fruit

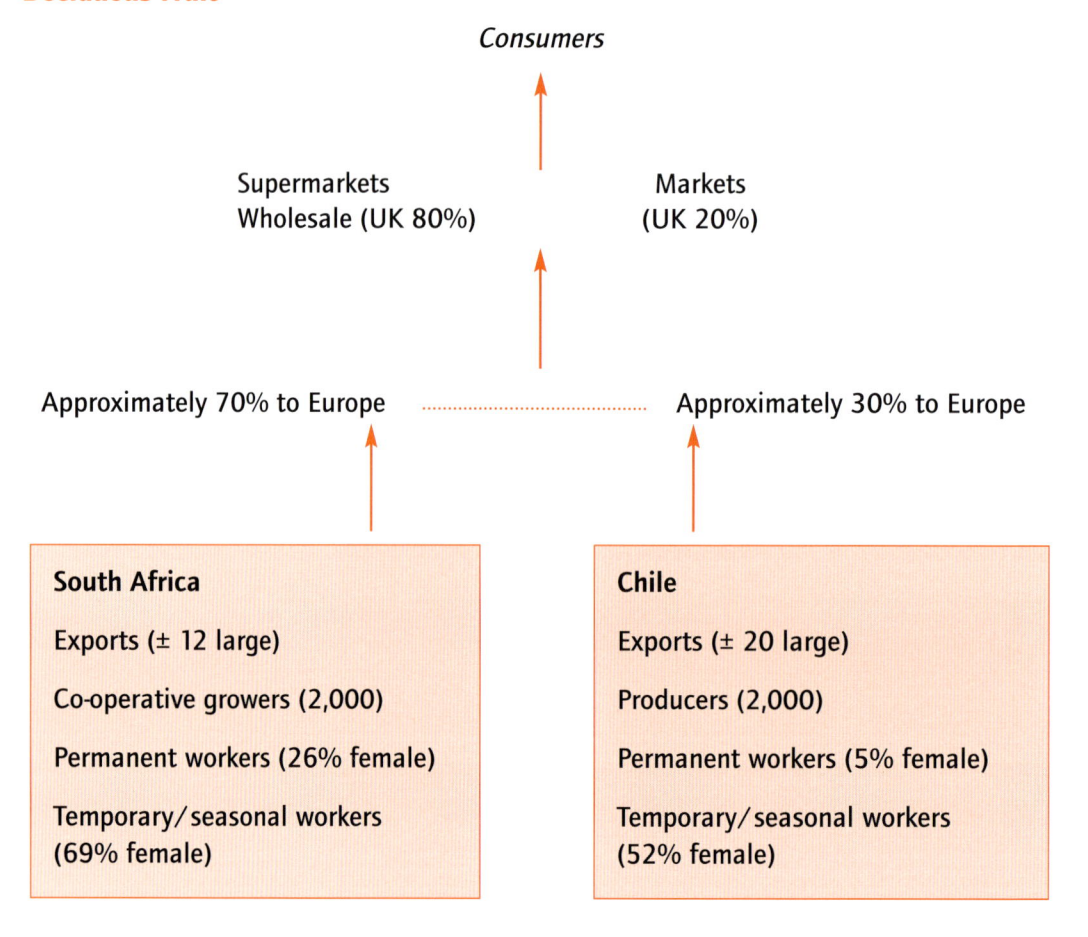

Consumers

↑

Supermarkets   Markets
Wholesale (UK 80%)   (UK 20%)

↑

Approximately 70% to Europe .... Approximately 30% to Europe

↑   ↑

South Africa

Exports (± 12 large)

Co-operative growers (2,000)

Permanent workers (26% female)

Temporary/seasonal workers (69% female)

Chile

Exports (± 20 large)

Producers (2,000)

Permanent workers (5% female)

Temporary/seasonal workers (52% female)

Employment in the horticulture sector

Continuum of employment relationships

At the production end of the value chain, employment is concentrated in growing and packing. Here, there is diversity and flexibility, with a relatively low level of formal employment and a high level of informal employment (see Box 5). The workforce is predominantly female. Once the produce leaves the packhouse, it enters the 'cool chain' distribution funnel, which is highly capital-intensive. The retail end of the chain is much more labour intensive. Here again, high levels of female employment dominate.

Box 5 Continuum of Employment Relationships: Horticultural Sector (Chile and South Africa)

Formal Employment

- Permanent work (a small core usually with contracts of employment);
- Regular temporary or seasonal work (with or without contracts of employment);
- Casual and irregular work for short periods of the season or on a daily basis (with or often without contracts);
- Contract labour employed by a third party labour contractor (often without contracts);
- Migrant labour employed directly or through a contractor (often without contracts);
- Small holder production, often involving family labour (paid or unpaid).

Informal Employment

Source: Lund and Nicholson, 2003:35

Estimates for the two countries suggest that most employment in the horticulture sector (from 65–85 per cent) is temporary or seasonal rather than permanent, and that most permanent

In the horticulture sector ... in South Africa, men form the bulk of permanent workers (74 per cent) while women form the bulk of temporary or seasonal workers (69 per cent).

workers are men (74 per cent in South Africa and 95 per cent in Chile) (see Table 7). Specifically, in South Africa, men form the bulk of permanent workers (74 per cent) while women form the bulk of temporary or seasonal workers (69 per cent).

Table 7: Estimates of Employment in Horticulture Retailing Value Chain in Chile and South Africa and Share of Temporary and Female Employment

	Number Employed	Per cent Temporary	Per cent Female
South African deciduous fruit	283,000	65–75%	26% of permanent 69% of temporary
Chilean fruit	336,700	85%	5% of permanent 53% of temporary

Sources: Kritzinger, Prozesky et al, 1995; Barrientos, McClenaghan et al, 1999; Barrientos, Dolan and Tallontire, 2001; de Klerk (date unknown) – as published in Lund and Nicholson, 2003.

Forms of wage payment

Forms of wage payment within the sector are varied and can change according to the individual employer, tasks performed, form of employment, productivity of specific groups of or individual workers or the stage in the season. An individual worker with the same employer could receive different forms and levels of payment as the season progresses.

Payments to workers can be based on:

- fixed weekly wage rates;
- fixed daily wage rates for days worked;
- minimum fixed wage, plus bonuses according to overall productivity of team or enterprise;
- minimum fixed wage, plus piece rate according to productivity of individual;
- piece rates only, based on productivity of work team or individual worker.

Only permanent workers receive payments all year round, and

they are more likely to be paid a standard weekly wage. Informal workers are more likely to be paid on a piece-rate basis. Also, they receive no income for the long periods of out of season unemployment. Temporary workers manage to work an average of four months per year in agriculture. Wages are low and variable, and workers complain that they are not always paid in full, so that income poverty is widespread, especially among women workers.

- In the Western Cape, South Africa (where deciduous fruit is dominant) average farm worker earnings in cash were approximately R720 per month. This was above the average cash wage for farm workers in the country as a whole of R544 per month. Contract workers earned between R440 and R1,320 per month depending on their task and the stage of the season. It is estimated that the wage needed to put an average household above the poverty line is R650 per month. Some contract workers, therefore, would be earning below the recommended minimum wage for their district and below the average wage necessary to keep a household above the poverty line. Supervisors in contract teams could earn up to R500 per week.[16]

- In Chile, half of the male and 60 per cent of the female temporary workers in agriculture receive wages below the set minimum wage.

Unemployment and underemployment

Unemployment and underemployment are very significant risks for those in informal employment in horticulture. There is a high incidence of unemployment among seasonal workers and, since production is concentrated in remote farm areas, there are few opportunities for off-season employment, making it difficult for temporary or seasonal workers to earn a livelihood. Unemployment is a particular problem in South Africa, which is shedding its permanent agricultural workforce.

Horticulture workers and income poverty

Income poverty occurs when income is insufficient to cover basic household needs. This risk affects all workers to a degree, but is particularly acute for households of informal workers, as this horticulture case study suggests. Compared to women permanent workers, women temporary workers are over-represented in the lower income quintiles and under-represented in the higher income quintiles: these quintiles are based on the nationwide income distribution. The difference in average per capita income between permanent and temporary workers captures the risks arising from informality.

A further measure of poverty risk is the proportion of women temporary workers whose per capita household income is below the *poverty line* (basic subsistence income) and the *indigence line* (basic food costs). In 1998, 20 per cent of women temporary workers in Chile had per capita household incomes below the poverty line and 4 per cent had per capita household incomes below the indigence line (Lund and Nicholson, 2003:39).

Gender Segmentation of the Informal Economy and Poverty

What this chapter has shown is the significance of informal employment in the work life of women and men and the differences in the situation of women and men in informal employment, both in terms of what they do and what they earn. This chapter has also provided a conceptual framework for thinking about the linkages between working in the informal economy, being a woman or man and being poor. While segmentation within the formal labour market has long been recognised, segmentation within the informal labour market is only now being appreciated. With the new, broader definition of the informal economy has come the understanding that there are different types of informal jobs as well as different types of informal enterprises.

As this chapter has also shown, the data available today on the relationship between working in the informal economy, being a woman or man and being poor are limited. What data are available confirm the relationship between working in the informal economy and being poor, with the notable exception of the employers who hire others, many of whom are quite well off. Also, the available data confirm that women who work in the informal economy are more likely than men to be poor because of where they are situated within it. There is, clearly, a need for more countries to collect data on informal employment and to link these data to earnings data and to data on household income and expenditure (as the studies summarised in this chapter have tried to do).

Our hope is that the conceptual framework presented here will be used: (a) to collect more data on the links between gender segmentation of the informal economy, poverty and inequality; and (b) to design appropriate policy and action responses to the 'hidden costs' of working informally. There is a need for improved data to capture these hidden costs. Such data would enhance our understanding of what it will take for the poor – and in particular the differential requirements for women and men – to work their way out of poverty and/or for their enterprises to be successful. But the lack of statistical data on the hidden costs of working informally should not stand in the way of taking the essential next step of formulating policy.

In sum, we see a need to integrate an understanding of both the gender segmentation of the informal economy and the 'hidden costs' of informal employment into poverty reduction strategies. Indeed, we see these hidden costs – or what the ILO calls the 'decent work deficits' of working informally – as key to fully understanding who is poor and why, and what can be done to reduce the various dimensions of their poverty. Chapter 3 will explore these relationships in the context of recent economic changes.

Notes

1 The formal or modern sector is comprised of regulated small and large enterprises (operating out of factories and/or offices) and of regular, stable and protected employment. Fifty years ago, most economists assumed that economic growth would lead to increased labour demand and eventual transformation of all economic activity into the modern or formal sector: classical economists assumed that surplus labour would be absorbed (Lewis, 1954); neo-classical economists assumed a shift to skilled labour and capital-intensive activities; and industrial economists assumed a shift in the location of production from households to small units to big firms.

2 Non-standard work is the general term used in OECD countries for forms of work that are not full-time wage employment for one employer on a known schedule or contract, including self-employment, part-time work, temporary work and various forms of casual day labour or contract work. The majority of these workers receive few (if any) employment-based benefits or protection. Informal employment is the general term used in developing countries for forms of work that are not protected by labour or social protection legislation, including self-employment, various forms of casual day labour, homework as well as 'employees' (full-time or part-time) of informal enterprises. In this Handbook, we use the term 'informal employment' to include those forms of non-standard work in both OECD and developing countries that are not covered by employment-based benefits or protections.

3 WIEGO is a global research and policy analysis network linked to the international movement of women in the informal economy. See Chapter 4.

4 Those temporary and part-time workers who are covered by labour legislation and statutory social protection benefits are not included in the informal economy.

5 What is presented here includes all readily available official data on the informal economy. While some key Commonwealth countries are included, notably India, Kenya and South Africa, the fact that more Commonwealth countries are not included reflects the fact that few countries have regularly collected official statistics on informal employment.

6 This section draws from a statistical booklet that Martha Chen and Joann Vanek prepared in 2002 for the ILO that includes data compiled by Jacques Charmes for anywhere from 25–70 countries, depending on the specific estimate, as well as case studies for India, Mexico, South Africa and OECD countries written by, respectively, Jeemol Unni, Rodrigo Negrete, Debbie Budlender and Francoise Carre (ILO, 2002b). Data available since 2002 were supplied by Jacques Charmes.

7 Unfortunately, the Task Force on Poverty of the Millennium Project has, to date, neither put employment in its recommended initiatives nor 'mainstreamed' the recommendations of the Task Force on Gender Equality in its own recommendations (see Millennium Project Task Force on Poverty, 2004).

8 A related phenomenon, which deserves more study, is the concentration of certain racial or ethnic groups, as well as immigrant populations, in the informal economy. For example, in South Africa, 85 per cent of all workers in the informal sector are black (NALDEI, 2003). Similarly, according to a 1989 household survey in Guatemala, indigenous workers are 4.3 times more likely to be working in the informal sector than in the formal sector (Funkhouser, 1996).

9 While the findings of both studies may not be surprising, there are very few empirical analyses linking household poverty and employment in this way.
10 These studies are co-ordinated by the Global Policy Network of the Economic Policy Institute in Washington, DC under a comparative workforce development project funded by the Ford Foundation.
11 While this Handbook takes up segmentation of the informal economy by gender, it is important to note that in many countries and contexts the informal economy is also segmented by race or ethnicity.
12 It should be noted that these studies did not differentiate between formal and informal employment within the employer and wage worker categories. The own account category was entirely informal, comprised of those who work on their own account and do not hire others.
13 Historically, in Bangladesh, most women were confined by norms of seclusion to work in and around homesteads, carrying out domestic chores and post-harvest activities for themselves or others. Unless forced to by necessity, they did not work in the public sphere – in fields, on roads or in markets. During and after the famine of 1974, significant numbers of women began to seek remunerative work outside their home, including – initially – in public works programmes (Chen and Ghuznani, 1979) With the establishment of the export garment industry in the 1980s, large (and visible) numbers of women began working in factories for the first time.
14 Global value chains are discussed more fully in Chapter 3 under 'The Production System'
15 This section is based on the summary of a case study in Lund and Nicholson, 2003. See Barrientos and Ware Barrientos, 2002 for the full-length case study.
16 The minimum wage for agriculture is currently under consideration and a key recommendation is a scale from R400 to R750 per month depending on the magisterial district.

3. The Changing World of Work: Linking Economic Reforms–Gender–Poverty

... the majority of workers in today's world do not work in what are still widely considered to be 'standard' jobs: those with secure contracts, mandated benefits and social protection.

In the last two decades many governments have undertaken a set of market-oriented reforms designed to restructure their economies and to integrate them globally. At the same time technological change, especially the spread of new information and communications technologies (ICTs) has accelerated the pace of reform and associated changes, including the reorganisation of production. The poverty and other social outcomes of these economic forces have been, and still are being, hotly debated. But there is growing recognition that they are two-edged forces, bringing both opportunities and constraints and creating both winners and losers. They can offer many opportunities for poverty reduction provided that steps are taken to enable the poor to gain rather than lose from the changes involved. On the other hand, they can leave poorer countries of the world – and the poorer sections of the population within them – worse off than before.

The consequences for the working poor depend on who they are, what they do and where they work. Most countries around the world have experienced profound changes in the nature of work, the employment arrangements of working women and men and the structure of the labour market. The net result has been that the majority of workers in today's world do not work in what are still widely considered to be 'standard' jobs: those with secure contracts, mandated benefits and social protection.

The connection between non-standard jobs, informal work and informalisation comes under the general heading of 'labour market flexibility'. While this is frequently advocated as a necessary economic adjustment strategy for economies in this era of global integration, the social costs are often ignored. This is not to argue that all forms of non-standard and informal work – or informalisation – necessarily imply a lack of or reduction in the welfare of working people. However, the variety of different work arrangements, and their poverty and inequality outcomes, underscores the need to identify and track context-specific changes in work arrangements as well as the associated costs and benefits.

In Chapter 3, we attempt to shed light on the linkages between economic reforms, the changing nature of work (particularly informal employment) and social outcomes (notably in terms of poverty and gender inequality). We focus primarily on the effects of trade liberalisation – i.e. the reduction of barriers such as quotas and licenses to the free flow of goods and services – and to a lesser extent on deregulation of labour markets and technological change. The chapter is divided into three parts:

- *Economic reforms and poverty.* Our analysis begins with a brief overview of three conceptual frameworks for considering the linkages between economic reforms, the changing nature of work and social outcomes: (a) neo-classical economics; (b) gender analysis; and (c) informal labour market analysis.

- *Trade and employment.* We then discuss two sets of common scenarios – one relating to the *quantity* of employment and the other to the *terms and conditions* of employment – associated with trade liberalisation. These scenarios highlight the risks and costs associated with trade liberalisation for the working poor.

- *The changing nature of work.* Building on examples of the changing terms and conditions of employment, our analysis concludes with a discussion of the effects economic reforms have not only on specific categories of workers but also on the nature of work itself. We focus on three key dimensions of the changing nature of work – (a) place of work, (b) employment status and (c) production system – each of which has direct implications for poverty and gender equality outcomes. To illustrate these various patterns of change, we use findings and concrete examples from recent studies on the working poor, especially women, in the informal economy.

While various forms of gender bias are found throughout these complex linkages, we give special focus to the gender dimensions of informal employment. Working poor women are

Women and men are positioned differently within the informal workforce, not just within households or within formal employment. Working poor women are affected differently than working poor men by economic reforms due to their disadvantaged 'position' on all fronts.

affected differently than working poor men by economic reforms due to their disadvantaged 'position' on all fronts. This includes not only: (a) their disadvantaged status due to gender hierarchies within households; and (b) their differential access and command over resources within the household and the wider economy; but also (c) their concentration in lower-paying and more risky segments of the informal economy.[1]

These different forms of gender bias interact and hinder the ability of women to respond to economic reforms and thus limit the hoped-for economic growth and poverty reduction effects of these reforms. But the literatures on trade and poverty – and on trade and gender – have not paid sufficient attention to the informal economy, much less to the gender segmentation within it (described in Chapter 2).

As noted in Chapter 1, within the international development community there has been a long-standing and often

Women working on the land, Papua New Guinea
WORLD WIDE FUND FOR NATURE SOUTH PACIFIC PROGRAMME/ PETER SOLNESS

heated debate about the links between economic growth and poverty. During the 1980s, the focus of this debate was on structural adjustment and its impact on poverty. Over the past 15 years, as countries have opened their economies, it has shifted to globalisation in general and trade liberalisation in particular. Part of the current debate focuses on whether to consider short-term versus long-term costs and benefits, and whether countries should conform to the international 'rules' of global integration set by the International Monetary Fund (IMF) and World Bank.

In a special contribution to the *Human Development Report 2003* on poverty, globalisation and growth, Joseph Stiglitz observes that the debate should not be whether globalisation or growth are good or bad. Sometimes these help poor people and sometimes they do not. Rather, he argues, the debate should be about which policies would lead to the kind of growth that improves the welfare of poor people. The debate should centre, that is, on "the appropriateness of particular policies for particular countries, on how globalisation can be shaped (including the rules of the game) and on international economic institutions, to better promote growth and reduce poverty in the developing world" (Stiglitz, 2003a).

What this Handbook brings to this debate is a focus on the effects of trade liberalisation, deregulation and technological change on the working poor, especially women, in the informal economy – both the new opportunities as well as the associated stresses and risks. Tracing these effects on informal labour markets, where most of the poor (especially women) work, should allow us to draw some conclusions about what types of policies and institutions are needed to ensure that trade liberalisation and other economic processes have the desired effects of reducing poverty and gender inequality.

Economic Reforms and Poverty

Economic reforms

To set the stage for our analysis, we start with a brief description of the various reforms, highlighting key linkages to informal employment.

> *... privatisation of public-sector enterprises is often associated with large-scale retrenchment of workers. This may lead in turn to reduced demand for informal goods and services ... and increased competition within the informal economy.*

Economic restructuring

The standard package of economic reforms, designed to control inflation and encourage investment, includes: (a) privatisation; (b) stabilisation; and (c) deregulation. All three processes are likely to have specific consequences for those who work in the informal economy. For example, *privatisation* of public-sector enterprises is often associated with large-scale retrenchment of workers. This may lead in turn to reduced demand for informal goods and services (as the purchasing power of former public sector employees declines) and increased competition within the informal economy (as many retrenched workers end up working there).

As part of economic restructuring and liberalisation, there has been a fair amount of *deregulation*, particularly of financial and labour markets. Deregulation is seen to have contradictory effects. Hernando de Soto, among others, has argued that the deregulation of costly and cumbersome government regulations, which inhibit the ability of informal entrepreneurs to operate a business and earn a living, would lead to increased economic freedom and entrepreneurship among working people, especially in developing countries (de Soto, 1989). More recently, he has advocated one form of regulation: the *formalisation* of property rights for the informal workforce to help them convert their informally-held assets into real assets (de Soto, 2000).

Deregulation of labour markets, however, is associated with the rise of informalisation or 'flexible' labour markets. Labour advocates have argued for some *re-regulation* to protect informal wage workers from the economic risks and uncertainty associated with flexibility. At the same time, the regulatory environment often overlooks whole categories of the informal economy. A *missing* regulatory environment can be as bad as an *excessive* regulatory environment. For example, city governments around the world tend to take either of two stances towards street trade: trying to eliminate it or turning a 'blind eye' to it. Either stance has a punitive effect: eviction or constant harassment (by police, municipal officials and other vested interests). Arguably, what is needed in such instances is *appropriate regulation*, not complete deregulation.[2]

Economic integration

The global integration of national economies includes the liberalisation of different markets: capital, goods and services and labour. In this Handbook, we focus on the liberalisation of the markets for goods and services – that is, on trade liberalisation – and on the liberalisation (or lack thereof) of labour markets. In regard to labour markets, it should be noted that workers are caught between two contradictory trends: *rapid flexibilisation* of the employment relationship (making it easy for employers to contract and expand their workforce as needed) and *slow liberalisation* of labour mobility (making it difficult for labour to move quickly and easily across borders).[3]

Technological change

Technological change contributes to – and is reinforced by – trade liberalisation and economic growth. Like other processes, it can have both positive and negative effects on the working poor. Increased mechanisation in the agricultural, manufacturing and construction sectors has led to the loss of jobs for millions of low-skilled workers, particularly women. At the same time, technological change can increase the demand for skilled workers. The net overall impact in terms of overall rates of employment (or unemployment) is thus hard to determine. Similarly, the impact of technological change on the relative wages of skilled and unskilled labour is not clear, though some studies suggest that it widens the wage gap between the two (Amadeo, 1998). The evidence presented in this chapter is on observed effects of technological change on specific groups of the working poor in the informal economy and thus offers only a partial picture.

By far the most profound – and publicised – technological change is the advent of global telecommunications and the widespread availability of the computer/Internet. These are altering in profound ways pre-existing economic, social, cultural, political and institutional arrangements. Again, this has had positive and negative effects for the working poor. Most notably, perhaps, information and communications technologies (ICTs) have facilitated outsourcing of jobs and industrial restructuring into global production systems. The new ICTs also hold out the promise of increased incomes for the self-employed in the informal economy – particularly in respect of

> *... workers are caught between two contradictory trends:* rapid flexibilisation *of the employment relationship (making it easy for employers to contract and expand their workforce as needed) and* slow liberalisation *of labour mobility (making it difficult for labour to move quickly and easily across borders).*

providing an increased source of information on domestic and global markets. But the working poor, especially women, have greater difficulties than the non-poor in benefiting from this resource because of their more limited access to computers, to training in their use and to education in general.

At the same time, the new ICTs hold out the promise of increased networking and solidarity between informal workers. This can be seen in their growing international alliances, including those of homeworkers and street vendors (HomeNet and StreetNet); the international network of trade unions and other membership-based organisations that are organising informal workers; and the global research policy network called Women in Informal Employment: Globalizing and Organizing (WIEGO) (see Chapter 4).

Conceptual frameworks

Conceptualising how economic reforms more generally – or trade liberalisation in particular – impinge on poverty is not straightforward. What follows is a brief comparison of three theoretical perspectives on these linkages: (a) neo-classical economics; (b) gender analysis; and (c) informal labour market analysis.

(a) Neo-classical economics

Most orthodox trade economists subscribe to what has been called the '*factor-abundance*' model of trade. According to this model, developing countries should specialise in producing goods that require their abundant factor of production (i.e. low skilled labour), while developed countries should specialise in producing goods that utilise their abundant factor (i.e. skilled labour or capital). According to the predictions of this model, demand for labour-intensive production would expand in developing countries, raising employment and wages. In developed countries, consumers would benefit from cheaper goods (and buy more of them). Similarly, developing countries would be able to import capital-intensive goods (or skill-intensive goods) at lower prices than could be produced without trade. In brief, according to this model, trade liberalisation will allow countries to leverage their comparative advantages, which will increase economic growth and lead to higher standards of living for their citizens. In particular, free trade will be good for low-wage workers in developing countries.

Over the last 20 years, many neo-classical economists have recognised that reality is more complex than this model would suggest and have begun to look at the role of social, political and economic institutions in the relationship between trade and poverty. What follows here is brief summary of a widely-cited analytical framework developed by L. Alan Winters for understanding how trade liberalisation is transmitted into poverty outcomes at the household level (Winters, 2000). There are three main pathways or channels: (i) *distribution* (i.e. changes in prices), (ii) *government* (i.e. changes in taxes and spending) and (iii) *enterprises* (i.e. changes in investment, production and employment) (see Figure 4).

To benefit the poor, policies complementary to existing trade policies may be needed to establish markets, improve competition and deepen market integration.

Figure 4: Trade Policy and Poverty – Pathways of Impact

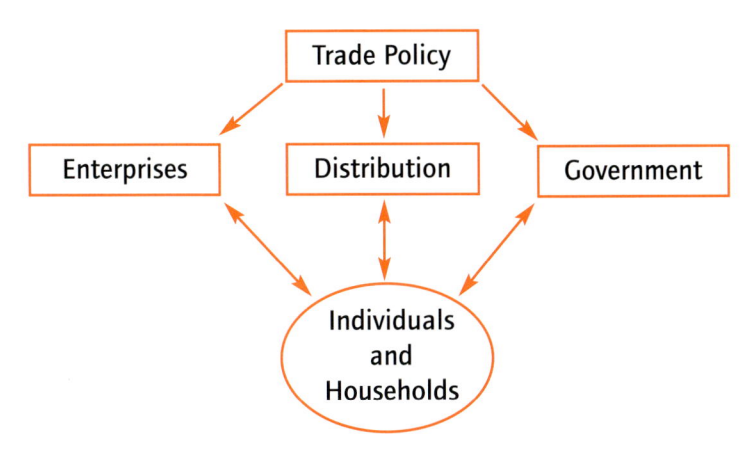

```
            Trade Policy
           /     |     \
          ↓      ↓      ↓
   Enterprises  Distribution  Government
          ↘      ↕      ↙
              Individuals
                 and
              Households
```

Source: Winters, 2000

(i) Distribution: The first effect of trade liberalisation is to change the relative world prices of both *imported* and *exported goods*. In the case of imported goods, these are transmitted from the border down to the household through wholesale and retail prices; in the case of exported goods, these are transmitted in the reverse direction. In general, assuming households both produce and consume goods, increased prices are seen to benefit net producers while decreased prices benefit net consumers. However, since some goods are used as inputs in the production of other goods, and since not all social groups are associated with products whose prices change, the net effect is often quite complicated (Winters, 2000; DFID, 2003). Moreover, the price changes associated with trade liberalisation are not always transmitted to the poor, and markets for goods may be created or destroyed. To benefit the poor, policies complementary to existing trade policies may be needed to establish markets, improve competition and deepen market integration (McCulloch et al, 2001).

(ii) Government: Trade liberalisation may also affect poverty through changes in the government's fiscal policies, particularly if trade taxation is an important source of revenue. This is because trade liberalisation is associated with reduced *trade-related taxes*. The net effect on the poor depends on the types of substitute taxes introduced, the subsequent level of government revenue and the level and pattern of government spending, especially pro-poor spending. The poor may not suffer if alternative sources of taxes do not target them, if the overall level of revenue is not cut and if social and anti-poverty programmes can be at least partially protected even if expenditure does decline. Moreover, good macroeconomic planning may well be more important for maintaining social spending than trade taxation (McCulloch et al, 2001).

(iii) Enterprises: Trade liberalisation also affects households through its impact on profits and hence on employment and wages. It is seen to encourage increased investment, which leads in turn to increased *production*. Orthodox economic theory suggests two scenarios regarding how increased investment and production affect wages and employment (the two variables of most relevance to poverty):

- in contexts where labour is fully employed and wages are flexible, the price changes caused by trade liberalisation will be reflected in changes in wages, with employment staying the same;

- where there is a large pool of workers who move in and out of employment depending on the circumstances, then trade liberalisation will cause changes in employment but not wages.

In reality, there will be a combination of these effects. How this affects poverty depends not only on how employment changes, but also on the types of labour that poor households can supply and whether the resultant changes in wage rates translate into per capital household incomes that fall above or below the poverty line (McCulloch et al, 2001).

In addition to these three main pathways, Winters suggests a fourth pathway between trade liberalisation and poverty outcomes: the effects of trade on the riskiness of household livelihoods. Households may become more vulnerable to risks as a result of switching their economic activities in response to trade liberalisation. Whether the change reduces or enhances welfare depends on whether or not the switch is voluntary and generates higher returns (McCulloch et al, 2001). The Winters framework also takes into account intra-household dynamics and gender in considering how changes in prices, taxes and spending, enterprises and risks translate into poverty outcomes at the individual level – though not to the degree that gender analysis does (see below).[4]

Finally, as Winters notes, the framework does not address the two other key ways in which trade liberalisation affects poverty: *economic growth* and *short-term adjustment costs*. Potentially the most important effect of trade liberalisation on poverty is through its impact on growth. Furthermore, the reason why trade liberalisation generates so much public controversy is often due to the short- and medium-term adjustments costs, including job losses in formerly protected sectors. Much of the public debate about trade and poverty has become unclear because of the confusion of issues of growth and adjustment with issues of trade. To avoid this confusion, the Winters framework focuses on the important channels through which trade liberalisation per se can affect the lives of the poor (Winters, 2000).

(b) *Gender analysis*

Gender analysis is the analysis of the social construction of the roles, relationships, power and entitlements of women and men. Applied to the field of economics, it starts with the premise that the standard notion of the 'economy' needs to be expanded to include non-market activities and unpaid work, notably the reproductive economy (Kanji and Barrientos,

> *Gender biases in the economic arena get transmitted through a variety of institutions – not only the family but also, less obviously, markets and the state. These often perpetuate gender bias through a host of economic policies, including macroeconomic, trade and labour-market policies.*

2001). It goes on to argue that neither the productive nor the reproductive economy is gender neutral. Rather, the entire economy is seen as gendered, as follows (Elson et al, 1997):

- ***macro level***: gender divisions in paid employment and unpaid time use;
- ***meso level***: gendered laws, norms and rules; gender-differentiated entitlements and access; gender-based price distortions and institutional biases; and
- ***micro level***: gender divisions in roles, responsibilities and power.

Gender analysis shows how the standard notion of the household in economics needs to be changed to incorporate (i) more than one breadwinner, (ii) gender-differentiated flows of income and consumption and (iii) gender (and age) hierarchies of preferences and bargaining power.

Gender biases in the economic arena get transmitted through a variety of institutions – not only the family but also, less obviously, markets and the state. These often perpetuate gender bias through a host of economic policies, including macroeconomic, trade and labour-market policies (see, for example, Cagatay, Elson and Grown, 1995; Grown, Elson and Cagatay, 2000; Whitehead, 2001). Gender biases in financial, labour and goods markets act as barriers to the working poor, especially women, being able to take up opportunities afforded by trade liberalisation (Elson and Evers, 1996). With particular reference to sub-Saharan Africa, these biases operate as follows:

- ***Financial markets*** tend to discriminate against women, with requirement for collateral and, in some contexts, male signatories. Despite the introduction of special credit schemes for women, disparities in credit allocation remain high.
- ***Labour markets*** tend to be segmented, with women's participation in both formal and more informal activities confined to particular areas, usually the less lucrative. At the informal end of employment, women tend to be concentrated in the easy entry, smaller enterprise, low start-up costs and low returns end of the market. In the agricultural labour force, women tend to be categorised as 'unpaid'

family workers rather than 'self-employed', which implies that women's labour is treated as a free good rather than a scarce resource.

- **Goods markets** tend to be biased towards exports rather than locally traded goods and services where women may be more engaged. Men tend to control mechanised means of transport and have greater access to market information than women. Despite women's labour inputs, in some contexts men control the cash for export crops.

Box 6 summarises some of the key points that gender analysis makes about the relationship between trade, gender and poverty.

Box 6 Key Points Raised in Gender Analysis

Some of the key points raised in gender analysis regarding the relationship between trade, gender and poverty can be summarised as follows:

- Economic reforms can lead to poverty outcomes because of the gendered structure of the economy.
- The price, tax/spending and employment effects of economic reforms work their way through institutions such as markets, enterprises and households in a gendered way.
- Gender bias in financial, goods and labour markets acts as a barrier to women's ability to take up opportunities afforded by economic reforms.
- Gender divisions in roles, responsibilities and power mean that women and men are not equally positioned to respond to opportunities or overcome constraints associated with economic reforms.
- Gender-differentiated entitlements mean that women tend to have less ownership of, control over or access to resources than men.
- The gender hierarchy within the household means that women tend to have less control over how income and food are allotted within the household.

One strand of gender studies has analysed the links between trade liberalisation and women's employment.[5] These links are quite complex. For example, in the manufacturing sector trade is associated with an increase in women's paid employment in developing countries and a decrease in women's paid employment in developed countries. However, the shifts in employment between the global North and South do not necessarily involve one-for-one gains and losses (Gammage et al, 2002). Employment in the manufacturing sector in the industrialised North is more likely to be *formal*: that is, workers are more likely to have contracts, to be covered by labour legislation and standards and to enjoy health benefits and pensions. Employment in the export manufacturing sector in the developing South is more likely to be *informal*: that is, workers are not likely to have contracts, fair wages or benefits. This is particularly true for homeworkers in global value chain production[6] and for contingent workers who get temporarily dismissed and rehired to meet the ebbs and flows of the production cycle. It is also the case for workers in the assembly factories in export processing zones (EPZs), where employers are often exempted from following labour standards and regulations or providing benefits.[7] Moreover, recent evidence suggests that the export-oriented manufacturing sector in many developing countries is becoming more skill-intensive and, in the process, is being defeminised (see sections on Manufacturing Sector and Production System below).

In predominantly agricultural economies, when the export of traditional crops increases, trade may disadvantage women compared to men. This is because trade tends to advantage large and medium producers. Small farmers, particularly women, often lack *access* to credit, new technologies and the marketing know-how needed to take advantage of new markets. Further, gender-based inequalities in *control* over resources such as land, credit and skills hinder women's ability to take advantage of new opportunities (Cagatay, 2001).

Reflecting these realities, there is often a negative relationship between feminisation of the workforce and relative wages (see Vasudeva-Dutta, 2004 for India; Dicken and Katz, 1987 for the US; Sequino, 1997 for the East-Asian 'Tiger' economies). Stephanie Sequino argues that feminisation of the labour force can increase the gender wage gap as women are disproportionately employed in 'footloose' or mobile industries, where the threat that the company will shift jobs to other sites makes it difficult for them to obtain higher wages (ibid). In addition to the mobility of the industries, the terms and conditions under which women are recruited – as unprotected workers in EPZ factories, as contingent workers or as homeworkers – further erodes their bargaining power.

In brief, gender analysis of the relationship between trade and women's employment highlights:

- the ways in which structural or cultural barriers constrain the free functioning of markets;

- the systemic gender biases that exist within financial, labour and goods markets, which limit the ability of women to take up new opportunities afforded by openness and growth of the economy; and

- the systemic gender biases that exist within the household, which mean that women are less well-positioned than men to seize opportunities and address constraints associated with trade and growth (Kanji and Barrientos, 2001).

However, the gender and trade literature tends to focus on women's work in export-oriented factories, especially in EPZs, to the relative neglect of homeworkers and self-employed women. Also, relatively few gender studies investigate the full sequence of gendered transmissions from trade through employment to poverty. They rarely adequately address changes in employment and production relations within the informal economy or trace the consequences of such changes through to poverty outcomes at either the individual or the household level. This Handbook seeks to help fill this gap by tracing the effects of trade liberalisation on working poor women through informal labour markets, thus adding an understanding of informal labour markets to the 'enterprises' channel in Winters' framework.

(c) Informal labour market analysis

Analysis of informal labour markets starts with the basic observation that labour markets in developing countries are often quite different from those in developed countries, with a far smaller formal economy and a large base of informal employ-

… labour markets in developing countries are often quite different from those in developed countries, with a far smaller formal economy and a large base of informal employment, including a relatively high share of self-employment.

ment, including a relatively high share of self-employment (Kurien, 1998). It suggests the need to:[8]

- distinguish between self-employment (and earnings) and paid employment (and wages), both formal and informal;

- question the relevance of unemployment (as opposed to under-employment) in countries that provide no unemployment insurance and few safety nets;

- recognise that labour markets are not perfectly integrated and competitive and that labour, as a factor of production, is not perfectly mobile – in this regard, there is a need to understand how both supply- and demand-side barriers may constrain the ability of labour to respond to new economic opportunities (especially when there are great asymmetries of knowledge, access and competitiveness); and

- extend the scope of labour market theory (and labour law) to apply to situations where the employer-employee relationship is disguised; where there is no fixed employer; or where there are multiple possible employers, such as in a sub-contracting chain or when an agency places workers with firms (ILO, 2003).

To illustrate, neo-classical economic theory suggests that as economies grow, the share of employment in informal enterprises (i.e. the informal sector) in total employment shrinks. Or, conversely, that employment in informal enterprises increases during business downturns. Generally, cross-country comparisons reveal a negative correlation between measured rates of informal employment (typically confined to employment in informal enterprises) and the level of per capital gross domestic product (GDP) (see, for example, Ihrig and Moe, 2000; Loayza, 1996). A recent review of official data in 14 Latin American and Caribbean countries supports this assumption: richer countries tend to have higher shares of formal employment, including public sector employment, while poorer countries tend to have higher shares of self-employment (a proxy for employment in informal enterprises) (Galli and Kucera, 2003).

Another recent review of official data for 20 countries in Asia, Africa and Latin America (compiled by Jacques Charmes) studied changes in the extent of informalisation (measured as informal employment over total employment)

Small farmer, Dominica
INTERNATIONAL FUND FOR
AGRICULTURAL DEVELOPMENT
(IFAD)/ROBERT GROSSMAN

with economic growth (Heintz and Pollin, 2002). It showed that growing informalisation is consistent with respectable levels of economic growth. Faster growth slows this rate of increase, and only at very high rates of growth does informalisation decline. While the review in Latin America and the Caribbean focused on the *absolute level* of informal employment, this review emphasised changes in the *extent* of informalisation. The authors conclude that various factors could contribute to these divergent observations, including variations in women's recorded labour supply, the composition of informal employment and the nature of the relationship between the formal and informal economies (ibid).

Similarly, a recent study in Tunisia, suggests the need to 'unpack' the informal economy to understand specific trends within these broader patterns. Business *upturns* in that country are associated with a rise in *informal wage jobs* (notably, homework under sub-contracts for large firms). Business *downturns* are associated with a rise in: (i) *independent informal firms*, as ties with formal firms are eroded or formal firms go out of business; and (ii) *survival activities*, as the newly unemployed and chronically underemployed compete for limited economic opportunities within the informal economy (Charmes and Lekehal, 2003: Table 11). In sum, this data suggests that different segments of informal employment – micro-enterprises, own account activities and homework – expand or contract under different economic conditions.

Box 7 Integrating Informal Labour Market and Gender Analyses

To integrate analysis of informal labour markets with gender analysis, the gendered propositions outlined in Box 6 would need to be amended, as follows:

- Economic reforms can lead to poverty outcomes because of imbalances in access, resources and power between capital and labour; between large, small and micro-enterprises; between formal and informal labour; and between women and men within each of these categories.

- The price, tax/spending and employment effects of economic reforms work their way through institutions such as markets, enterprises and households in different ways for capital and labour; for large, small and micro-enterprises; for formal and informal workers; and for women and men within each of these categories.

- Biases against labour, especially informal labour, within financial, goods and labour markets act as barriers that limit the ability of the working poor, notably informal workers and especially women, to take up opportunities afforded by economic reforms.

- Gender and class divisions in roles, responsibilities and power mean that capital, large enterprises, formal workers and men (within each of these categories) tend to be better-positioned than, respectively, labour, micro-enterprises, informal workers and women to respond to opportunities or to overcome constraints associated with economic reforms.

- Gender- and class-differentiated entitlements mean that capital, large enterprises, formal workers and men (within each of these categories) tend to have greater ownership of, control over or access to resources and to have greater bargaining power than, respectively, labour, micro-enterprises, informal workers and women (within each of these categories).

In regard to gender analysis, an understanding of informal labour markets points to the need to focus on several inter-linked and mutually-reinforcing biases, not just gender bias, in order to understand the linkages between gender and poverty. Integrating informal labour market and gender analysis suggests that:

- four inter-linked biases – favouring capital, formal enterprises, formal workers and men (over labour, informal enterprises, informal workers and women) – are likely to be reflected throughout the transmission process from economic reforms through the various pathways to poverty outcomes (see Box 7); and

- all of these biases affect policy outcomes in regard to both reducing poverty and increasing gender equality (see Box 29 in Chapter 5, which provides a framework for assessing these mutually-reinforcing biases in policies).

Thus the reality in developing countries is somewhat more complicated than prevailing neo-classical models would suggest, particularly if one takes into account gendered patterns of employment in informal labour markets. Most developing countries, more so in Asia than in Africa or Latin America, have an abundant supply of labour that, if not formally employed, moves in and out of *self-employment* and *informal paid employment*, depending on the circumstances. Moreover, since most developing countries do not provide universal unemployment insurance or social safety nets, most of the working poor cannot afford to remain unemployed and are, instead, *under-employed* (seeking additional work) and *over-worked* (working long hours). It is also the case that labour, especially female labour, is often not mobile across industries or sectors. In other words, labour in most developing countries is neither fixed nor flexible.

Types of evidence and analysis

Some of the differences between the perspectives of neo-classical economists, gender analysts and informal labour market analysts stems from the fact that they use different units of analysis and different time-frames, and they see markets as operating in quite different ways (Kanbur, 2001).

... most of the working poor cannot afford to remain unemployed and are, instead, under-employed (seeking additional work) and over-worked (working long hours). It is also the case that labour, especially female labour, is often not mobile across industries or sectors.

- Neo-classical economists tend to look at the incidence of poverty at the national or global level; to consider the medium- and long-term impact of economic policies; and to subscribe to the standard economic model of perfectly competitive market structures.

- Gender analysts tend to look at gender inequality and biases rather than poverty outcomes; to highlight the gendered structure of the economy as a whole and of specific markets; and to identify gender biases in macroeconomic policies and gender hierarchies in the household.

- Informal labour market analysts tend to look at the relationship between informal employment and poverty; to consider the short-term consequences of economic trends and policies on specific groups of the informal workforce; and to see markets as riddled with market power exercised by big corporations over small corporations and by employers over employees.

Some of the difference between the three perspectives also stems from the fact that they use different types of evidence.

Statistical analyses of macro data

Most economists tend to look at the linkages between trade liberalisation, growth and poverty at the aggregate or macro level, using countries as their unit of analysis. While some focus on country-specific experiences, collecting primary data as needed, many carry out cross-country comparisons by running regressions of secondary data.[9] Analysts who treat countries as the unit of analysis fail to differentiate outcomes for different groups at the micro-level (Kanji and Barrientos, 2001), and there are several methodological challenges to assessing the impact of trade on poverty at the aggregate level. In addition, as noted earlier, Joseph Stiglitz points out that the debate should not be whether trade and/or growth are good or bad but what kind of growth improves the welfare of poor people (Stiglitz, 2003b). This question cannot be answered by statistical analyses of aggregated macro data. What is needed are types of analysis and data that can isolate the impact of particular policies on specific groups of the population or workforce.

Analyses of micro data

In this chapter, we analyse findings from recent micro studies to trace how trade liberalisation is likely to affect specific categories of the informal workforce and with what consequences. The studies used several types of field research, notably livelihood analysis and value chain analysis.

Livelihood analysis: Livelihood analysis looks at the assets, vulnerabilities and capabilities of specific households or groups of people and their strategies to earn a livelihood. For example, the sustainable livelihoods framework, popularised by the UK Department for International Development (DFID), defines five types of assets – human, social, natural, physical and financial – that are affected by the vulnerability status of households or groups. Vulnerability is thought to take three forms: periodic shocks, regular seasonality and longer-term trends. The livelihoods framework can be used to look at the processes and institutions that are most likely to help poor households or groups deal with their vulnerability and translate their assets into improved well-being. In the context of our analysis, it contributes to an understanding of how different households or social groups (and women and men within them) are likely to be affected by the dominant economic processes.

Value chain analysis: Value chain analysis begins by mapping the distinct groups of firms within specific supply chains and the types of workers engaged in them. It then focuses on transactions between firms and, more recently, on the relationship of workers to firms. It provides a framework for assessing the power of the lead firm in structuring chains, and the consequences of this for the autonomy of other firms to upgrade and for workers to bargain for wages, rights and benefits (Nadvi, 2004). It thus challenges orthodox economic theory that assumes free markets in which buyers and sellers meet each other as independent agents (Kanji and Barrientos, 2001).

When applied to *global* value chains, the analysis provides critical insights into the operations of the global economy. For instance, global value chain analysis suggests that the international system of outsourcing production is not as decentralised or fragmented as it would seem. While the functions of

> *... global value chain analysis suggests that the international system of outsourcing production is not as decentralised or fragmented as it would seem. While the functions of production are fragmented and the sites of production are scattered, the lead firms exercise significant control over the chain of interconnected firms.*

> *Value chains can be used to trace profits or benefits ... Most importantly, value chain analysis can be used to trace appropriate points of intervention.*

production are fragmented and the sites of production are scattered, the lead firms exercise significant control over the chain of inter-connected firms. Value chain analysis can be – and is being – extended as an important methodology for analysing poverty outcomes of the global economy, to assess:

- how value added is passed up along the chains;
- how risk and uncertainty are passed down along the chains;
- how far benefits and protection are passed down the chains;
- what small informal firms need to upgrade and access the chains; and
- what different types of workers – employees, seasonal workers and homeworkers – need to upgrade their wages and working conditions.

Such assessments help identity points of leverage for different stakeholders linked to the chain that could improve labour standards of wage workers, access and competitiveness of small firms and farms and social protection for the working poor (ibid).[10]

Value chains can be used to trace *profits* or *benefits* (see Box 8). Most importantly, value chain analysis can be used to trace *appropriate points of intervention*. Thus, in garment manufacturing, it may be impossible for owners of small workshops to pay their workers higher wages because they have minimal profit margins themselves as a result of pressures from further up the chain. However, it could be quite feasible for Northern retailers to add a tiny amount to the sales price of garments with little hardship to consumers and great benefits to producers (McCormick and Schmitz, 2002). This type of analysis has been used to great effect by those involved in fair or ethical trade initiatives who monitor corporate investment and marketing practices, particularly of transnational corporations (TNCs).[11]

One final note on the micro-evidence presented here. Since the unit of analysis is not the country as a whole, the micro-findings do not provide an aggregate account of net overall gainers and losers. Instead, they provide a partial, context-specific picture. However, when analysed in combination with related macro data – as in the horticulture case presented

> **Box 8 Using Value Chain Analysis to Trace Profits and Benefits**
>
> *Tracing profits:* In the case of coffee in Uganda, one value chain study interviewed many suppliers along the chain – the farmers, the millers and the exporters – to trace the rising price of coffee beans as they made their journey from the farmer's trees to the jars sitting on supermarket shelves (Oxfam, 2002b). If the beans had ended up in a US supermarket, the farmer would have received only 4.5 per cent of the retail price of the coffee. In the case of UK markets, the farmer received just 2.5 per cent of the retail price.
>
> *Tracing benefits:* In the case of the garment sector in Thailand, two case studies investigated the access of different categories of workers to social protection. One chain involved lingerie production in large urban factories for export to North America and Europe; the other involved home-based production of jackets and women's clothing for middle level export markets in Europe. As a woman moves down the chain of production from being a regular worker in a registered factory to being a homeworker, it becomes less and less likely that she will obtain social protection from either her employer or the government. Even in those contexts where she is entitled to social insurance benefits, it is hard for her as an individual worker, without the backing of an organisation, to guarantee that she receives them (Lund and Nicholson, 2003). However, "the cases also show that a small, home-based workshop in a rural province can also – like large urban factories – provide its workers with social insurance benefits through the SSO (national Social Security Organisation) if the homeworkers are organised" (ibid:99).

in Chapter 2 – they can present an in-depth yet generalisable picture. By tracing the impact of trade on different categories of the working poor in the informal economy, using recent micro data and concrete examples, we hope to contribute to a better understanding of the 'enterprises' channel of the Winters analytical framework. More importantly, we hope to

> *Even if one assumes that trade liberalisation leads to growth, the impact on employment is not straightforward as some patterns of growth are capital-intensive rather than labour-intensive.*

identify the conditions under which trade works for and against the welfare of specific groups of the working poor. To answer the central question posed by Stiglitz – namely, which policy prescriptions would lead to the kind of growth that will improve the welfare of the poor – is not straightforward or easy and will require additional such analyses based on both macro and micro data and the use of both statistical and qualitative techniques.

Trade and Employment

Those who support trade liberalisation tend to stress that it generates economic growth and creates jobs that can be of benefit to the poor and to women in particular. Those who are against trade liberalisation stress that it destroys jobs – especially of the poor and women – and that even if jobs are created they exploit the workers concerned and do little if anything to contribute to growth and poverty reduction. Even if one assumes that trade liberalisation leads to growth, the impact on employment is not straightforward as some patterns of growth are capital-intensive rather than labour–intensive.

The analysis is further complicated by the fact that the poor earn their livelihoods through both self-employment and wage employment, each of which is impacted differently by these processes. While wage workers are affected by changes in employment and wages, the self-employed are affected by changes in markets and prices. In reality, it is difficult to determine the net overall impact of trade and/or growth on employment because outcomes vary considerably according to employment status, economic sector and gender.

What follows here is an analysis of commonly-observed effects of trade liberalisation on women's employment, particularly in the informal economy. The analysis begins with a discussion of two sets of common scenarios:

- the first set relates to the *quantity* of employment generated; and

- the second set relates to the *terms and conditions* of the employment generated.

The complex interplay of these two sets of possible effects will then be examined by looking at trends in: (a) women's employment in three major economic sectors – manufacturing, agriculture and services; and (b) international migration, including why international migrants should be seen as a major category of the global informal workforce.

Admittedly, the following analysis will seem quite pessimistic. This is because we simply cannot say how many jobs and opportunities have been created, either in absolute terms or relative to those that have been destroyed or to the number of jobs needed to employ the growing working age population. This is also because we draw on the first-hand knowledge and experience of members of WIEGO and the wider movement of informal workers (see Chapter 4) who have studied or worked with specific groups of the working poor, some of whom have suffered a disproportionate share of the costs associated with trade liberalisation.

Quantity of employment

The empirical evidence on trade and employment, or even growth and employment, is ambiguous at best. Also, many of the existing studies on the labour market effects of trade or growth deal only with the manufacturing sector, and then too only with formal wage jobs, making it difficult to draw conclusions about overall employment effects. However, three broad patterns have been identified. Trade and/or growth can either:

- create enough jobs and other employment opportunities to keep up with growth in the working age population;
- create an insufficient number of jobs or employment opportunities to keep up with the growth in the working age population;[12] or
- lead to a loss of jobs or other earning opportunities.

The fact that all three patterns may occur within a given country, depending on the nature of growth in different sectors, complicates the analysis of the net aggregate impact. The experience of the fast-growing Asian economies, including Hong Kong, Singapore and Taiwan, shows how sustained long-term growth can expand employment, reduce unemployment

MAINSTREAMING INFORMAL EMPLOYMENT AND GENDER IN POVERTY REDUCTION

... economic growth does not necessarily create as much employment as might have been expected or enough to match growth in the working age population.

and raise productivity and wages. This can, in turn, reduce poverty and inequality. Such growth was led by small-scale agriculture in Taiwan and by labour-intensive export manufacturing in Hong Kong and Singapore (UNDP, 1996).

> ### Box 9 India: An Example of Growth without Increased Employment
>
> During the 1990s, India enjoyed a growth rate in GDP of about 6.5 per cent per annum. This consistent growth sustained the reduction in headcount poverty that began in the mid-1980s (Deaton and Dreze, 2002). However, a recent Task Force on Employment Opportunities set up by the Planning Commission in India in 2001 pointed out that even a continuation of the GDP growth at this rate is not likely to bring about a significant improvement in the employment situation. This is because much of the growth has been capital-intensive (in the manufacturing sector) or information-intensive (in the service sector) rather than labour-intensive. Also, some of the growth has been associated with informal rather than formal wage jobs.
>
> As a result, the – already large – proportion of the Indian workforce that is in the informal economy has continued to grow. Without an appropriate policy environment, it is difficult for the benefits of economic growth to reach these categories of workers. For example, the policies that have spurred the rapid vertical growth of the food industry in India, involving heavy investments and associated technological modernisation, are essentially aimed at large corporations. No serious attention is being paid to small-scale and micro-businesses, which account for more than 75 per cent of those employed in the industry and provide employment for large numbers of women (ILO, 2003).

However, economic growth does not necessarily create as much employment as might have been expected or enough to match growth in the working age population (Unni, 2002; Desai and Das, 2004). This has happened, for example, in India (see Box 9). Economic growth has also outstripped employment growth in recent years in South Africa, although it is not clear how much of informal employment is captured in employment figures there and how much remains 'disguised' as unemployment.

Finally, and most problematic of all in terms of poverty reduction, there is the fact that economic reforms are associated, in some sectors and countries, with the contraction or destruction of jobs and other economic opportunities. While the net overall impact in terms of the creation versus the destruction of jobs and opportunities is not known, it is important to understand how, when and where the contraction and destruction take place.

First, as noted earlier, technological change associated with trade liberalisation can lead to the destruction of waged jobs when unskilled workers are replaced as a result of the introduction of capital-intensive technologies. For example:

In India, many large international companies, bringing mechanised technologies, have recently entered the construction industry under the global tendering requirements of the World Trade Organization. The Government of India has responded by assisting Indian companies to compete through upgrading their own technological capabilities. The net result is a significant displacement of unskilled labour, particularly of women who have traditionally been deployed in soil digging and brick carrying (Jhabvala and Kanbur, 2002).

In the coir industry in Sri Lanka, export promotion policies, including the supply of coconut husks, have led to a shift to mechanised units owned by men with access to credit and away from manual units operated by women with little access to credit (Bajaj, 2000).

Second, competition from inexpensive imports can undermine the domestic market for many micro-enterprises and own account operations (see Box 10). Third, in many countries, governments have actively encouraged foreign investment to process local raw materials/natural resources for export in order to earn foreign exchange. This is often done without any consideration for the impact on the domestic economy and on the thousands of informal enterprises and smallholders.

A related concern is that of the loss of potential economic benefits in rural communities through the appropriation of intellectual property rights by foreign companies. Under the

... economic reforms are associated, in some sectors and countries, with the contraction or destruction of jobs and other economic opportunities.

> **Box 10 Job Loss Due to Inexpensive Imports**
>
> With trade liberalisation, many micro-enterprises and own account operations can lose out due to competition from inexpensive imports. For example,
>
> - In many African countries, small-scale oil processing plants have closed owing to competition from imports of cooking oil from South-East Asia (ACGD/WIEGO, 2002).
>
> - In India, an estimated 3 million jobs have been lost as a result of the closure of small oil mills producing mustard seed oil following the influx of cheap soya-based cooking oil from North and South America. In addition to the destruction of jobs, this shift prevents consumers from using the cooking oil of their choice (Shiva, 2000).
>
> - In Mexico, maize production fell following the North American Free Trade Agreement (NAFTA), leading to an estimated loss of almost 1 million livelihoods (Madeley, 2000).
>
> - In Zimbabwe, the import of clothing from Asia effectively wiped out the domestic manufacturing of clothing, done mainly by women workers (Carmody, 1998).

Trade Related Intellectual Property Rights (TRIPS) Agreement of the WTO, it is now possible for corporations and others to patent life forms if they have been altered in some way for new and innovative uses. This has resulted, for instance, in the patenting of *brazzein*, a substance found in a West African berry and which is 500 times sweeter than sugar, by American researchers with no plans to share the estimated $100 billion a year worldwide market with the communities in which it was found (Kaihuzi, 1999). Protecting communities' rights over their traditional knowledge would benefit women in particular since they play a key role in preserving and enhancing genetic resources (Appleton et al, 1995).

Finally, it is important to note that corporate business practices – not just economic trends or policies – have been another cause of the *contraction of existing waged jobs*, notably when employers decide to trim the size of their core workforce and maintain a 'reserve army' of peripheral workers to meet peak periods of production or specialised orders.

The effects of trade and growth on employment are thus clearly multifaceted, making them difficult to measure or predict. Furthermore, in some countries, even if economic growth is associated with employment growth, population growth may outstrip employment growth, making the effect on the aggregate rate of employment more difficult still to predict. A recent study on the effects of NAFTA on women and men's employment illustrates the complexities involved in understanding employment effects (see Box 11).

... corporate business practices – not just economic trends or policies – have been another cause of the contraction of existing waged jobs, notably when employers decide to trim the size of their core workforce and maintain a 'reserve army' of peripheral workers ...

Box 11 NAFTA'S Impact on the Female Workforce in Mexico

A study of the impact of the 1994 North American Free Trade Agreement (NAFTA) on Mexico looked specifically at the processes of liberalisation and structural reform on the labour force, and especially on the female labour force. It found that, as a result of changing economic and social conditions during the years prior to and following the signing of NAFTA, women joined the labour force at a faster rate than men. However, women's jobs tended to be low paying, in services and in the informal economy. The growth in women's employment did not necessarily lead to an improvement in their living standards. Women found more jobs in the vegetable and fruit export sector in agriculture but, with an increase in working hours and in employment on a piecework basis, their general labour conditions often worsened.

In addition, while women's employment in the maquiladoras (or in-bond processing export industry) grew in absolute terms, it fell in relative terms. Men took many of the new manufacturing jobs created in the maquiladoras due both to push factors, as employment

> **Box 11** (continued)
>
> opportunities were limited outside the sector, and to pull factors, as the industry and companies began to value higher-skilled workers. In 1988 women had 63 per cent of the jobs in the maquiladoras, but by 1997 their share had fallen to 58 per cent. Women were forced to look for other types of employment, often accepting lower wages and poorer labour conditions. Jobs in the informal sector increased greatly, with a larger share of the female workforce (41%) than the male workforce (37%) employed in this sector.

In sum, while there is a growing concern about those who become *unemployed* as a result of trade or other macro-economic trends and policies, much less attention has been paid to those who lose their source of livelihood or those who remain in or join the informal economy. What follows illustrates the ways in which the working poor are absorbed into the global workforce and on what terms and conditions.

Terms and conditions of employment

We provide concrete examples in this section of three common ways through which the working poor, especially women, are inserted into the global workforce. Each of these common scenarios indicates that, while new economic opportunities are being created, the terms and conditions of employment generated often mean that the working poor may not be able to take advantage of them or may not benefit fully from their involvement.

The three common scenarios are:

1. Creation of new jobs – but without rights and benefits;

2. Opening up of new markets – but with unequal access and competitiveness;

3. Increased risk and uncertainty – but without adequate protection.

The first two scenarios relate to the nature and the quality of economic opportunities associated with economic reforms. The third relates to generalised effects commonly associated with economic reforms, seen from the perspective of the working poor in the informal economy.

Scenario 1. Creation of new jobs – but without rights and benefits

While trade liberalisation has provided jobs to large numbers of people in developing countries, available evidence suggests that women are concentrated in low-technology manufacturing where wages and benefits are relatively low and working conditions are generally poor. According to official agreements in many countries, employment in assembly factories in EPZs is not subject to government regulation, with the result that national labour laws are often not adhered to, hygiene and safety fall short of international standards, working conditions are harsh, benefits are not paid and overtime is often mandatory (Gammage et al, 2002). Also, due more to business strategies than to policy design, industrial outwork or homework falls outside of government regulation and is associated with the lack of labour standards, worker benefits and protection.

Evidence suggests that in countries that have large supplies of labour relative to national demand and high rates of unemployment or under-employment, wages may not rise as a result of expanded production and increased exports. In the garment industry in Bangladesh, for example, real wages for the lowest skilled workers declined by 28 per cent between 1990 and 1997 even as value-added per worker rose over the same period (Bhattacharya and Rahman, 1999). By contrast, in countries where the supply of labour is not so abundant, wages are more likely to increase. For example, since 1985 Mauritius has experienced an expansion of employment opportunities, particularly in its EPZ where wages rose consistently between 1985 and 1995 (World Bank, 1995b; ILO, 1996). Given the overall growth in employment opportunities in the country, the EPZ faced labour shortages and high turnover rates and, in response, increased wages to attract higher-skilled labour and improve the retention rate (ibid).

Similarly, in sectors where workers' bargaining power is weak and where collective contracts are not negotiated,

While trade liberalisation has provided jobs to large numbers of people in developing countries, available evidence suggests that women are concentrated in low-technology manufacturing where wages and benefits are relatively low and working conditions are generally poor.

Vegetable vendor, Kenya
MARTHA CHEN

"workers are less likely to be able to capture some of the gains from these increased export revenues" (Gammage et al, 2002: 20). The latter is the case both in EPZs, where workers are typically not allowed to unionise, and (more so) for homeworkers, who remain isolated and have little (if any) bargaining power.

Scenario 2. Opening up of new markets – but with unequal access and competitiveness

Trade liberalisation and growth are offering new economic opportunities through the opening up of export markets. However, this often takes place in the absence of a level playing field in terms of market knowledge, access and competitiveness. The smaller and more remote an economic unit is, the less likely it is that the owner or operator will know about new market opportunities or have direct access to them. Even with knowledge or access, small and remote enterprises are less able to compete effectively than larger, more strategically-located enterprises. This disadvantaged status translates into either of two outcomes:

- lack of access to or competitiveness in global markets; or
- integration into global markets on dubious terms.

(a) Lack of access to or competitiveness in global markets: There are a great many barriers that constrain own account operators and micro-entrepreneurs from linking with global markets and, in general, women face more constraints than men do (see Table 8).

For the main part, these barriers relate to:

- exclusion from factor markets and lack of access to land, credit, training, technology, infrastructure and information on markets and prices and other economic inputs that are necessary for integration into the global economy;
- lack of organising into co-operatives or associations;
- lack of voice and representation; and
- lack, in the case of women, of mobility (cultural restrictions) and time (domestic responsibilities).

The lack of a conducive policy and regulatory environment for micro-enterprises can also exclude entry to export markets. These barriers are to be found in all sectors: agricultural, manufacturing and services (including ICT-related businesses such as 'telekiosks').[13] They also serve to constrain women wishing to increase productivity/quality to meet higher standards in export markets, diversify into new products in order to enter export markets or set up an export business for the first time.

(b) Integration into global markets on dubious terms: At the same time, many own account workers are being absorbed into export-oriented production – often without their knowledge or against their will – and on terms that are not entirely favourable to them. This is happening, for example, with many forest workers who earn their living from gathering and selling non-timber forest products (NTFPs) such as medicinal plants, mushrooms, nuts and spices. By definition, these workers live in remote areas and can only link with markets – even domestic ones – through a chain of middlemen. As the demand for such products is growing in global markets (there are now 150 NTFPs of major significance in international trade), there is

There are a great many barriers that constrain own account operators and micro-entrepreneurs from linking with global markets and, in general, women face more constraints than men do.

Table 8: Levels of Mutually-reinforcing Constraints on Female Micro-enterprises

Enterprise Constraints	Macro-level	Household Level	At Level of Individual
Resources and property	Unequal inheritance laws, inequality in marriage contract and community access to land	Male appropriation of household/family property	Lack of individual property
Income	Legal systems that treat women as dependants rather than individuals, also reflected in tax and benefit systems	Male appropriation of incomes	Lack of control over income
	Lack of public welfare provision or recognition of costs of reproductive services	Female responsibility for family provisioning and male withdrawal of income	Prioritisation of investment in household
	Low female wages		Low incomes for investment
Credit	Financial system discriminating against women	Male appropriation of credit	Lack of collateral
Skills	Lack of opportunities for apprenticeship	Lack of investment in female education and skill acquisition	Lack of confidence and ability to enter new areas of activity
	Gender-stereotyped training and education that devalues women	Low valuation of female skills	
	Discrimination in access to education system and training		
Marketing	Lack of access to marketing support	Concern with family honour and restrictions on female mobility	Lack of information and networks
	Lack of marketing support for female-dominated industries		
	Harassment of female informal sector workers		
Labour	Unwillingness of men to work under a woman entrepreneur	Limited claim to unpaid male family labour	Lack of networks and authority
		Women's responsibility for unpaid family labour	Lack of time
General underlying constraints on change	Institutionalised discrimination and violence	Opposition to female independence and autonomy	Lack of autonomy
	Lack of women's participation in decision-making	Domestic violence	Lack of confidence

Source: Mayoux, 2001

increasing interest on the part of foreign companies in commercialising these commodities (IIED, 1997). One example is shea nuts in West Africa (see Box 12).

> ### Box 12 Joining Global Markets on Unfavourable Terms
>
> In the case of shea nuts in West Africa, there is a growing and profitable market for processed shea butter in Europe, North America and Japan for use in cosmetics and, more recently, in chocolate manufacture. While demand for shea butter is growing in the North, with a consequent rise in the final price in Northern markets, women who collect shea nuts are often totally unaware of this trend and continue to sell to their existing brokers/middlemen who then supply the nuts into the ever more profitable global markets, as well as continuing to supply domestic and regional markets. Thus, women shea nut collectors are now integrated in global value chains but without any knowledge of these chains or their position and rights within them, and without any means of exploiting more profitable markets to their own advantage.

Scenario 3. Increased risk and uncertainty – but without adequate protection

Insertion into the global economy is associated with three broad types of risks for the working poor:

- fluctuations in the level of work and income;
- changes in the terms and conditions of work;
- sudden loss of work.

(a) Fluctuations in the level of work and income. This risk is associated with the fluctuation in and the seasonal nature of global demands for goods and services. To offset these factors, companies or employers often opt to retain a contingent workforce of 'long-term seasonal' workers – who are temporarily dismissed and then rehired to match increases in the demand for goods – or to sub-contract work to suppliers who, in turn, pass on the uncertainty and risk to units and workers further down the chain.

Of critical importance for poverty and gender equity outcomes is the fact that the risk and uncertainty associated with trade liberalisation and economic restructuring are likely to be more significant for labour (than capital), for informal workers (than formal workers), for informal enterprises (than larger, more formal enterprises) and for women (than men) within the informal economy.

(b) Changes in the terms and conditions of work. The working poor face the risk of having to shift to more disadvantaged forms of work, even within the same sector of the economy. For example:

- In the case of export-oriented manufacturing, women – who were the early winners in the globalisation process – are now beginning to lose out. They are losing hold in factory production, both in terms of jobs and work-related benefits, and are increasingly reliant on industrial outwork or homework in the same sector or marginal own account activities in other sectors, such as vending.

- In the case of the export of primary products or commodities, many smallholders have had to forego their independence and become dependent on very uncertain wage work as casual labourers. These include smallholders in Asia who now work as contract workers for multinationals producing baby corn and other vegetables for export (Shiva, 2000; *Thai Development Newsletter*, 1998); and women who used to have their own fish smoking and marketing businesses in Africa but are now dependent day labourers in export-oriented fish-processing plants (set up by foreign investors encouraged by local government policies). Many of these women must wait for two or three days at factory gates to obtain work (Carr and Chen, 2004).

(c) Sudden loss of work. There is a risk of a sudden loss of employment due to the ease and speed with which capital can move the location of production within and between countries. For example:

- The long-term security of jobs in the information-based industries is causing concern as they become increasingly 'footloose' or mobile in nature, with firms seeking the lowest wages across countries and continents. For instance, recent evidence suggests that some data entry work is moving from India (with relatively high wages of $1,250 per annum) to countries in Africa such as Ghana (with relatively low wages of $480 per annum).

- New technologies – such as the bar code – have facilitated what is called 'lean retailing' and 'just-in-time' production in the textile and garment industry. To meet the demand for 'just-in-time' production, companies have shifted production to the periphery of Europe and the United States, leaving thousands of workers in Asia and elsewhere without jobs or even severance pay. For instance, The Limited, the manufacturer of Victoria's Secret underwear, recently opened a plant in Mexico. Despite the fact that wages are three times higher in Mexico than in Sri Lanka, it was more economical to produce in Mexico because of savings in time, transport costs and duties. In fact, there has been a steady reduction in apparel imports from Asia to the US from 83 per cent of the total in 1980 to 41 per cent in 1996. Not only is it cheaper and quicker to operate within the Western Hemisphere, but it also allows US textile manufacturers to supply the bulk of the fabric, something they cannot do with Asian suppliers (ILO, 1998).

Illustrative cases

The following section outlines the complex interplay of these common scenarios in three major sectors of the economy – manufacturing, agriculture (including horticulture) and services – and in international migration, from the perspective of women workers, particularly those in the informal economy.

Manufacturing sector

The current wave of globalisation is associated with a dramatic increase in the share of manufactured goods in total exports from developing countries: from 24 per cent in 1970 to 66 per cent by 1999 (World Bank, 2001). A related fact is the massive creation of jobs in export-led manufacturing in developing countries – particularly in South-East/East Asia and in Central and South America. Starting in the 1960s, this was encouraged through the creation of EPZs, which offered incentives to foreign corporations in terms of tax holidays, cheap labour rates and lack of unionisation of the workforce. Estimates for the mid-1990s suggest that perhaps 27 million jobs had been created in these zones – of which 70 to 80 per cent were for women – mainly in labour-intensive industries such as garments, footwear and electronics (ILO, 1998). In addition to EPZs, a sizeable share of global manufacturing is sub-con-

> *While export-led industrialisation has created new jobs for women in many countries, the quality of this employment has been questioned. Typically, wages are very low, working conditions are poor, written contracts are rarely involved and workers are unlikely to receive any benefits such as health insurance or leave (maternity, sick or annual leave).*

tracted to domestic companies, many of which further subcontract to homeworkers, most of whom are women.

Informality of women's employment in manufacturing: While export-led industrialisation has created new jobs for women in many countries, the quality of this employment has been questioned. Typically, wages are very low, working conditions are poor, written contracts are rarely involved and workers are unlikely to receive any benefits such as health insurance or leave (maternity, sick or annual). Young women are preferred because they are seen as docile and unlikely to take union action and agitate for improved wages and working conditions. Yet employers who express a preference for young women in factory jobs normally terminate employment once a worker gets married or becomes pregnant. Furthermore, employers are turning towards hiring labour on a contingent basis, whereby workers can be hired and fired without prior notification or temporarily dismissed with each production lull and rehired to meet production deadlines. The position of homeworkers in export-oriented production is even more precarious as they are more isolated than factory workers and have a more tenuous link with their employer (see Box 13).

Defeminisation of employment in manufacturing: In recent years, there are signs that some markets for labour-intensive products produced in export-oriented industries are becoming flooded and highly competitive. Large corporations have dealt with this in two ways: by moving across borders in search of the cheapest labour and thus promoting a 'race to the bottom' that drives wages ever lower and increases the insecurity of work; or by diversifying into higher technology and higher profit markets. With the switch from working 'harder' to working 'smarter', there is evidence that export manufacturing is being defeminised in certain sectors and certain countries as companies hire men for the higher-skilled jobs. While women tend to be concentrated in low technology manufactures, men tend to be concentrated in higher-technology manufactures (Fleck, 2001; Mehra and Gammage, 1999).

For example, in Malaysia, the proportion of women workers in EPZs fell from 75 per cent in 1980 to 54 per cent in 1990 (Joekes, 1999). And, in Mexico, the proportion of women in maquiladoras fell from 77 per cent in 1982 to 60 per cent in

> *Box 13* **The Precarious Position of Homeworkers**
>
> Almost without exception, homeworkers are paid less than informal factory workers and receive no benefits from their employers (who in any case often hide their links to such workers in an intricate network of contractors and sub-contractors, thus divorcing themselves from any responsibilities). Typically, homeworkers are at the lowest end of the production chain, receiving less than 10 per cent of the total sale price of what they produce and lacking the means to redress the balance of power and returns. Further, as noted earlier, they typically have to bear the non-wage costs of production, including workspace, equipment and utilities. This has been shown by recent research in seven countries in Asia (Bangladesh, China, India, Pakistan, the Philippines, Sri Lanka and Thailand) as well as Bulgaria and the UK (Hurley, 2004). In China, women homeworkers are even expected to pay a down payment amounting to one month's income to the agent who gives them work (ibid). Homeworkers also often have to absorb the temporary costs associated with delayed payments.

... there is evidence that export manufacturing is being defeminised in certain sectors and certain countries as companies hire men for the higher-skilled jobs.

1990 (Ghosh, 1995) and to 58 per cent in 1997 (UNIFEM, 2000), while the proportion of women in the export sector as a whole fell from 45 per cent in 1991 to 35 per cent in 1993 (Ghiara, 1999). In Mexico, this is due not only to the requirement of higher skills, which men are more likely to have, but also to the lack of sufficient employment opportunities elsewhere in the economy (see Box 11).

Agriculture

While Africa has largely been excluded from export-led industrialisation – mainly because it is more abundant in land than in unskilled labour – it has become incorporated in global value chains of a different type: those involving agricultural exports, including non-traditional agricultural exports (NTAEs) such as fresh fruits and vegetables and cut flowers aimed mainly at the European markets. The effects on the working poor, especially women, are perhaps more complex than in manufacturing because of the need to distinguish between smallholders and labourers and between those who grow food crops as opposed to cash or export crops – and between women and men within each of these categories.

Smallholder agriculture: Smallholder agriculture in sub-Saharan Africa is often highly segmented by gender. "Typically, but not exclusively, women are engaged in the production of domestic staples, or in processing and sale of domestic foodstuffs in national markets whereas men focus their activities primarily on cash crop production" or export production (Gammage et al, 2002:33). Also, almost without exception, "women seem to have access to smaller and less numerous plots with more precarious usufruct rights" (ibid: 34). Available evidence suggests that, as the volume of agriculture products that is traded increases, less land is available for domestic and household production, with the result that food security and women's control over agricultural production is undermined. Furthermore, the likelihood that women can increase their output and gain from trade or price liberalisation is constrained by their lack of access to credit, storage and transport facilities (Baden, 1998). In some countries, women may find alternative job opportunities in agriculture as *labourers* in the production of export cash crops on their husbands' or relatives' land or as *seasonal or contract workers* in the production of NTAEs (Seguino and Grown, 2002; Carr, Chen and Tate, 2000).

Horticultural labourers: "Over the last few decades there has been a rapid increase in the trade of fresh products, which can now be sourced from around the world…. In sub-Saharan Africa, horticultural exports have doubled since 1980, and in 1996 they exceeded the region's exports for coffee, cotton and all other individual commodities other than cocoa" (Lund and Nicholson, 2003:25). Women represent up to 90 per cent of the workforce of this fast-growing sector (UNDAW, 1999). In many ways, these chains replicate the labour-intensive manufacturing chains in Asia and Central America, with large corporations dominating and with women working on large-scale 'factory' farms at very low wages, in bad working conditions and without benefits of any sort (see horticulture case study in Chapter 2).

In fact, the terms of inclusion of women workers in these

horticultural chains are perhaps worse than those of women workers in manufacturing chains for two reasons. First, as noted earlier, for all but a small proportion of (mainly male) workers, employment is seasonal or temporary as employers attempt to reduce costs and their contractual commitments to workers – and women comprise the majority of temporary or seasonal workers. Second, the health risks involved in horticulture production (including the use of toxic products without protective clothing) are higher than in the garment and other labour-intensive manufacturing industries (Lund and Nicholson, 2003). Consumer pressure in the North, however, is forcing supermarkets to buy from growers who take measures to reduce health risks and are more environmentally sound (Dolan and Tewari, 2001; Barndt, 1999).

Service sector

One distinguishing feature of the present wave of globalisation is that countries have become increasingly connected through trade in 'digitised' information. With increased digital processing of information, it has become possible – and generally cost-effective – to transfer information processing work to offices and work units that are remote from main premises, within and across national boundaries. Like manufacturing, the growth of the service industry seems to be female-led in many countries (UN DAW, 1999; Gammage et al, 2002). In some developing countries, women represent the major share of recruits to this globally distributed work (Mitter, 2003).

For example, the global digital economy is recruiting large numbers of young women to work in call centres. But, as with manufacturing, service jobs are often 'informalised' as they are exported and governments are setting up EPZs for data processing, which means that many services jobs are associated with poor working conditions and low wages (White, 2001). In call centres, most contracts are short-term and unionisation is discouraged. Although more skills are required in this sector than in manufacturing and NTAEs, women still tend to be clustered in the low-skilled end of the hierarchy with little chance of career progression. For instance, they are more likely to be employed in data entry and customer care centres than in the software sector. Initially, data entry was considered promising work for women: all of the workers in 'digiports'[14] in

... as with manufacturing, service jobs are often 'informalised' as they are exported and governments are setting up EPZs for data processing, which means that many services jobs are associated with poor working conditions and low wages ...

Jamaica are women, and the majority of data entry jobs for airlines, banking and insurance companies in India are filled by women. However, technological changes could lead to 'defeminisation' in the service sector, as in the manufacturing sector, if women do not have the necessary training and skills to adapt. Data entry jobs are also becoming 'footloose': that is, companies have begun to shift the site of call centres from Asia, notably India, to Africa, presumably in the interest of lowering labour costs (as noted earlier).

International migration

There is a nexus between international migration and informal employment. Since international labour mobility has not been liberalised, many migrant workers remain irregular. At the same time, since employment relationships have been liberalised, most low-skilled migrant workers – even those who emigrate through legal channels – end up working under informal employment relationships: without a secure contract, workers' benefits or social protection.

The migration of workers from developing countries to developed countries has been on the rise for a number of years. In Organisation for Economic Co-operation and Development (OECD) countries, the number of migrant workers from developing countries is estimated to have more than doubled between 1988 and 1998: from 8.4 to 17.3 million (OECD, 2003).[15] Moreover, a large share of reported migrants moves from one developing country to another. The full global magnitude of this phenomenon, like the other phenomena we have been discussing, is hard to ascertain. It is estimated that there are over 80 million economically active migrants around the world today, of whom some 28 million are in the developing regions (ILO, 2004b).

The forces driving migration are many and complex, but it is widely recognised that lack of employment and decent work as well as increasing differences in wage levels between countries help explain a large share of contemporary international migration (ibid). It should be noted that migration is driven not only by push but also by pull factors. While many workers migrate in search of better jobs and higher wages, employers often prefer to hire migrant workers in order to reduce labour costs, avoid the demands of organised labour or have them undertake work that nationals are no longer willing to do. For example, in developed countries, companies hire immigrants (even those without legal status) for jobs that cannot be outsourced overseas, such as in restaurants, hospitals and farms; and households often hire immigrants as domestic workers.

Women account for a large proportion – probably nearly half – of international migrants (ILO, 2004b). While many women migrants enter other countries for the purpose of uniting with their families, especially in more developed countries, more and more women are migrating on their own to earn money for their families back home. For example, in Asia, hundreds of thousands of women emigrate each year in both unskilled and skilled occupations, mainly in domestic service and entertainment and, to a lesser extent, in nursing and teaching (ibid). Recent estimates suggest that each year about 100,000 women leave Asia's developing countries to work in its newly industrialising countries as domestic servants and hotel workers, and another 75,000 leave to work in Australia, Canada, Western Europe and the USA as nurses, service industry workers and domestic servants (Seager, 2003).

Those migrant workers who enter other countries legally do so through one of three channels: as permanent migrants (primarily highly-skilled migrants), as temporary migrants (commonly known as 'guest workers') or as temporary migrants for time-bound employment (i.e. seasonal workers). An estimated 10–15 per cent of migrants, however, are 'irregular', having entered other countries without legal authorisation.[16]

The well-being of migrant workers relates not just to whether they have a clear and secure legal status but also to the nature of the work they find, whether the work generates a sufficient income and whether they have access to social services and social protection. Other than the high-skilled professionals, migrant workers tend to be concentrated at the bottom of the occupational scale. Even if they enter the country through legal channels, they tend to end up doing what are referred to as '3-D' jobs: *dirty*, *dangerous* or otherwise *difficult* (ILO, 2004b). They are not likely to be unionised or to fall under the protection of labour legislation or labour inspectorates. They also tend to occupy temporary jobs, which are the first to be closed down during periods of economic recession. Irregular migrants are extremely vulnerable to exploita-

> *... migration is driven not only by push but also by pull factors. While many workers migrate in search of better jobs and higher wages, employers often prefer to hire migrant workers in order to reduce labour costs, avoid the demands of organised labour or have them undertake work that nationals are no longer willing to do.*

... women migrants, whether temporary or irregular, have particular difficulties securing basic rights as workers and are particularly vulnerable to exploitation ...

tion of various kinds (see Box 14). And women migrants, whether temporary or irregular, have special difficulties securing basic rights as workers and are even more vulnerable to exploitation.

> **Box 14 Examples of Migrants' Vulnerability to Exploitation**
>
> - In British Columbia, Canada, farm workers are excluded from important labour laws. Eighty per cent of farm labourers are from India (of which 75 per cent are women) – mostly recent immigrants. They are hired by contractors (mainly Indian men), work long hours on low piece rates and are often cheated out of overtime pay (Oxfam, 2004).
>
> - In the UK, a government investigation in 2003 revealed that contractors are illegally charging immigrants high recruitment fees to work excessive hours, picking fruits at piece rates below the minimum wage (ibid).
>
> - More recently in the UK, the deaths of 19 Chinese immigrants working as cockle pickers led to widespread questions being raised about the circumstances of immigrant workers in general (*Economist*, 2004).

In principle, all regular migrant workers in developed countries should have access to basic education and emergency health care. But other entitlements may be linked to employment and contributions to social security benefits. And the level and quality of services and benefits available vary greatly among and within countries. Also, immigrants are often not aware of what they are entitled to or how to access services and benefits. Of course, irregular immigrants are the most vulnerable in this regard. Further, the lack of legal recognition of countless migrant workers around the world means that they are not able to engage in the civic and social life of their new communities.

The Changing Nature of Work

While our analysis has focused on the 'downside' of economic integration, there are clearly both winners and losers in the process of economic integration and economic reforms, even among the working poor. What is also clear is that the world of work itself being changed because of these economic processes. In what follows, we focus on three key dimensions of the changing nature of work and on the consequences of these changes for working poor women and men in the informal economy:

- the place of work;
- the employment status of individual workers; and
- the production system.

The place of work

The conventional view of 'the work place' is of a factory, shop or office. Yet more and more people, especially in the informal economy, are working in non-standard work places. In India, for example, the 1999–2000 Informal Sector Survey of the National Sample Survey Organisation found that 36 per cent of informal enterprises were home-based and 22 per cent had no fixed location; only 42 per cent of informal enterprises had a designated business place, and of these 6 per cent were in temporary structures (Unni and Rani, 2003b). The following classification (adapted from ILO, 2002b) distinguishes between the different non-standard locations of work:

- **Dwellings:**
  own dwellings (at home)
  client's or employer's home
  attached or adjacent to dwellings

- **Open Spaces:**
  street adjacent to home
  street
  door to door
  construction sites
  agricultural areas, including pastures and forests

... there are clearly both winners and losers in the process of economic integration and economic reforms, even among the working poor. What is also clear is that the world of work itself is changing because of these economic processes.

Security of tenure is directly related to income security for people working at home, whether self-employed or industrial outworkers.

- **Unregistered Premises:**
  workshops
  shops

Each place of work is associated with specific costs, risks and benefits. Consider, for example, home-based work.[17] For some women workers, there are advantages to working at (or near) home as this can be combined with domestic chores as well as child care, and the home may be seen as a safe place to work. However, home-based workers often have to interrupt their paid work in order to look after a child or cook a meal, and this is likely to lead to lower productivity. Moreover, home-based work may increase vulnerability as the producer or worker is less visible and not usually legally recognised. This is likely to undermine her capacity to claim any social protection measures or other benefits for which a worker may be eligible. Further, home-based workers are harder to reach and organise than those who work in small factories or even those who work on the streets (Lund and Unni, 2004).

Many informal workers, particularly in urban areas, live in informal settlements or low-income housing and often do not have title or legal ownership rights to the house they live in. Security of tenure is directly related to income security for people working at home, whether self-employed or industrial outworkers. The amount of space that can be used for work and for storage, the cleanliness of the home and access to electricity influence the type and amount of work that can be undertaken (ibid). In one study in India, low-income women who lived in dilapidated shelters on the streets reported that they would like to undertake piece-rated garment work at home, but no one was willing to give them this work because of the condition of their homes (Unni and Rani, 2003b). Where would they store the raw material and finished products? In spite of their having the rudimentary skills needed to undertake garment work, they had to resort to work as casual labourers or as garbage pickers, living off what they could collect and sell from garbage dumps (ibid).

Around the world, a large and perhaps growing share of the informal workforce operates on streets and sidewalks and in public parks, outside any enclosed premise or covered workspace. This includes not only those street vendors who sell goods but also a broader range of street workers who sell services and produce or repair goods. In Kenya, the Swahili term *jua kali* – which means 'under the burning sun' – is the traditional name for the informal economy. This is because so many informal activities, not just street trade, take place in the open air (King, 1996).

Even when used in the narrower and precise sense of informal traders who sell goods from the street or outside, street vending is a large and diverse activity: from high-income vendors who sell luxury goods at flea markets to low-income vendors who sell fruits and vegetables alongside city streets. Vendors also work under a number of quite different economic arrangements: some are truly self-employed and independent, others are semi-dependent (e.g. agents who sell products for firms against a commission), while still others are paid employees and fully dependent.

As noted in Chapter 2, evidence shows that women are more likely to sell perishable goods while men sell non-perishable and higher value goods. In addition, women are more likely to sell from the ground while men sell from carts, stalls or kiosks. It is important to note, however, that this division of labour is usually not a matter of choice on the part of women but a consequence of their more limited access (than male vendors) to credit and productive assets that would enable them to run more profitable and less risky vending operations.

Depending on the regulatory environment, street vendors may face great insecurity in regard to their place of work as they often are not entitled to a secure site from which to trade. They are often viewed as a nuisance or obstruction to other commerce and the free flow of traffic. Since street vendors typically lack legal status and recognition, they may experience frequent harassment and evictions from their selling place by local authorities or competing shopkeepers. Historical patterns of urban settlement or current pressures on limited urban land force many people to trade in marginal locations that are not economically viable. Their goods may be confiscated and arrests are not uncommon. The places where they work are often dirty and hazardous. Nevertheless, street vending may be the only option for many poor people.

In thinking about the linkages between employment and

> *... street vendors may face great insecurity in regard to their place of work as they often are not entitled to a secure site from which to trade. ... Nevertheless, street vending may be the only option for many poor people.*

... a large and increasing share of workers worldwide is not protected under labour laws or collective bargaining agreements.

social outcomes, the location and security of the work place are key issues. Proposals to address these issues can be found in Chapter 5.

Employment status

'Employment status' is a conceptual framework used by labour statisticians to refer to two key dimensions of the contractual arrangements under which economically active persons work, namely the *allocation* of:

- *authority* over the work situation and the outcome of the work done; and

- the *economic risks* involved (ILO, 2002a).

Historically, labour statistics classified all economically active persons into one of five employment statuses: employers, employees, own account workers, unpaid contributing family members and members of co-operatives. However, this does not clearly identify two large categories of the informal workforce: a) a whole range of wage workers who are not standard employees; and b) industrial outworkers or homeworkers. Also, this classification assumes that all the self-employed – both employers and own account workers – are fully independent and all employees are fully dependent. Recently, labour statisticians and other observers have therefore sought to expand the employment status classification to encompass the full range of work arrangements in today's world.

The employer-employee relationship has represented the cornerstone – the central legal concept – around which labour law and collective bargaining agreements have sought to recognise and protect the rights of workers. This concept has always excluded those workers who are self-employed. But some of the self-employed are dependent, if not on an employer *per se*, on a dominant counterpart such as the trader from whom they buy raw materials (if they are producers) or goods to sell (if they are vendors). Also, increasingly, some categories of wage workers have found themselves to be, in effect, without labour protection because their employment relationship is disguised, ambiguous or not clearly defined. The net result is that a large and increasing share of workers worldwide does not fit neatly into existing categories of labour statistics or labour law and is not protected under labour laws or collective bargaining agreements.[18]

Industrial outworkers, or homeworkers, represent a prime example of workers who fall into a grey intermediate zone between being fully independent and being fully dependent. Their intermediate status is illustrated in Table 9.

Table 9: Characteristics of the Self-employed, Homeworkers and Employees

Characteristics	Self-Employed	Homeworkers	Employees
Contract	Sales contract	Production contract	Employment contract
Remuneration	From sale of goods/services	For work (typically piece rate)	For work (time or piece rate)
Contract with	Self	Employer/intermediary	Employer
Means of Production	Provided by self	Provided by self	Provided by employer
Workplace	Provided by self	Provided by self	Provided by employer
Supervision	Autonomous	Indirect or no supervision	Direct supervision

As noted above, homeworkers typically have to absorb many production costs and associated risks, often without help from their employers. Thus their net remuneration may be significantly less than indicated by the piece rates that they are paid. For instance, most garment homeworkers have to buy and maintain their own sewing machines, replace needles and oil and pay for the electricity to run their machines and light their workspace. Most of them are also not directly supervised by those who contract work to them, although they are subject to delivery deadlines and to quality control of the products or services they deliver. For these reasons, they should be considered semi-dependent, not dependent, wage workers.

A second issue in understanding the employment status of the homeworker is identifying the specific firm for which he or (usually) she works and determining the characteristics of that firm. Existing labour statistics and labour laws treat the intermediary – the contractor – who supplies raw materials and receives the finished goods against payment for the work done as the 'employer'. However, analytically, it is not clear which firm should be considered as the employer of the homeworker: the intermediary that directly places work orders, the supplier that puts out work to the intermediary, the manufacturer that outsources goods from the supplier or the retailer that sells the goods. There is a parallel legal problem, namely which unit in the chain should be held accountable for the rights and benefits of workers down the chain? Many labour lawyers and activists argue that the lead firm that initially put out the work should be considered the equivalent of the employer.

Depending on the number of intermediaries in any given sub-contracting chain, however, the links between the homeworkers and the lead firm for which they work are often obscure, and the homeworkers often do not know which firm puts out the work or sells the finished goods. In long complex chains of intermediaries, the lead firm is a multinational firm based in an industrialised country and the homeworkers are scattered across one or more countries. In such cases, the bargaining for higher wages is complicated by the distance between the homeworker and the lead firm and the ambiguity over who is responsible for increasing wages. The case in Box 15 illustrates how complicated things can be in negotiating payment or wages due for completed work.

Box 15 Who Employs the Homeworker?

When a trade union organiser in Canada tried to help an immigrant Chinese garment worker get her back wages, she found that the garment worker did not know who she worked for as the man who dropped off raw materials and picked up finished garments drove an unmarked van. When the garment worker eventually found a tag with a brand label on it among her raw materials, the trade union activist was able to trace the label from a retail firm in Canada to a manufacturing firm in Hong Kong to an intermediary in Canada: in this case, the global value chain began and ended in Canada. When the local intermediary was asked to pay the back wages due to the garment homeworker he replied: "Put me in jail, I cannot pay. The manufacturer in Hong Kong who sub-contracted production to me has not paid me in months."

Source: Stephanie Tang, personal communication

The production system

Only a few categories of informal workers – including employees of informal enterprises and domestic workers – are dependent workers who work under the direct supervision of a given employer in his or her enterprise or home. Another category of the informal workforce – casual day labourers – is made up of dependent workers who work under the direct supervision of an employer but, by definition, do not have a fixed employer. Most other groups of informal workers operate under varying degrees of dependence or independence in a variety of production systems.

To understand the relative dependence or independence of these workers – the degree of authority they have over various aspects of their work and the share of work-related risks that they have to absorb – it is important to consider the nature of the production system under which they work. This is because the same type of worker within different production systems would be subject to different controls and risk. For instance, a home-based own account garment worker producing for a co-operative would face different controls or risks from one producing for the open market. Similarly, a homeworker producing garments for a local trader would face different controls or risks than one who produces for a supply firm linked to a multinational company. Types of production systems include:

- **Individual transactions:** Some categories of informal workers exchange goods and services in what might be characterised as open or pure market exchange (in the sense of independent units transacting with each other). In such cases, the dominant counterpart – in terms of market knowledge and power – controls the exchange or transaction. This is true for some self-employed persons, both employers and own account operators. It is also true for some paid workers, notably casual day labourers who sell their labour services to different employers.

- **Sub-sectors:** Many self-employed persons produce and exchange goods and services in what are called sub-sectors, that is, networks of independent units involved in the production and distribution of a particular product or commodity. In such networks, individual units are involved in a series of transactions with suppliers and customers. The terms and conditions of these transactions are governed largely by dominant counterparts in the individual transactions but also by the 'rules of the game' for the sub-sector determined by dominant firms in the network.

- **Value chains:** Some self-employed persons and, by definition, all homeworkers produce goods within a value chain. The terms and conditions of production in value chains are determined largely by the lead firm. However, the major suppliers to whom the lead firm sub-contracts work also help determine the terms and conditions of work that they sub-contract to firms and workers down the chain.

EPZs and global value chains

The reorganisation of production as part of economic globalisation has taken place at the national level by the creation of export processing zones and at the global level by the creation of global value chains. Most EPZs are established and governed by national governments in the South, whereas most global value chains are driven and governed by lead buyer or producer firms in the North. From 1970 to mid-1990s, the number of countries with EPZs grew from ten to over 70 (ILO, 1996). While most countries created industrial enclaves of export-oriented factories, others simply extended the EPZ incentives and protections to designated export-oriented firms scattered around the country. In real life, the distinction between global value chains and EPZs becomes blurred because many EPZ firms are sub-contracted as suppliers to specific global value chains.

In both types of system, there are marked shifts in focus:

- from *intra-firm* (or employer-employee) relationships to *firm-government* relationships (in the case of EPZs) or to *inter-firm* relationships (in the case of value chains); and

- from concerns of production (and workers) to concerns of distribution (and consumers).

These shifts have associated consequences for the workers within each system. For instance, as part of the EPZ package of incentives and protections, some governments offer exemption from national labour laws, including those that mandate a minimum wage and union representation. In global value chains, the lead firms tend to negotiate directly only with the first-tier of their suppliers, thereby retaining power and control within the chain and excluding those down the chain from direct negotiations and associated benefits.

There are basically two types of global value chains: producer-driven and buyer-driven chains. These apply mainly to manufactured goods, ranging from automobiles to garments. In producer-driven value chains (e.g. automobiles), large, usually transnational manufacturers play the central role of co-ordinating production networks (including their backward and forward linkages). The lead companies have considerable control over how, when and where manufacturing will take place, and how much profit accrues at each stage.

Buyer-driven value chains, by contrast, are characterised by highly competitive and globally decentralised factory systems with low entry barriers (Gereffi, 1994). The lead firms, such as fashion designers or private label retailers, control the functions that generate the most profitable returns – such as product design and brand name. Buyer-driven chains have been used more recently to analyse the global horticultural export industries (see Chapter 2). In both of these types of chains, the subcontracted workers and enterprises have little control over their terms of involvement (see Box 16).

Buyer-driven global value chain production tends to erode external patterns of socio-economic regulation and favour internal regulation and control by lead companies (Perret 1998). It also takes a toll on the bargaining position of labour relative to management. This is visible in the decreasing share of the value added being taken by wages in particular sectors or industries (Grunberg, 1998). In addition, given that a large share of workers in global value chains work from their homes, this pattern of work serves to undermine the socialisation function of work and to complicate efforts to unionise workers (Perret, 1998).

When production takes place through buyer-driven global value chains, the lead company usually outsources or sub-contracts production to, but does not set up operations in, the countries where production takes place.[19] This form of production undermines external regulation in two ways: (a) the local supply firms feel more accountable to the lead firm, as that firm provides them with work orders, than to local regulations; and

> *... given that a large share of workers in global value chains work from their homes, this pattern of work serves to undermine the socialisation function of work and to complicate efforts to unionise workers.*

> **Box 16 Buyer-driven Value Chains: A Classic Example**
>
> The garment or apparel industry is a classic example of a buyer-driven value chain that employs large numbers of women in developing countries. The ease of setting up clothing companies, coupled with the prevalence of developed country protectionism in this sector, has led to an unparalleled diversity of garment exporters in the developing world. From the perspective of the workforce, these chains are associated with high volatility and insecurity, long overtime working hours (during peak seasons), sudden cancellation of work orders and sudden closures of firms as production is shifted to another location or country. More recently, as noted earlier, the introduction of the electronic bar code in garment retailing and the associated system of 'just-in-time production' has led many manufacturers to shift the locus of production from Asia closer to Europe and the United States.

(b) the lead firm does not feel it is accountable to domestic laws and regulations in the countries that supply goods. In such contexts, efforts to make voluntary corporate codes of conduct legally binding and enforceable up and down the supply chain are important. This would include holding the lead firms responsible not only for the operations of their supply firms in EPZs and other such export enclaves but also in subcontracting relations outside such enclaves, all the way down to the homeworkers in their supply chains.

Attempts have been made to extend this type of analysis to chains for 'traditional' primary commodities through introducing the concept of a third type of chain – one that is trader-driven (Gibbon, 2001). Trader-driven chains link producers of these commodities to local processors-cum-traders who then export the commodities through buyer-driven chains (see Box 17). They do not use their power to co-ordinate the activities of other enterprises in the chain, but take a less proactive approach and are mostly interested in maximising their volume of output and their trading opportunities. Thus trader-driven chains are less structured and less controlled but result in greater price volatility and greater economic uncertainty for producers than would be the case in more tightly controlled chains that are co-ordinated from the top down.

> **Box 17 Value Chains and Non-timber Forest Products**
>
> Industries involving non-timber forest products – such as shea nuts or cashew nuts – are good examples of trader-driven chains in which large numbers of seemingly own account workers/independent producers (predominantly women) are, in fact, linked through a series of intermediaries (or traders) to local processors who in their turn supply global retailers in the North. Planters, a subsidiary of R J R Nabisco, is the world's largest single distributor of final-processed and branded cashews. The quality demands that distributors place on cashew nut processors makes the market very competitive for large-scale distribution. Thus, the relationship between processors in India and Brazil and final markets can be described as being more buyer-driven. In contrast, the chain down from local processors in India and Brazil to producers and suppliers is trader-driven, with intricate, multi-tiered networks of buyers.
>
> Source: Gibbon, 2001; Cambon, 2003

While both EPZs and global value chains are credited with creating new jobs, the employment created is often precarious.

While both EPZs and global value chains are credited with creating new jobs, the employment created is often precarious. In global value chains, lead companies are likely to shift the location of production from one country to another depending on competitive advantages, including the incentive packages offered by different countries. Similarly, EPZs in several countries have recently shifted to more capital-intensive production processes that require either fewer or more skilled workers.

It is important to note that self-employed/own-account workers operating outside EPZs are also involved in global production systems to varying degrees. Some are absorbed into these against their will and on terms unfavourable to themselves. Others actively seek out links with higher-value export markets – inevitably through some sort of production chain –

Paper bag makers, India
MARTHA CHEN

but they are not always successful in achieving this objective because of barriers to entry. Also, investment by large corporations in export-oriented production/processing activities using local resources and raw materials may deplete the supply or raise the price of these natural resources, forcing previously self-employed persons – e.g. small farmers or fisher folk – to become dependent wage workers without independence or security.

Conclusion

There have always been profound differences between formal and informal employment in terms of the place of work, employment status and production system. In developing countries, these facets of work have always been non-standard for the majority of workers. Over the past few decades, the process of informalisation of formerly 'standard' or formal jobs has been associated with changes along each of these dimensions. The net result is that the majority of the global workforce now works in so-called non-standard places of work, employment relationships and/or production systems. Some of these non-standard arrangements may have benefits for the workers involved, such as higher earnings, but they may also be associated with specific costs and risks, such as lack of benefits or long-term security. Effective poverty reduction requires maximising the benefits and minimising the costs associated with the employment opportunities available to the poor. As such, it needs to be built on an understanding of the costs and benefits associated with different work arrangements.

In our analysis of what is driving these changes, we have focused on macroeconomic trends and policies of various kinds. But the driving forces include not only economic policies and processes – treated as abstractions – but also various economic actors and agents. While we will discuss the role of these actors in Chapters 4 and 5, we feel it is important to highlight that transnational corporations (TNCs) are one of the driving forces behind global integration, given their control over resources, access to markets and development of new technologies (Oxfam, 2002a). In the manufacturing sector, for example, TNCs and (less so) their suppliers decide whether production takes place under direct hire or sub-contracting arrangements; in factories, small workshops or homes; and under sweatshop conditions or less precarious forms of employment. Clearly, the investment and labour policies of host countries provide legal support to – or constraints on – the strategies of TNCs; and clearly, global competition drives many of the decisions taken by companies. But, in the end, TNCs adopt their own business strategies. In sum, both macroeconomic trends and policies as well as corporate practices – particularly the practices of TNCs – serve to determine employment and associated welfare outcomes.

We hope that the preceding analysis has shown that who wins and who loses from trade liberalisation and growth depends on who they are, what they do and where they work. The analysis may seem quite pessimistic. This is so for various reasons. To begin with, while we acknowledge that jobs and economic opportunities are being created, we simply cannot say how many jobs and opportunities have been created even in absolute terms, much less in relative terms: that is, relative to the number of economic opportunities destroyed and, more importantly, to the number of economic opportunities needed,

> *Effective poverty reduction requires maximising the benefits and minimising the costs associated with the employment opportunities available to the poor. As such, it needs to be built on an understanding of the costs and benefits associated with different work arrangements.*

especially given the growing numbers in the population seeking work. Secondly, we discussed the 'downside' of the opportunities that are being created. This is because our analysis and findings are based on first-hand knowledge of specific groups who have struggled to benefit from the new opportunities associated with economic reforms. We acknowledge that, in many cases, the new opportunities are better than previously existing opportunities. But by pointing out the 'downside', we wanted to highlight how they could be improved to meet the standards of decent work.

In Chapters 4 and 5, we take up the challenge of what can be done to ensure that the working poor in the informal economy, particularly women, benefit more fully from the new opportunities. Chapter 4 presents a set of strategies with promising examples of how to increase the opportunities, rights, protection and voice of the informal workforce, especially those of women. In addition to governments, as the examples will illustrate, a range of actors can – and should – be involved in these initiatives. And in Chapter 5, we outline a strategic policy approach to the gender segmentation of the informal economy. What is required is a comprehensive policy approach, informed by an understanding of the economic contributions of the informal economy and premised on the notion that all policies affect women and men working in the informal sector.

Notes

1 For a discussion of the first two of these issues, see *Gender Mainstreaming in Poverty Eradication and the Millennium Development Goals* in this series (Kabeer, 2003). This Handbook is concerned with the third issue.

2 Given the diversity of the informal economy, all three perspectives on regulation are appropriate in regard to the specific components they refer to: de Soto focuses on informal *enterprises* (or informal *commercial* relationships); the labour advocates focus on informal *jobs* (or informal *employment* relationships); and those concerned about street vendors focus on the regulation of *urban space* and *informal trade*.

3 Liberalisation of labour markets implies: (a) wage flexibility; (b) flexibility in contractual arrangements; and (c) limited regulation in terms of the conditions under which labour is exchanged. It should be noted that international labour mobility is often excluded from discussions of labour market flexibility (James Heintz, personal communication).

4 See Whitehead, 2001 for a gender critique of the Winters framework.

5 Another strand of gender analysis, supported by the Commonwealth Secretariat, focuses on the 'government' channel of the Winters framework: namely, gender budget analysis that looks at the differential impacts of government taxes and expenditures by gender (see Budlender et al, 2002; Budlender and Hewitt, 2002; and Budlender and Hewitt, 2003). A parallel strand of informal labour market analysis looks at the differential impacts of government taxes and expenditures by size and type of enterprises and labour (formal and informal): see write-up on informal budget analysis in Chapter 5.

6 Global value chains are sub-contracting or out-sourcing chains that disperse the production process globally across different countries. While the site of production is spatially dispersed, the control of the different functions or operations is often quite tightly controlled by the lead firm. Global value chains are discussed more fully below under 'Production System'.

7 EPZs, which have been established in various developing countries since the 1960s, offer special incentives and protections to attract foreign direct investment and promote exports.

8 Some of these perspectives on labour markets have been identified by economists who study formal labour markets. But self-employment and informal wage employment have not been systematically integrated into mainstream labour market theory.

9 Regression analysis is a statistical technique used to test the tendency of a given variable in different countries to conform to a mean value.

10 For a particularly effective use of value chain analysis to assess how risk and uncertainty are passed down along the chains and how far benefits and protection reach down the chain, see Lund and Nicholson, 2003.

11 See the set of recent publications by Oxfam International that look at trade and poverty by considering three key export sectors: agriculture, garment manufacturing and coffee (Oxfam, 2002a; 2002b; 2004).

12 The *Human Development Report 1996* (UNDP, 1996) distinguished between growth that is employment-generating (which it termed 'job-led growth') and growth that does not generate sufficient employment opportunities to match growth in the economy or in the working age population (which it termed 'job-less growth').

13 A telekiosk, also called a community telecentre, is a community access point for information and communications services.

14 Digiports are the equivalent for the information and communication industries to EPZs for manufacturing. They are the base from which data entry for airlines and other service industries is provided.

15 These statistics cover 19 OECD countries. Recent members – the Czech Republic, Hungary, Iceland, Mexico, Poland, Republic of Korea and Turkey – are not included.

16 An International Symposium on Migration held in Bangkok, Thailand in April 1999 recommended the use of the term 'irregular', rather than 'illegal' (which connotes criminality), since irregularities in migration may be committed *against* the migrant not just by the migrant (ILO, 2004a).

17 This discussion of 'place of work' draws on Lund and Unni, 2004. The term 'home-based' is used to refer to work that takes place in or around the home and, as such, may include a wide range of activities, including post-harvest processing, beekeeping, poultry rearing and animal husbandry.

18 The WIEGO network has initiated a project to develop a unified conceptual framework for labour statistics and labour law that includes all categories of non-standard and/or informal employment status.

19 Outsourcing of sub-contracting production is, arguably, the ultimate form of capital mobility. We suggest that the term 'foreign *indirect* investment' (FII) be used for the sub-contracted or outsourced mode of foreign investment, as opposed to foreign direct investment (FDI) when a foreign company sets up a branch or unit in another country.

4. Decent Work for Informal Workers: Promising Strategies and Examples

Around the world, there has been a range of responses to the opportunities and risks associated with trade liberalisation and the changing nature of work detailed in Chapter 3. Many different actors – international agencies, governments, the private sector and civil society – have been involved in these initiatives, sometimes working individually but often working together and hand-in-hand with organisations of informal workers and producers. In Chapter 4, we present a selected set of these promising examples drawn from different corners of the world and involving different actors. We use the four pillars of the Decent Work agenda of the International Labour Organization – opportunities, rights, protection and voice – to organise these examples in a meaningful way.

As noted earlier, the ILO has played a lead role in making the case for putting employment creation and the concept of 'decent work' firmly on the development agenda in an attempt to inform and influence the economic policies of national and local governments. As part of this wider effort, they have promoted the notion of decent work for all workers, including those in the informal economy. In 2002, the International Labour Conference – comprising governments, employers and unions – approved the Conclusions to a General Discussion on 'Decent Work and the Informal Economy' that provide a mandate for the ILO to integrate a focus on the informal economy into its work (ILC, 2002d).

Under the four goals of the Decent Work agenda, we have identified a number of key strategies and grouped the examples according to which of these they illustrate, as follows:

… the ILO has played a lead role in making the case for putting employment creation and the concept of 'decent work' firmly on the development agenda in an attempt to inform and influence the economic policies of national and local governments.

Goal 1: **Promoting opportunities**
Strategy 1.1 – promoting employment-oriented growth
Strategy 1.2 – promoting a supportive environment
Strategy 1.3 – increasing access and competitiveness
Strategy 1.4 – improving skills and technologies

> *Governments in several countries have recognised the importance of putting employment at the centre of the development process and have developed and implemented policies to reflect this change of focus.*

Goal 2: **Securing rights**
Strategy 2.1 – securing rights of informal wage workers
Strategy 2.2 – securing rights of the self-employed

Goal 3: **Promoting protection**
Strategy 3.1 – promoting protection against common contingencies
Strategy 3.2 – promoting protection for migrant workers

Goal 4: **Promoting voice**
Strategy 4.1 – organising informal workers
Strategy 4.2 – promoting collective bargaining
Strategy 4.3 – building international alliances

We have also indicated the importance of collecting statistics on the informal economy as a strategy to support all these goals.

Goal 1: Promoting Opportunities

Promoting employment-oriented growth

In order to promote growth that creates new jobs and earning opportunities, explicit employment-oriented decisions are required in regard to which sectors, technologies, production sites and sizes of enterprises should be supported. Ideally, governments and policy-makers at both the national and local levels should put employment on the macroeconomic policy agenda as a priority goal, rather than as a hoped-for outcome – a residual – of other policies, and should be supported in this endeavour by the policies and programmes of the international development agencies and financing institutions.

Governments in several countries have recognised the importance of putting employment at the centre of the development process and have developed and implemented policies to reflect this change of focus. There are examples of this at the national, state and local municipal levels.

Since 1999, many heavily-indebted countries have developed national poverty reduction strategy papers, which are meant to provide a blueprint for growth, poverty reduction and human development. While these are supposed to be developed through participatory processes, trade unions and workers' organisations have not always been involved. As a result of this and other factors, most PRSPs do not pay sufficient attention to employment as a key pathway to poverty reduction. However, in some countries, trade unions have been involved and employment issues have been incorporated in the PRSPs.

In addition, several national and provincial governments have been experimenting with policies that aim either to revive economic sectors that have suffered a decline as a result of economic restructuring or to promote those for which there are growing markets internationally.

Tripartite action on poverty reduction, Tanzania

The ILO is working with trade unions and employers' associations in Tanzania to enhance their role and contribution to the PRSP process as part of a pilot programme in five countries. Workshops have been held with unions and employers to familiarise them with the process and engage them in the setting of policies, strategies and targets. Concerns raised by the unions included inadequate emphasis on the agricultural sector (where most people work), lack of gender mainstreaming targets, lack of attention to health and safety in the workplace and the low quality of vocational training. (Source: DFID, 2003)

Unions fight for employment not welfare, Bolivia

With the loss of jobs in the formal sector, following privatisation in 1985, people in Bolivia moved out of the formal into the informal economy, seeking to earn their living in areas such as small-scale mining, artisanal manufacture and the transport sector. In doing so they lost job security and welfare benefits. In the search for new alternatives in the framework of a liberal market economy, trade unionists have brought with them the values, norms and strategies of the old trade union movement. Although self-employed, they refer to themselves as 'workers' and couch their political activity as a struggle for rights. The Comite Enlave, founded in 1999, is a confederation of associations of micro-enterprise workers that aims to give stronger political voice to those working in micro-enterprise so as to deliver policy outcomes in their favour, for example, the rights to tender for local government contracts or to benefit from tax incentives for mining experts. Both these groupings were active during the PRSP consultation process, challenging a government model of poverty reduction that conceived poverty primarily as lack of access to basic social services. As a result, the final PRSP gave some recognition to livelihood as a poverty issue, and the associated legislation gave a voice to producers in the machinery of local government. (Source: DFID, 2003)

Government support to small export industries, Mozambique

When the Government of Mozambique reduced the export tariff on raw cashew nuts as part of its structural adjustment programme in the 1990s, most of the country's processing factories closed down because of the reduced availability of raw nuts on the domestic market. In order to revive the industry and to create employment, the Government is supporting the private sector in its use of smaller-scale, semi-mechanised technology, which provides many more jobs – especially for women. It also gives much better quality products (and thus higher demand and price in export markets) as the less capital-intensive methods are not so likely to break the cashews during processing. This policy has involved co-ordinated effort at three levels:

- *production*, through increased spending on research and development, which increases the incomes of smallholders and the thousands of people who survive through sale and processing of nuts in local markets;

- *increased processing*, through loans to the private sector to establish small-scale factories processing for export, which create jobs in rural areas; and

- *commercialisation*, through raising export taxes on cashew nuts, which discourages sale of raw nuts overseas and encourages local processing, thus creating more jobs. (Source: Kanji et al, 2004)

State government promotes employment in horticulture, India

The government of Andhra Pradesh in India aims to establish and rapidly expand a food processing industry and attract foreign investment. It anticipates that, by 2020, Andhra Pradesh will have a thriving horticulture sector and will be the country's leading supplier of fruits and vegetables to both domestic and international markets. Horticulture is expected to account for 10 to 15 per cent of the state's GDP and contribute convincingly to higher per capita agricultural incomes. The strategy for achieving this growth in horticulture is through private sector investment in infrastructure and food processing. It also includes strengthening of the fresh produce value chain through farmer co-operatives and the provision of institutional support. This includes the establishment of Agricultural Export Zones (AEZs). Companies locating within AEZs are offered incentives to enter contract-farming arrangements with producers, with a view to improving standards and cutting wastage. Companies benefit by accessing an assured supply of low-cost, high quality produce, and farmers will have an assured market and technical and financial support. Companies, farmers and the government are to enter into a tripartite contract. The employment-generating potential of horticulture is not treated as a direct objective, but may be the major benefit. Employment generation through vegetable production creates more jobs than traditional crops. (Source: Deshingkar et al, 2003)

Promoting a supportive environment

In several countries, including India, Kenya and South Africa, the national or local government has adopted policies on the informal economy.

Policy support to artisans, India

India has a rich tradition of handicrafts and artisanal production. While industrialisation has displaced most handicrafts in many other countries, the Government of India has followed a deliberate policy for more than 40 years to promote artisans. Most of the assistance has gone to master crafts persons who produce for both the domestic and international market. Government measures to promote artisan production included setting up ministries for handicrafts, reserving raw materials and markets for designated products, undertaking research on designs and technologies and providing special budgets and subsidies. When India liberalised its economic policies, many of its artisans were able to take advantage of global markets. The sector nearly doubled in size from 1991 to 1998. Recent estimates suggest that there are nearly 10 million skilled crafts persons in the country, contributing $5.6 billion to India's GDP. The artisanal sector is also a major contributor to India's export earnings. (Source: WIEGO, 2002)

National policy on street vendors, India

This policy, jointly drafted by the Government of India and the National Association of Street Vendors, was officially adopted in early 2004. The overarching objective of the policy is to provide and promote a supportive environment for earning livelihoods to the street vendors, as well as ensure absence of congestion and maintenance of hygiene in public spaces and streets. The following are the basic objectives of the policy:

- **Legal:** To give vendors legal status by amending, enacting, repealing and implementing appropriate laws and providing legitimate hawking zones in urban development/zoning plans.

- **Facilities:** To provide facilities for appropriate use of identified space, including the creation of hawking zones in the urban development/zoning plans.

- **Regulation:** To not impose numerical limits on access to public spaces by discretionary licenses and instead move to fee-based regulation of access.

- **Role in distribution:** To make street vendors a special component of the urban development/zoning plans by treating them as an integral and legitimate part of the urban distribution system.

- **Self-compliance:** To promote self-compliance among street vendors.

- **Organisation:** To promote organisations of street vendors, e.g. unions/co-operatives/associations and other forms of organisation to facilitate their empowerment.

- **Participation:** To set up participatory mechanisms with representation by urban vendors' organisations (unions/co-operatives/associations), voluntary organisations, local authorities, the police, Residents Welfare Associations (RWAs) and others for orderly conduct of urban vending activities.

- **Rehabilitation of child vendors:** To take measures for promoting a better future for child vendors by making appropriate interventions for their rehabilitation and schooling.

- *Social security and financial services:* To provide/promote social security (pension, insurance, etc) and access to credit for street vendors through promotion of self-help groups, co-operatives and micro-finance institutions. (Source: Government of India (Ministry of Urban Development and Poverty Alleviation), 2004)

Fishmonger, Kenya
MARTHA CHEN

National policy for micro and small enterprises development, Kenya

Recognising its contribution to economic prosperity, the Government of Kenya has for many years incorporated the informal economy into its national economic planning, initially through a Sessional Paper in 1986 that detailed direct assistance to entrepreneurs and small businesses. This included the provision of credit, training and marketing services as well as government procurement from the informal economy. Since 1986, the Government has continued to address the informal economy through a number of specific policies and its five-year Development Plans. The 1997/2001 Development Plan highlights the promotion of the micro and small enterprises (MSE) sector by addressing:

- developing and reviewing the legal framework and regulatory environment;
- formulating and developing programmes to improve access to credit and finance;
- supporting women and youth involvement in the small/medium scale and informal sector through special programmes;
- encouraging strong backward linkages with the manufacturing sector; and
- reviewing and harmonising licensing procedures for informal sector enterprises

The 2002/2008 Development Plan moves beyond the previous plan and points out that measures will be taken to:

- decentralise registration of business names to district level;
- eliminate trade licensing at central government level and harmonise, rationalise and implement a Single Business Permit system;
- review laws and regulations;
- enact an MSE Act; and
- ensure control and regulation of hawking within the Central Business District (CBD) in urban areas.

Although prior to 2000 many of the national policies on the small and medium-enterprise (SME) sector were not implemented, there has been a concerted effort since 2000 to implement the national SME policy. For example, most of the provisions in the 1997/2001 and 2002/2008 Development Plans are being implemented. The Single Business Permit has been implemented in all local authorities, street vendors have been relocated, laws and regulations are being reviewed and a Draft Sessional Paper on MSE has been prepared through a participatory approach. Other Draft Sessional Papers that have been prepared include: Gender and Development, Micro Financial Institutions, Labour Laws and a Local Government Bill. Kenya is going through a transition where most legal and regulatory provisions, including the Constitution are being reviewed. In sum, the National Rainbow Coalition (NARC) government has renewed the national commitment to small and medium-enterprise development. (Source: Dorothy McCormick and Winnie Mitullah, personal communication)

Local government policy, South Africa

In recognition of the significant contribution of the informal economy to economic and social life, the Durban (now called eThekwini) Metropolitan Council decided in 2000 to develop a comprehensive policy approach to the informal economy. This is an excellent example of policy-making for the urban informal economy, from elaborating a vision for its role in the long-term economic plans for the city, to turning that vision into policy and moving to set up an implementation strategy with institutional structures.

In 1994, with the advent of democratic government and Nelson Mandela as President, the new South African Constitution mandated local government to promote local economic development and adopt pro-poor urban policies emphasising participation and consultation. In 1999, Durban/eThekwini embarked on a one-year process of policy development to both support and control the informal economy. Early in the process the policy team adopted a shared vision of the role and importance of the informal economy as an important job creator and contributor to the city's economy, organically linked to the formal economy. They saw street traders as workers who were an integral part of the city's life and economy, not survivalists or welfare cases. Research on informal trade sectors – including clothing and accessories, traditional medicine, fruits and vegetables – supported the making of policy. The team consulted with poorer traders and their organisations. In workshops, mass meetings and other settings, workers identified their priority needs and expressed their views on possible mechanisms for integrating the informal economy into local government structures. The policy development process benefited from the existence of a number of pilot projects in urban renewal and in city health, through which officials learned the importance and cost-effectiveness of negotiated change.

Some aspects of the policy and its implementation include:

- simplification of registration costs for vendors and home-based workers, with incentives for registration;

- representation of informal trader organisations on planning and policy committees;

- provision of support to trader organisations (e.g. meeting places, legal advice and secretarial help), using existing municipal assets;

- city officials and traders working together to improve the image of the informal economy. (Source: Durban Metropolitan Council, 2001)

The establishment of an implementation team followed the 18-month policy development process. The South African economy is fragile, and local governments are under pressure to deliver on a number of fronts. Nevertheless, the policy process continues to build, including the strengthening of organisations of informal traders so that government has strong partners with whom to negotiate. Positive aspects of the policy include:

- It is pro-development and dovetails with the economic development policy set by the city government.

- The policy process was widely consultative with all major stakeholders.

- It is pro-poor, targeting the poorest segments of the informal economy (street vendors and homeworkers).

- It combines area-based management with sector-based support to micro and small enterprises.

- It promotes a co-ordinated approach among the various city departments dealing with informal economy issues.

- It seeks to promote complementarity and synergies between the formal and informal parts of the economy – including through dealing with formal and informal economy issues in the same institutional structures and processes.

- It integrates support for enterprise development with a supportive regulatory framework, environmental and occupational safety and health measures, promotion of safety and security through local action and organisation of informal actors. (Source: ibid)

Examples of two support programmes offered by the municipality for two quite different categories of the informal workforce – the traditional medicine sector and waste collectors – can be found in Box 18.

Increasing market access and competitiveness

As we saw in Chapter 3, many of the working poor, and especially women who are involved in micro-enterprise or own account activities, are unable to take advantage of new opportunities being opened up as a result of privatisation and trade liberalisation because they lack access to credit, skills and business training, improved technologies (including ICTs), markets and market information, infrastructure and other economic resources. In addition, the economic policy environment tends to be biased in favour of large and medium enterprises and ignores or discriminates against micro-enterprises and own account workers.

Business development services aimed at increasing the access to markets and economic resources and competitiveness of micro-enterprises and own account workers have frequently been tried both by governments and by non-governmental organisations (NGOs). Government services have generally failed to successfully reach the smaller enterprises and own account workers and, while NGOs have had some successes,

Box 18 Two Support Programmes Offered by the Durban/eThekwini Municipality

Traditional medicine support programme: A significant component of the informal economy in South Africa is the traditional medicine (or muthi) sector. Eighty per cent of black South Africans use traditional medicine, often in parallel with modern medicine. It is estimated that 61 million rand (+- US$8.7 million) of medicinal plant material is traded in KwaZulu-Natal (KZN) annually, with Durban/eThekwini the primary trading and dispensing node. Over 30,000 people work in this sector, mostly as rural gatherers who are largely women. Collecting and dispensing of traditional medicine occurs almost entirely in the informal economy.

The muthi demand and turnover figures cited above convinced the Durban/eThekwini City Council to take this industry seriously. Consequently the Council, in consultation with existing traders, developed a dedicated built market, with shelter, storage, water and toilet facilities, which accommodates 550 stallholders. The market facilities, which also include a product processing plant, have significantly improved the working environment for traders. There are also initiatives aimed to address environmental sustainability issues. These include: (a) training gatherers in sustainable harvesting techniques, which has led to the establishment of a sustainable bark harvesters association (the first organisation of its kind in South Africa); and (b) a cultivation drive, including a dedicated medicinal plant nursery that produces seedlings to supply farmers and trains traditional healers in growing methods.

In the next phase of the support programme a black empowerment company, consisting predominantly of existing healers and traders, will be established. The company will procure plant material from existing industry role players and contract growers, process it in partnership with an existing pharmaceutical operation and market the

Box 18 (continued)

products. The objective is not only to service existing clients better, but also to access more middle class South African consumers of all races as well as an international market.

Source: Mander, 1998; Institute for Natural Resources, 2003

Buy-back centres for waste collectors: Waste collectors are amongst the poorest of those working in the informal economy. In South Africa, since legislated racial segregation of urban areas was abolished, there have been increasing numbers of waste collectors operating throughout its cities. These are largely black women whose incomes are extremely low. In the mid 1990's the Self Employed Women's Union (SEWU) organised cardboard collectors in the inner city of Durban/eThekwini. The union found that these collectors were innumerate and often exploited by unscrupulous middle men, and it lobbied local government to assist them.

Through SEWU's activism, and the understanding by the City Council that waste collection provided a livelihood for many residents, a buy-back centre was established in the inner city. This is a public-private-community partnership. The Council provided a small plot of centrally located land that was converted into the centre, and a large private sector recycler provided the scales, storage containers for the cardboard and trolleys for the collectors. SEWU worked alongside city officials to design the intervention and trained the cardboard collectors on how to weight their cardboard. Through this intervention, the collectors sold their cardboard directly to the recycling company. This has substantially increased the (albeit still low) incomes of these waste collectors. The success of the inner city buy-back centre has led to the Council establishing a number of similar centres throughout the city.

Source: Mgingqizana, 2002

The global Fair Trade movement has two distinct components: one that seeks to improve labour standards for wage workers, the other that seeks to increase market access and competitiveness for small producers.

their outreach has been extremely limited. More recently, there is evidence that lessons have been learned from past experiences and that both governments and NGOs – and particularly now the private sector and civil society organisations and associations – are beginning to have more success. Some selected examples are outlined below, which cover:

- alternative and Free Trade;
- other strategies for linking producers with markets;
- markets and ICTs;
- skills training and improved production technologies.[1]

Informal producers organising for alternative trade, international

The global Fair Trade movement has two distinct components: one that seeks to improve labour standards for wage workers, the other that seeks to increase market access and competitiveness for small producers. Under the second component, efforts are made to provide better trading conditions and to raise consumer awareness. The goals of this component of Fair Trade are to:

- improve the livelihoods and well-being of producers by improving market access, strengthening producer organisations, paying a better price and providing continuity in the trading relationship;
- promote development opportunities for disadvantaged producers, especially women and indigenous people, and protect children from exploitation in the production process;
- raise awareness among consumers of the negative effects on producers of international trade so that they exercise their purchasing power positively;
- set an example of partnership in trade through dialogue, transparency and respect;
- campaign for changes in the rules and practice of conventional international trade; and
- protect human rights by promoting social justice, sound environmental practices and economic security.

There are several key networking or membership organisations that seek to bring Fair Trade organisations together (see Box 19).

> **Box 19 Fair Trade Organisations**
>
> The following are the key networking organisations in the area of Fair Trade. Each services a different group of Fair Trade organisations and therefore takes a different perspective on the nature of the issue:
>
> **The International Federation for Alternative Trade (IFAT):** is a global network of 13 Fair Trade organisations in 47 countries. The members include: alternative trading organisations (ATOs) helping disadvantaged producers toward equity in trading relationships; marketing organisations designed to benefit producers rather than to maximise profits; and handicraft and agricultural production groups based in developing countries.
>
> **The Fairtrade Labelling Organisation (FLO):** is responsible for ensuring co-operation between independent Fair Trade certification bodies on monitoring and standards. Monitoring of the producers is paid for by the consumer. Products for which a register exists are coffee, tea, cocoa, sugar, bananas, orange juice and honey.
>
> **The Network of World Shops (NEWS):** co-ordinates co-operation between World Shops, where fairly traded products take up most of the stock, all over Western Europe. Consists of 15 national World Shops associations in 13 countries and a total of 2,500 World Shops.
>
> **The European Fair Trade Association (EFTA):** enables co-operation between 13 European ATOs to assist them in taking co-ordinated and effective action.
>
> **FINE:** was established by the other four networks in an effort to unite standards and approaches. A major achievement was the agreement on the definition of Fair Trade (see above).
>
> Source: Redfern and Snedker, 2002

Fair Trade partnership with local co-operative, Ghana

A good example of how Fair Trade works in practice is that of the Kuapa Kokoo cocoa co-operative in Ghana. A UK Fair Trade organisation (Twin Trading) joined with an NGO in the Netherlands (SNV) to assist the co-operative, with its 45,000 members, to join the FLO cocoa producers' register. This enables importers and chocolate companies to source beans from the co-operative under Fair Trade conditions. These markets give the smallholders a guaranteed fair price plus a premium of $150 per tonne. The premium is then used by the co-operative members to invest in community development projects such as wells, corn mills and schools, which are priorities for women in their everyday lives. In addition, the co-operative has established the Day Chocolate Company as a joint venture in the UK that markets Divine brand chocolate to retailers. The co-operative provided 33 per cent of the equity stake in the company and receives 66 per cent of the profits. (Source: Tiffen P et al, 2004; Redfern and Snedket, 2002)

Multinational corporation sources from informal producers, South Africa

Sourcing of commodities and products from informal producers is not limited to the Fair Trade market. For example, in collaboration with the South African Council of Scientific and Industrial Research, Daimler Chrysler is using natural fibres from small farms in South Africa to make interior car parts. The project matches the environmental needs of the company and is a social and environmental win-win for the local communities. Daimler Chrysler was under regulatory pressure to increase the amount of recoverable materials in its cars to meet the European Union directive that requires vehicles to become at least 95 per cent recoverable by 2015. Regenerative natural fibres are a good choice for such dilemmas, as they are lighter than glass-based fibres for interiors and require much less energy to manufacture. Furthermore, their production generates income for poor farmers. Daimler Chrysler has recently transferred the experience to Brazil, including stakeholder dialogue and engagement. Working with Daimler Chrysler, the Poverty and Environment in the Amazon Programme (POEMA), a local NGO, and the University of Pará have developed a method to stuff car headrests and seat parts with coconut fibre, which is a waste product that the poor villagers can collect. (Source: Maya Forstater et al, 2003; *www.daimlerchrysler.com*)

Social entrepreneur links rural beekeepers with export markets, Kenya

Another way in which informal producers can reach export markets is through social entrepreneurship. A good example of this is the social entrepreneur who set up Honey Care Africa about four years ago in Kenya. Since then the company has enabled almost 12,000 rural beekeepers to improve their incomes by linking them with markets in Europe with the help of funds from almost 20 donors. It does this through a tripartite model that involves a private sector company (Honey Care), a development organisation and the rural communities. Honey Care guarantees to purchase every kilogram of honey a beekeeper can produce at a fair and fixed price and to pay in cash on the day of collection. It then processes and packs this honey and sell it at a profit to export markets. It also provides the necessary training for the rural communities and, where economically viable, it provides extension support. While its main product at the moment is honey, for which it has International Organic and Fair Trade Certification, Honey Care is also exploring higher value products such as royal jelly, pollen and beeswax as well as doing research on developing better beekeeping technology. The development organisation has experience in working with rural communities and has extensive outreach into the rural areas, thus providing a conduit to beekeepers and ensuring that an exploitative relationship does not develop between the private sector organisation and the beekeepers. In some instances, it also provides loans to beekeepers to acquire improved beehives. The loans are recoverable at the time that the honey is sold to Honey Care. (Source: Jiwa, 2002)

Women's cashew business creates market linkages for informal women producers, Senegal

A Dakar-based company owned by two women from Benin holds the single largest market for processed cashew nuts. The first company to formally commercialise cashew kernels in

Senegal, it has been buying all its kernels from women's associations based in the Kaolack and Farick regions for over ten years. Through close linkages over time with 12 of these groups, which involve an estimated 300 women in six villages, they have developed a product that sells well in key markets north of The Gambia. They distribute an elegantly packaged brand of artisanally-processed nuts in a chain of petrol stations in Dakar and other major urban centres. They enjoy strong name recognition in Dakar, having been recently brand marketed. (Source: Cambon, 2003)

NGO helps to link local producers with supermarkets, international

NGOs are also active in linking local producers with global markets. For example, Technoserve, an international NGO, has been experimenting with ways to enable local producers to benefit from the rapid spread of supermarkets in the global South. Between 1990 and 2000, throughout Latin America and South Africa, supermarkets grew from 15 to 55 per cent of the total food retail sector. In Kenya, supermarkets now account for between 20 and 30 per cent of this sector. For other African countries – such as Ghana, Mozambique, Tanzania and Uganda – the growth of supermarkets has not been as dramatic, but researchers predict swift changes in the next five years. Shifts in demographics are creating the critical mass of consumers that supermarkets need in order to be profitable. A growing urban middle class can now afford to buy packaged foods, brand names and gourmet items, and more working class residents are in need of 'one stop' shopping.

Technoserve believes that, for rural entrepreneurs in developing countries to sell their products to urban supermarkets, they need to (a) understand how supermarkets procure products and (b) use post harvest methods that meet the needs of the companies they want to sell to – or that give them a competitive advantage over other suppliers. This involves going far beyond traditional washing and crating of products to include packaging, labelling – even bar-coding and refrigerated delivery. It also means that most entrepreneurs will need investment capital to make this giant leap forward. In Ghana, in 2002, Technoserve trained 322 small-scale pineapple and citrus fruit farmers in organic production, helped them to become organically certified and then established a commercial link to Athena Foods, a local juice processing plant. Athena, in turn, processed and bottled $400,000 of organic juice for a new supermarket client in the Netherlands. All over Africa, it is hoped that the development of supermarkets may provide a stepping stone to supermarkets in the US and Europe for other producers and entrepreneurs who succeed at becoming part of the farm-to consumer chain in their own countries. (Source: Technoserve, 2002)

Trade union obtains marketing license for informal women producers, India

Trade unions have helped their members to link with markets in a variety of ways. For example, during the agricultural off-season about 80–90 per cent of women in Gujarat, India, engage in gum collection from the forest areas where they live. Although there is a thriving open market for gum that includes textile and pharmaceutical companies, the collectors have historically been restricted by law to selling their products to the National Forest Department. The Self Employed Women's Association (SEWA) negotiated with the Gujarat State Forestry Development Corporation to obtain a license for their members to collect gum and to sell it to private traders who pay higher prices.

SEWA Marketing now sells about 60,000 kilograms of gum per year to the textile processing, pharmaceutical, fire cracker and printing industries at the rate of 20 rupees per kg for black gum, 35 rupees per kg for red gum and 60 rupees per kg for white gum. The Forest Development Corporation continues to procure gum at the rate of 9 rupees per kg. SEWA Rural has also worked extensively to facilitate the transfer of appropriate technology and skills so that gum collectors can increase their yields and secure a better price for their products. In addition, SEWA has partnered with the Centre for Science for Villages to provide training for women on improved collection techniques and the production of various gum-derived products, such as chocolates, chewing gum and a variety of Indian sweets. (Source: Chen, Jhabvala and Nanavaty, 2003)

Access to markets is only half of the battle in assisting small producers to benefit from the opening up of markets. They must also be able to compete in these markets in terms of quality, price and delivery.

Women fishworkers union uses ICTs as marketing tool, Senegal

In Africa, many women entrepreneurs who are traders, ranging from micro-trading in foodstuffs to large-scale import-export trade, are in need of market information and are beginning to use ICTs to access this. In Senegal, the Grand Coast Fishing Operators Union, an organisation of women who market fish and fish producers, uses ICTs to exchange information on supply and demand between their different locations along the Atlantic coast. The women feel that this tool has improved their competitiveness in the local market. They are planning a website to enable the nearly 7,500 members to promote their produce, monitor export markets and negotiate prices with overseas buyers before they arrive in Senegal. (Source: Hafkin and Taggart, 2001)

Improving skills and technologies

Access to markets is only half of the battle in assisting small producers to benefit from the opening up of markets. They must also be able to compete in these markets in terms of quality, price and delivery. Normally, this will mean assistance with skills training, improved production technologies and credit. The following examples show that NGOs and women's membership associations and trade unions have been particularly active in this field. As will be seen, skills training has in all cases been linked with market considerations.

Training for self-employment, Bangladesh

The Centre for Mass Education in Science (CMES), an NGO that was founded in Bangladesh in 1978, uses a flexible skills training programme that leads to immediate income generation. The programme is directed at adolescents and youth who can afford education only in terms of learning while earning. It now serves 20,000 students in 17 rural areas and has a specific gender empowerment programme aimed at helping young women to shake off discrimination and stereotypes and to take an active part in the economy in terms of more challenging, skilled work. A crucial aspect of the programme is the careful examination of the present state of the economic and technology scenario, especially in the informal economy and its interface with the formal economy. It identifies and pilots small income-generating activities that have not been tried before in the villages, including soap and candle making, solar electrification and computer use. (Source: ILO, 2002)

Skills upgrading and marketing services for informal clothing manufacture, South Africa

In 1999, the City Garment Project was initiated to support the nearly 2,000 informal clothing manufacturers operating in the Johannesburg inner city. This project is a collaboration between the Johannesburg Development Agency – set up by the City Council to redevelop the inner city – a local businessman and a development consultancy, Bees Consulting Group (BCG). There are two inter-related components of the project: skills upgrading and securing access to new markets. The local businessman has established a sewing training and display centre that offers subsidised sewing courses. So far over 300 garment operators have been trained. A system of business mentorship has been established in which second and third year business science students from CIDA Business School, a college located in the inner city, assist individual entrepreneurs in business strategy. In terms of accessing new markets, the project focuses on establishing business linkages, particularly between garment operators and designers. It also actively seeks orders from institutions such as schools. Further, a number of fashion shows have been held, giving exposure to the garments being made in the district. A recent impact assessment concluded that those who had been involved in the project had improved the quality of their garments and their production process and manufactured a much greater variety of products. It was also demonstrated that they now kept business records and were able to market their products. In addition, they secured more orders because of the variety of their products. (Source: Jocum and Cachalia, 2002)

NGO links women with improved technology to produce for export markets, Samoa

In addition to skills training, the introduction of improved production technologies can also be necessary to compete in export markets. Women in Business Development Incorporated, an NGO, assisted several rural communities in Samoa to acquire an improved processing technology that has enabled them to access export markets for organic virgin coconut oil and associated value-added products. In addition to assistance with technology transfer, the NGO has helped with credit for the purchase of equipment and with training of village women and their families in the operation of the new technology. It has also helped to identify markets, to obtain organic certification and monitor standards and to establish a central purchasing export company. (Source: Cretney and Tafuna'i , 2004)

Trade union obtains marketing license for informal women producers, India

ICTs can also be used by informal producers to increase productivity and competitiveness. The National Development Dairy Cooperative, whose 10.7 million member-owners produce the major share of processed liquid milk marketed in India, introduced a computerised system to measure and evaluate the milk that small producers delivered to their local collection centres. In the past, the fat content in the milk was calculated through a cumbersome measurement process hours after the milk was received. Farmers were paid every ten days based on the co-operative society staff's manual calculations of the quality and quantity of milk. Malfeasance and underpayment to farmers, although difficult to substantiate, were commonly alleged.

With the new computerised system, dairy farmers receive immediate payment and save considerable time. Farmers delivering milk to the collection centres drop their identification card into an electronic reading machine that transmits the identification number to a computer. The farmer's milk is then emptied into a steel trough, and the weight is instantly displayed to the farmer and communicated to the computer. A sample is also fed into a machine that determines the milk's fat content in seconds, displaying it to the farmer while electronically recording it. The total value of the milk is then printed on a payment slip and issued to the farmer, who collects the payment at an adjoining window. In many centres the entire transaction takes no more than 30 seconds from delivery to payment. The system is currently installed at 2,500 milk collection centres, benefiting more than 50,000 dairy farmers. (Source: Jhabvala and Kanbur, 2002)

Goal 2: Securing Rights

Securing rights of informal wage workers

As we saw in Chapter 3, even when economic reforms lead to the creation of jobs there are often concerns expressed as to the quality of these jobs. Specific areas of concern, as the examples in Chapter 3 illustrate, include the situation of informal workers, especially women, in labour-intensive manufacturing, commercial agriculture, horticulture and globalised service provision. Within and across these sectors, there are important differences between informal workers, both women and men, who work in export processing zone factories, other units in EPZ enclaves, domestic factories or workshops, commercial farms and home-based sub-contracted production.

Strategies that have been adopted in an attempt to deal with this issue include:

- the development and ratification of international labour standards and conventions and the development, implementation and monitoring of codes of conduct;

- changes in national labour legislation, including extending the scope of the employment relationship; and

- collective bargaining agreements and grievance mechanisms.

Labour standards and codes of conduct, international

In 1988, the ILO produced the Declaration on the Fundamental Principles and Rights at Work. In the Declaration, the ILO's Member States agreed that, regardless of their level of development, they should all respect, promote and realise:

- freedom of association and the effective recognition of the right to collective bargaining;

- the elimination of all forms of forced or compulsory labour;

- the effective abolition of child labour; and

- the elimination of discrimination in respect of employment and occupation.

Together, these are known as the core labour standards that

MAINSTREAMING INFORMAL EMPLOYMENT AND GENDER IN POVERTY REDUCTION

The work of a number of activist organisations led to the elaboration of the only ILO Convention specifically targeted to the informal economy – the 1996 ILO Convention on Home Work ... which sets out minimum standards as to pay and working conditions for homeworkers.

should, in principle, apply to all workers. However, with the increasing globalisation and changing employment relations described in Chapter 3, many workers find themselves excluded.

ILO Convention for Homeworkers, international

For example, as the number of homeworkers has increased, labour standards and collective bargaining have been bypassed, leading to unacceptable standards of work. The work of a number of activist organisations led to the elaboration of the only ILO Convention specifically targeted to the informal economy – the 1996 ILO Convention on Home Work (Convention No 177) – which sets out minimum standards as to pay and working conditions for homeworkers. A related Recommendation, also passed in 1996, details a full programme to improve the conditions of homeworkers. To date, only Finland and Ireland have ratified the Convention, although several other countries are considering national legislation in line with the Convention and its Recommendation, and the EU has encouraged its member states to consider ratification. The text of the Convention can be found in Appendix 1.

Voluntary codes of conduct

Closely associated with core labour standards are voluntary codes of conduct. Over the past three decades, as corporations have grown both in size and in terms of influence over all aspects of economic and social development, there has been an associated shift of power from governments to large corporations. This growth in the size and influence of corporations is now accompanied by calls for companies to act responsibly. One mechanism through which this is achieved is the implementation and monitoring of voluntary codes of conduct. These are voluntary agreements drawn up at a company, industry or multi-sector level to outline basic social or ethical standards. A popular issue around which codes of conduct have been developed is that of labour standards in global supply chains. Many companies have their own code covering issues such as health, safety and child labour. However, other basic human rights in the workplace, particularly the right to organise and bargain collectively, remain controversial and do not feature in many codes.

Trades unions and campaigners have developed 'model codes' as a benchmark for acceptable practice. They concentrate on five key areas within the ILO Conventions:

- forced and bonded labour (No 29 and 105 and recommendation 35);
- freedom of association (No 87);
- the right to collective bargaining (No 98);
- no discrimination (No 111 and No 100).

Health and safety in the workplace is also a key demand. A more recent and controversial addition to the content of codes is that workers should receive a living wage. This recognises that legally set minimum wages, which are included in many company codes, are often not adequate to meet the basic needs of workers. (Source: Burns and Blowfield, 2000)

Ethical Trading Initiative, UK

Codes of conduct and ethical trade are closely linked, and an interesting and influential example relating to the development and implementation of codes of conduct between business interests and civil society is that of the Ethical Trading Initiative (ETI) in the UK. This was formed in 1998 to bring together companies, NGOs and trade unions in a joint approach to labour codes of conduct, using the ETI Base Code (which corresponds closely with the ILO core conventions). The ETI works with local stakeholders in developing countries and has a number of working groups to develop learning on the monitoring and verification of codes of conduct for different sectors and groups of workers (including homeworkers). It is also currently running a series of pilot programmes around the world – China, South Africa and Zimbabwe being the first to report – that test different ways of monitoring and verifying codes of conduct. (Source: ILO, 2002a; Redfern and Snedker, 2002)

Application of ETI Base Code, South Africa

A good example of codes of conduct in practice comes from South Africa. Here, with increased exposure to global pressures following liberalisation, farmers growing deciduous fruits for the UK market have become subject to the implementation of the Base Code of Conduct of ETI to which most UK supermarkets belong. Combined with new national labour legislation, this has led to better conditions for some women workers, especially those with permanent contracts. However, a downside of this initiative is that, under pressures of global competition to keep costs low, some growers are shedding on-farm labour and rehiring the same women as off-farm workers, making it easier to avoid paying benefits. The lack of unions for rural workers in general and women in particular makes it difficult for women to make their case for retribution. (Source: Barrientos et al, 2004)

National homeworkers code of conduct, Australia

Another example at the national level is that of codes of conduct applied to homeworkers in Australia. For each factory worker in the garment industry in Australia, there are 15 homeworkers. In their work to organise homeworkers, the Textile, Clothing and Footwear Union (TCFUA) launched a consumer campaign to encourage retailers to sign up to a code of good practice. Homeworkers were defined as persons who manufacture products at home or in premises other than a registered factory. The trade union also won a binding, industry-wide agreement on the terms and conditions of home-based employment. A unit within the union monitors the situation of garment homeworkers and files cases against companies that fail to comply with the conditions of the agreement. TCFUA worked with consumer, church, community and student groups to encourage signatories to the code of good practice.

Parties to the code agreement – including the union, the Council of Textile and Fashion Industries Ltd, the Australian Chamber of Manufacturers and the Australian Business Chamber – agreed on issues such as pay rates, hours of work, workers' compensation and payments to a retirement pension fund. Homeworkers, who are union members, also receive advance notice when work is no longer available for a period. In 1996, TCFUA lobbying led to the passage of a federal law protecting their pay and working conditions. When a backlash tried to remove the legal protections for clothing homeworkers, it was defeated in court in 1999. The same year, the union successfully pursued legal actions against a number of major textile companies that had been ignoring the federal law. (Source: TCFUA, 1996)

> ### Box 20 Effectiveness of Codes of Conduct and Ethical Trade Initiatives
>
> Despite the data limitations, there is evidence of ethical trade delivering on social/environmental goals. Examples include:
>
> - reductions in child labour in Central American garment manufacture;
> - workers being reinstated and allowed to unionise in garment factories in Central America;
> - improvements in environmental management in electronics factories in Thailand;
> - improvements in health and safety conditions in footwear factories in South-East Asia;
> - reductions in water and air pollution emissions from factories in Asia.
>
> However, relatively successful consumer campaigns – such as the growth of Fair Trade coffee – are overshadowed by the larger number that have little or no impact. Voluntary mechanisms to encourage reporting on social and environmental issues by big firms have led only a small percentage of firms to comply. Where self-regulated initiatives, such as codes of conduct, have been accepted by firms, they have come in for criticism as window-dressing: "to date such initiatives have had a more visible effect on their firms' market image in the North than on the actual pay and conditions of workforces in the South".
>
> Source: Heeks and Duncombe, 2003

Extending labour legislation to agricultural and domestic workers, South Africa

Through a combination of union campaigns and negotiations in a statutory tripartite (plus community) forum, workers rights and protections have been extended to large numbers of vulnerable women workers in South Africa. This includes the right to organise, bargain collectively, access the dispute resolution processes and be protected from dismissal. It includes minimum conditions of employment such as leave, sick leave, maternity leave (although unpaid), overtime pay, prevention of discrimination, affirmative action and access to skills development. It applies not only to workers with full time-employment and a single employer, but also to part-time workers and those with multiple employers. Recently, minimum wages were legislated through sectoral determinations for domestic and agricultural workers. Such determinations are made for 'vulnerable' workers, where collective bargaining forums are not in place. (Source: Chris Bonner, personal communication)

Unemployment insurance for domestic workers, South Africa

In 2003, after a 15-year struggle, domestic workers in South Africa were finally brought under the Unemployment Insurance Act covering employed workers. This requires employers to register their domestic workers and pay a monthly levy to a Fund. Workers also contribute. The Fund covers unemployment, maternity, sickness and death. Enforcement of the law is a problem, but there is evidence emerging of positive results in some areas. Statistics from the official disputes resolution body, the Commission for Conciliation, Mediation and Arbitration (CCMA), show fairly extensive usage of the disputes resolution machinery by the domestic sector. Latest statistics (April-December 2003) show that 12 per cent of all referrals were from this sector, second only to the retail sector. The majority of cases referred are about dismissals – 85 per cent between 1999 and 2003. (Source: Chris Bonner, personal communication)

Industry-specific welfare funds for informal workers, India

In India, the Government has set up a number of welfare funds for workers in specific industries, including building and construction, *bidi* (cigarette) and cigar rolling and mining. These funds are created by enactment of special Acts of Parliament. For example, the Building and other Construction Workers' (Regulation of Employment and Conditions of Service) Act was passed in 1996. Unlike previous legislation, this bill extended coverage to construction sites previously excluded: those sites that "employ, or had employed on any day of the preceding twelve months, ten or more building workers in any

> ### Box 21 Welfare Funds for Bidi Workers in India
>
> A constraint that governments face in providing social protection to informal economy workers is the difficulty of identifying workers who do not work in formal factories or other institutional settings. One solution to providing coverage for workers in the unorganised sector is through taxing not the employers but the revenue that the sector generates. Termed 'welfare funds', the funds raised from these levies are used on the welfare of the workers producing the taxed products. For instance, India uses this system for the benefit those who produce *bidis* (hand-rolled cigarettes). There are estimated to be over four million *bidi* workers in India, 90 per cent of whom are women. Most of them work under a sub-contract from their homes for a low piece rate and without access to health insurance or social security.
>
> The Bidi Workers Welfare Act (1976) provides the national labour legislation that taxes the revenue generated by the sector (but not employers) to create a welfare fund administered by government. Taxes of 50 paise (or half a rupee) per 1,000 *bidis* are levied. The welfare fund operates hospitals and dispensaries, awards scholarships and provides school supplies and uniforms. However, the expenditures are limited and do not cover standard aspects of social protection such as sickness, occupational injury, maternity, disability, old age or survivors and unemployment coverage. Recently, welfare funds have been extended into group insurance for which the welfare fund pays half. The remainder is subsidised by the Life Insurance Corporation Insurance Scheme. While some 2.7 million workers are covered by the Bidi Welfare Fund, estimates put the number of *bidi* workers at 4.3 million, which reveals the problems in getting employers to issue ID cards.
>
> Source: Jhabvala and Tate, 1996

building or other construction work". Among the requirements of this law are: the issuance of identity cards and attendance cards; the creation of a welfare fund; the provision of insurance coverage and payment of medical expenses; and the payment of minimum wages. Additionally, building sites with more than 50 workers are required to set up crèches for the children of workers.

Another sector specific law is the Bidi and Cigar Workers (Conditions of Employment) Act, 1996. This bill expanded the definition of 'employee' to those who work under the 'sale-purchase system'. The Act also created a national minimum wage to be adopted by all states in India. Welfare funds for *bidi* workers, 90 per cent of whom are women, are also generated by the Bidi Workers Welfare Cess Act (see Box 21). (Source: Jhabvala and Kanbur, 2002; Subrahmanya, 2000).

Unorganised Sector Workers (Employment and Welfare) Bill, India

At present, the Government of India is actively reviewing a national bill on workers in the unorganised sector, drafted by the National Commission on Labour and submitted to Parliament in 2002. This Bill has the objectives of regulating " the employment and conditions of service of unorganised sector workers and to provide for their safety, social security, health and welfare".[2] It defines a worker as " a person engaged in Scheduled Employment whether for any remuneration or otherwise" (122 occupations are listed as Scheduled Employment). The Bill:

- provides for the establishment of Workers' Facilitation Centres to support and assist unorganised workers, which:
  - are responsible for registration of workers and for guidance on a range of issues, such as dispute resolution, self help groups and schemes available for their benefit;
  - will maintain a register of workers and provide an identity card and social security number;
  - will be responsible for formulating safety and social security schemes, including health and medical care, employment injury benefit, maternity benefit, old age pension and safety measures;

- provides for the setting up in the states of an Unorganised Sector Workers' Welfare Fund, with funds from government and contributions by employers and registered workers; and

Basket weaver, Ghana
INTERNATIONAL FUND FOR
AGRICULTURAL DEVELOPMENT
(IFAD)/ROBERT GROSSMAN

- sets out minimum conditions of service, including hours of work and minimum wages.

There is an attempt to safeguard the rights of women. Wage discrimination on the grounds of gender is prohibited and a women worker is entitled to "such maternity benefits with wages as prescribed". Employers are liable also to pay compensation for injury on duty (see Appendix 2 for the details of the bill). (Source: Government of India, 2003; Shalini Sinha, 2004)

New Labour Act, Ghana

The Ghana Trade Union Congress (TUC) recently undertook a review of labour laws. It found that the these laws were outdated, fragmented and did not fit with either work realities or the Ghana Constitution. The resulting New Labour Act (2003) was negotiated through a tripartite process, involving the government, trade unions and employers. The Act applies to all workers (excluding armed forces, police, etc). A key objective of the TUC was to extend important protective elements secured by formal workers to informal workers. The Act contains special provisions relating to temporary and casual workers that allow them to benefit from the provisions of collective agreements, such as equal pay for work of equal value, access to the same medical provisions available to permanent workers, full minimum wage for all days in attendance (even if the weather prevents work) and public holidays. In addition, a temporary worker employed by the same employer for a continuous period of six months or more must be treated as a permanent worker. (Source: Owusu, 2003; Asemoah, 2004)

Supreme Court judgements, India

The Supreme Court of India has recognised street vending and hawking as a fundamental right. In 1985, in *Bombay Hawkers Union vs Bombay Municipal Corporation*, the Court directed that each city should formulate schemes that would include hawking and non-hawking zones. This was followed by the 1989 judgement of *Sodhan Singh Etc. vs New Delhi Municipal Committee* where hawking was declared to be a fundamental right under Article 19(1)g, subject to reasonable restrictions.

The Supreme Court has also recognised the employment relationship in situations where this relationship is disguised. In the case of *Saruspur Mills Co. Limited and Ramanlal Chimanlal and Others* in 1973, the Court held that even the employees employed by the Co-operative Society that managed the canteen of a factory were the employees of the factory and were entitled to all benefits. In the same year, in the case of *Silver Jubilee Tailoring House and Others and Chief Inspector of Shop and Establishment and Others*, the Court held that if an employer has the right to reject the end product, the element of control and supervision is also present. In 1978, the Court held that if the livelihood of the workers substantially depends on labour rendered to produce the goods and services for the benefit and satisfaction of an enterprise, the absence of direct relationship cannot snap the real life bond. (Source: Renana Jhabvala, personal communication)

Box 22 Extending National, State or Provincial Legislation to Informal Workers: Further Examples

At the national level:

- The UK recently passed a national minimum wage law that covers homeworkers. The law put the burden on employers to show that the worker is an independent contractor and not an employee, thus addressing the problem of 'disguised workers'.

- In 1994, legislation was introduced in Chile that explicitly defined a category of temporary workers. Employers are required to issue a written labour contract for workers, and to register this in the Labour Office after 28 days of continuous employment (Lund and Nicholson, 2003).

- A recent policy change in Chile was aimed at extending coverage of health insurance to temporary workers. Workers in Chile are required to contribute 7 per cent of their earnings to a public or private health insurance plan. However, because a high proportion of the temporary workers work without contracts, they could only access basic health care as indigents for most of the year, which provided a strong disincentive for affiliation. On his election, President Ricardo Lagos asked the government's women's service SERNAM to negotiate with FONASA (Ministry of Health) to extend coverage for outpatient and secondary health care for 12 months to temporary workers with three months of payroll contributions. To overcome some of the administrative problems in implementing this programme, temporary workers were provided with a card that, on presentation to health-care providers, guarantees their access to health care. These cards were introduced in January 2002.

- In January 2001, SERNAM set up four tripartite commissions in Chile to consider ways in which the welfare of temporary workers in horticulture could be improved.

> **Box 22** (continued)
>
> - Also in Chile, the Labour Protection Act of 1997 is intended to improve working conditions for informal workers, including spelling out the rights of women, child, and migrant workers.
>
> **At the state or provincial level:**
> - The state of Kerala in India has introduced old-age pensions for agricultural workers with below-poverty incomes.
>
> - In Madeira, an autonomous region of Portugal, the Portuguese statutory social security system has been extended to cover home-based embroiderers for old age, disability, maternity and sick days.
>
> - In the Rizal province of the Philippines, if proven need is show to the hospital's social service department, patients can receive a 50 per cent discount. If they still cannot afford the bill, they can approach the Municipal Social Welfare and Development Office, which can pay the remainder through the disbursement of municipal funds. This process can also be used by pregnant homeworkers who cannot afford delivery charges.
>
> - In some states in the US, domestic workers (those who work in other people's homes as housekeepers or babysitters) receive some but not all protections that protect formal economy workers.
>
> Source: compiled by WIEGO

Trade union encourages multinational company to establish grievance mechanism, international

What can workers do to ensure that employers adhere to labour legislation? A lead firm that has implemented a grievance mechanism is the banana company Chiquita. In 2000, the company signed an international framework agreement with the International Union Federation for Food, Agriculture and Allied Industries (IUF) that creates a forum for addressing workers' rights violations arising in the company's operations and supply chains. According to the Communications Manager of IUF, "Multinational companies make strategic decisions at the global level, but most refuse to accept global responsibility for industrial relations … that is why agreements like this one are a valuable tool for bringing industrial relations into the new environment of globalised production." (Source: Oxfam, 2004)

Export company promotes rights of women workers, Kenya

In Kenya, a company that is involved in exporting and that employs part-time and temporary women workers has set up a Gender Committee specifically to address the concerns of these workers. Representatives from all areas of the workforce are elected onto the committee where they meet with senior management to raise issues and seek solutions. Among other things, they have instituted training on women's rights and private counselling sessions for sufferers of domestic violence. (Source: Sally Smith et al, 2003)

Securing rights of the self-employed

While self-employed or own account workers benefit from many of the initiatives outlined above, they also have particular concerns and needs that do not relate to wage workers. These include the right of access to economic resources including credit, land and natural resources and the right to a fair share in the benefits of their intellectual property.

The right of access to credit has been written about at length and there are numerous books and articles that supply a wealth of examples of how this issue has and is being dealt with – particularly in terms of ensuring that women producers have the financial means to support their enterprise activities. Here we give examples of protecting access to land and intellectual property rights.

Grassroots union lobbies for land rights for rural women, Mozambique

The absence of legal property rights means that potential entrepreneurs are not able to use, build, recombine or exchange their assets in the most productive way in order to generate additional value. For example, if informal operators

> … self-employed or own account workers … have particular concerns and needs that do not relate to wage workers. These include the right of access to economic resources including credit, land and natural resources and the right to a fair share in the benefits of their intellectual property.

held title to their land, they would be able not only to build on the land but also to use it as collateral. Without being able to convert assets into productive capital, they do not have the means for entrepreneurship, innovation, business growth or development. This also means that a country is not able to effectively harness capital from domestically available assets. In many developing countries where secure title to land does exist, it is men who own and control the land. In several countries, women cannot even hold title to land. In Mozambique, the National Farmers Union (NFU), an association of some 430 local co-operatives and farmers groups led by a woman grassroots leader, lobbies the Government to issue land-ownership deeds to rural women. Despite resistance from the male-dominated bureaucracy, the NFU has helped some 95 per cent of its members to secure deeds of ownership. (Source: ILO, 2002a; UNCTAD, 2001)

Indigenous people win rights to share in commercialisation, Southern Africa

Hoodia is a succulent plant that has long been chewed by the San people in southern Africa to suppress hunger. The active ingredient, known as P57, was isolated and patented in 1996 by scientists from the South African Council on Scientific and Industrial Research (CSIR). In 1997, CSIR licensed Phytopharm, a UK-based drug development company, to develop and commercialise P57, though CSIR retained the patent. In 1998, Phytopharm in turn sold the rights to license the drug for $21 million to the US-based pharmaceutical giant Pfizer. Given current concerns about obesity, the potential for an appetite-suppressing drug based on P57 is great. In 2001, media reports on the deals between CSIR, Phytopharm and Pfizer led to a huge increase in the share price of Phyopharm. They also alerted the San to the potential use of their traditional knowledge.

A few months later, the South African San Council was selected to represent the interests of more than 100,000 San people in Angola, Botswana, Namibia, South Africa, Zambia and Zimbabwe in discussions with the CSIR on options for sharing the benefits emanating from their traditional knowledge. In March 2002, a Memorandum of Understanding (MoU) was signed between the CSIR and the San under which the CSIR formally acknowledged the San as the custodians of their traditional knowledge. In return, the San acknowledge the CSIR's need to protect its investment in isolating *hoodia*'s appetite-suppressing ingredient by patenting it in CSIR's name. The MoU led to an agreement in March 2003 outlining how any benefits will be shared. The potential income for the San – which could exceed $7 million per year for the 15 to 20 years before the patent expires – will be deposited in a San Hoodia Sharing Trust established by the CSIR and the San and will be used for the "general upliftment, development and training of the San community". (Source: Scheckenberg, 2003)

Goal 3: Promoting Protection

Promoting protection against common contingencies

Social protection, including safety nets, health insurance and pensions, is a major element in reducing risk for the working poor. Different types of strategies for providing these services to women and men have been tried in several countries. They include those that extend existing government schemes to informal workers, those that combine government and voluntary schemes and those that are established by the voluntary sector.

Pension scheme for the elderly poor, South Africa

With its 40 million people, South Africa has a healthy private pension regime. It is a vastly unequal society, however, and for the many poor people who cannot make private provision for their retirement, there is an additional social assistance scheme, which gives elderly people (women from 60, men from 65) a monthly means-tested cash transfer, payable from general revenue. The benefit, which goes to more than 80 per cent of all poor elderly people – about 1.5 million people – has interesting characteristics: it goes disproportionately to women (who receive it earlier, live longer and spend it better), it reaches rural areas and it has an important poverty alleviation effect in the three generation households in which most elderly people live, as it is pooled as general household income. The pension is a vitally important source of household security and plays a role in the promotion of small enterprises. It has a household income-smoothing function: it is spent on 'social'

Social protection, including safety nets, health insurance and pensions, is a major element in reducing risk for the working poor.

items such as children's schooling and transport to health services, and it is used for agricultural inputs and for small enterprise development. There are a number of signs of its importance in local and rural economies: major hire purchase firms have changed their collection schedules to coincide with pension days; and clients of a micro-finance organisation have asked for co-ordination between pension payment dates and dates of micro-finance loan repayments. (Source: Lund and Srinivas, 2000)

A government-initiated voluntary scheme for health and pension provision for informal workers, Costa Rica

An increasing proportion of the labour force in Costa Rica is not covered by occupationally related social insurance. However, voluntary insurance is available for independent workers, own account workers and non-remunerated workers (family workers, housewives and students). It is aimed at those who have either never contributed to a health or pension plan or who did not do so for long enough to accumulate adequate benefits. To join, it is necessary to have a per capita family income that is lower than the basic basket of food products determined by the Statistics Institute. Although joining is voluntary at present, it will become statutory in 2005. It is funded by the contributions of the state and the individuals who join. That so many independent workers are reached by the system is remarkable and is in marked contrast to the old age benefit system. This is an interesting example of where a country with a good history of social provision is attempting to adjust in flexible ways to change in the labour market (i.e. increasing numbers of informal workers). (Source: Martinéz and Meso-Lago, 2003)

Unorganised Sector Workers' Social Security Scheme, India

Over 90 per cent of India's workers are in the informal economy (including agricultural workers), with little – if any – statutory social security. Most are casual labourers, contract and piece-rate workers and self-employed own-account workers. The Government of India recently launched the Unorganised Sector Workers' Social Security Scheme on a pilot basis in 50 districts. The scheme provides for three basic protections: old age pension, personal accident insurance and

DECENT WORK FOR INFORMAL WORKERS: PROMISING STRATEGIES AND EXAMPLES

> ***Box 23* Examples of Social Protection Systems**
>
> In **Bolivia**, a Mutual Health Insurance Scheme covers basic health services for its members, half of whom are informal economy workers excluded from other social security systems. The programme is run by an NGO and financed through member contributions and grants from development agencies.
>
> In **Brazil**, the Rural Social Insurance Programme is a rare Latin American example of state-sponsored social protection for those outside the formal sector. The programme is a non-contributory pension and disability programme for the rural poor, instituted by the 1988 Constitution that extended basic pension benefits to the old and disabled in informal rural employment. It has not only alleviated poverty but has also lead to recipients moving from subsistence agriculture to sustainable household production. Ancillary social benefits include increased school enrolment among children in beneficiary households.
>
> The National Pension System in **Japan** provides health and pension insurance for more than 90 per cent of people, including informal workers. Japan does not distinguish between the formal and informal economy or between self-employed workers and those in micro-enterprises.
>
> Source: Lund and Srinavas, 2000

medical insurance. It is compulsory for registered employees and voluntary for self-employed workers. Workers contribute to the scheme, as do employers. Where self-employed workers join the scheme they pay worker and employer contributions. Government also contributes. Workers Facilitation Centres are being set up to assist workers (see above under Securing Rights of Informal Workers). The scheme will be administered through the already existing Employee Provident Fund Organisation offices around the country. (Source: Government of India, 2004a)

SEWA's integrated social insurance scheme, India

At present, the largest comprehensive contributory social security scheme in India for informal economy workers is the Integrated Social Security Programme set up by the Self Employed Women's Association (SEWA) (see Box 24). SEWA's insurance programme insures more than 100,000 women workers and covers health insurance, including a maternity component, life insurance and asset insurance. The scheme requires that subscribers have a SEWA bank account and that they take out all three parts of the package. Women have a choice of contributions and coverage, which can incorporate husbands and children. The premium structures, including lifetime, annual and monthly payments, are designed to suit different income groups among the very poor. SEWA is decentralising its operations to accommodate the large number of poor rural women who want to join the scheme.

SEWA has shown that it is possible to create schemes that are adaptable, reproducible and profitable. This scheme demonstrates that workers are willing to pay for insurance in increasing amounts, as long as the service is appropriately designed and sensitive to their needs. SEWA is planning to expand its health benefits as well as trying to increase private sector and government participation. (Source: Chatterjee and Vyas, 2000; Lund and Srinavas, 2000)

Government sponsored social protection, Thailand

The formal social insurance programme in Thailand, administered by the Social Security Office (SSO) has been changing and expanding in recent years, with the benefits increasingly being extended to smaller enterprises and informal workers. The programme covers sickness, maternity, disability, death and survivor grants, maternity benefits for 90 days, old age pensions and child allowances. In the late 1990s and early 2000s, it covered only about 15 per cent of the workforce and mostly formal workers. It may cover a larger percentage now as compulsory participation was extended to establishments with one or more workers in April 2002 (and will finally be extended to the agricultural, fishery and forestry sectors in succession). Apart from the contributory SSO scheme and additional programmes covering pensions and health care for civil servants, the Thai Government has social assistance programmes for targeted groups, voluntary subsidised health cards for those not covered by the SSO programme and labour protection laws. The aim is to provide universal health coverage within 10 to 15 years, and the Government has instituted a '30 Baht Health Scheme' to begin moving in this direction. (Source: Lund and Nicholson, 2003)

Promoting protection for migrant workers

While all of the above schemes deal with local populations, it is often those who have crossed borders (either legally or illegally) who are most at risk and most in need of protection, as we saw in Chapter 3. Actions have been taken in support of these types of workers also.

Migrant care workers programme, Canada

The demand for foreign household and care workers has grown in the OECD countries, with rising female employment rates, changes in family structures and an ageing population leading to higher dependency ratios. A good number of these workers, who are primarily women, have 'irregular' status. In 2002, Citizenship and Immigration, Canada, established the 'Live-in Caregiver Program for employers and caregivers abroad', based on labour market shortages of Canadian or permanent residents to fill the need for live-in care for children, elderly people or persons with disabilities. Prior to this programme, Canada was providing permanent resident status for housekeepers, servants and others providing personal services to only a very limited number of people. The Live-in Caregiver Program offers the possibility of applying for permanent residence in Canada after two years of employment. (Source: ILO, 2004b)

Model contracts to safeguard migrant domestic workers, several countries

In many countries domestic work is excluded from the scope of national labour and/or other laws. The ILO's approach has been to regulate the recruitment process and introduce model contracts incorporating basic issues such as salary, hours of work and weekly rest. The approach has been used in several countries. For example, Hong Kong has adopted a model con-

... several international alliances of informal workers have been formed which together constitute a growing international movement of informal workers and their advocates.

tract for domestic workers and has established a 'hotline' to receive complaints from domestic workers. Jordan has included in a model contract entitlements to life insurance, medical care, rest days and repatriation upon expiration of the contract, and reiterates migrant women's right to be treated in compliance with international human rights standards. Other countries also use model contracts in relation to particularly vulnerable occupations such as domestic work, manual labour and agricultural work (e.g. Sri Lanka and Tanzania). (Source: ILO, 2004b)

Goal 4: Promoting Voice

Organising informal workers

Throughout the Handbook, we have referred to the importance for women and men in the informal economy to be organised in unions, co-operatives or other membership-based organisations through which they can gain representation and voice in local, national, and international policy-making or rule-setting fora. There are two basic paths to organising in the informal economy:

- when new organisations are set up by informal workers themselves (self-organisation); and

- when an existing union or union federation extends its field of activity to include informal workers (Gallin, 2002).

Over the past three decades, organisations of informal workers have been established in different corners of the world. And, over the past decade or more, existing trade union federations and trade unions have begun to recruit and/or provide services to informal workers. In addition, several international alliances of informal workers have been formed which together constitute a growing international movement of informal workers and their advocates.

1. New organisations of informal workers
Trade unions

The largest trade union of informal workers is the Self Employed Women's Association (SEWA) of India, which has over 700,000 members (see Box 24).

Box 24 The Self-Employed Women's Association (SEWA) of India

SEWA, established in 1972, is a trade union of low-income working women who earn their livelihoods by running small businesses, doing subcontracting work or selling their labour. With over 700,000 members in 2003, SEWA is the first trade union of workers in the informal economy not only in India but around the world. It is also the largest trade union in India. SEWA's objectives are to increase the self–reliance as well as the economic and social security of its members.

SEWA groups its membership into four broad occupational categories:

- *hawkers and vendors*, who sell a range of products including vegetables, fruit and used clothing from baskets, push carts or small shops;

- *home-based producers*, who stitch garments, make patchwork quilts, roll hand-made cigarettes (bidis) or incense sticks, prepare snack foods, recycle scrap metal, process agricultural products, produce pottery or make craft items;

- *manual labourers and service providers*, who sell their labour (as cart-pullers, head-loaders or construction workers), or who sell services (such as waste-paper picking, laundry services or domestic services); and

- *rural producers, including small farmers*, milk producers, animal rearers, nursery raisers/tenders, salt farmers and gum collectors.

Within these four broad occupational groups, some women are self–employed, others work as casual day labourers and still others are homeworkers who produce goods on a piece rate under a sub–contract.

To promote its objectives, SEWA pursues a mix of what it calls 'struggle' and 'development': that is, unionising activities to address constraints and demand change and

Box 24 (continued)

development interventions to provide services and promote alternative economic opportunities. To pursue these complementary strategies, SEWA organises its membership into trade organisations and co-operatives and builds service-specific institutions to manage and sustain its activities.

Over the years, SEWA has built a sisterhood of institutions, as follows:

- SEWA Union (which is the primary membership-based organisation to which all of SEWA's members belong and which provides the overall governance of the organisation);
- SEWA Bank (which provides financial services, including both savings and credit);
- Gujarat Mahila Cooperative Federation (which is responsible for organising and supporting SEWA's membership in several types of co-operatives);
- Gujarat Mahila Housing SEWA Trust (which provides housing services);
- SEWA Social Security (which provides health, childcare and insurance services);
- Rural and Urban Branches of SEWA (which oversee, respectively, its rural and urban activities, including the recruitment and organising of members);
- SEWA Marketing (which provides product development and marketing services);
- SEWA Academy (which is responsible for research, training and communication).

The first three are democratic membership-based organisations, governed by elected representatives. The others are support institutions that provide services of various kinds to SEWA members.

Source: SEWA, 2003

Other trade unions of informal workers include the Self Employed Women's Union (SEWU) in South Africa and SIBTTA, the union of embroidery, tapestry, textile and handicraft workers on the island of Madeira, Portugal. SEWU was launched in Durban/eThekwini, South Africa in July 1994 and is a membership-based organisation composed of women who work informally in both urban and rural areas of the country. While the national office is based in Durban/eThekwini, SEWU has offices in the Western and Eastern Cape regions of South Africa, as well as the Free State and Mpumalanga regions. It empowers its members through workshops aimed at building self-reliance through savings, providing leadership training and teaching negotiating and many other skills that aid them in becoming "key agents of change in South African society". Additionally, SEWU has worked to help members obtain soft loans as well as assisted them with opening savings accounts at post offices and commercial banks. As of late 2003, SEWU had some 25,000 members.

Sindicato Dos Trabalhadores da Industria Bordadoros, Tapecarias, Texteis e Artensanato (SIBTTA), based on the island of Madeira, has been organising home-based workers for more than 30 years and has a membership of roughly 8,000 workers. SIBTTA first began as an organisation of workers from a single textile plant but has branched out considerably since then. Most recently, it began organising home-based wicker workers, most of whom are male. It has won the recognition, under national law, that home-based producers are workers with rights to health benefits, unemployment insurance and retirement pensions. (Dan Gallin, personal communication)

In addition, there are national trade unions of domestic workers in several countries (see Box 25).

Street vendors' associations, several countries

Street vendors associations provide a good example of how informal workers can organise initially at the local level and then federate eventually into national and international organisations. At the national level, an important function of street vendor organisations is to proactively litigate in order to establish important precedents that can protect street vendors' legal rights. In some European countries there is a long history

Box 25 Domestic Workers' Unions

Federación Nacional de Trabajadoras del Hogar, Peru, is a union of women domestic workers with some 10,000 members. In 2003, after more than 30 years of struggle, the union secured a new law regulating working conditions for domestic workers, including social security, breaks for breastfeeding, health coverage, vacation time and an eight-hour working day. It has created a support organisation, the Centro de Capacitación para Trabajadoras del Hogar (CCTH), which acts as a lobby and a vocational training centre. It is affiliated with the Latin American federation of domestic workers (formed in 1988 and based in Cochabamba, Bolivia) and also works with the national trade union centres in Peru.

National Union of Domestic Employees (NUDE), Trinidad and Tobago, initially established in 1982 to organise domestic workers, since 1992 also includes other low wage workers without protection and guaranteed benefits. In 2002, the union had 450 members, of whom 65 were men, and an all-female executive. The union has been campaigning against discrimination against domestic workers in labour legislation and for having women's housework counted in the national budget. It has convened several meetings of domestic workers' organisations at Caribbean regional level, which defined common demands, and has hosted meetings on domestic workers' issues involving unions, NGOs, government agencies, UN agencies, universities and individual researchers.

The United Workers' Association, UK, is a union of migrant domestic workers formed in 1987. It has 4,000 members (almost all women) from 30 different countries – with the majority from the Philippines. It works closely with the Transport and General Workers' Union and is supported by Kalayaan, an NGO that in 1996 also became the base for Rights, Equality, Solidarity, Power, Europe Corporation Today (RESPECT), a European network of

> **Box 25** (continued)
>
> organisations of migrant domestic workers. This was initially supported by SOLIDAR, the international organisation of labour movement and welfare organisations. The United Workers' Association and Kalayaan have successfully campaigned in the UK to change the immigration rules tying a domestic worker to a named employer and for the regularisation of undocumented migrants. United Workers' Association members are encouraged to become members of the Transport and General Workers' Union.
>
> Source: Global Labour Institute, 2003

of such activism: the Associazone Nazionale Venditore Ambulantore (ANVA) in Italy, for example, was started in 1947 and now has about 80,000 members and 180 branches.

There are fewer such national-level institutions in the developing world. One example is the National Alliance of Street Vendors of India (NASVI). Established in 1998, its membership includes vendors from 27 cities and towns across the country. As a result of a series of national and regional meetings, NASVI has been able to raise awareness and lobby for change across India.

2. Existing trade unions organising informal workers
Informal economy recruitment policy, Ghana

In 1996, the Ghana Trade Union Congress (GTUC) adopted six policies – one of which was organising – to help the organisation confront challenges of declining membership. Since an estimated 85 per cent of the economically active labour force is in the informal economy, the GTUC policy included a strategy to target these workers for recruitment. The objectives of the informal economy recruitment policy are to:

- create a desk in the Organisation Department of the GTUC and within the national unions for the informal economy;
- develop links with existing informal economy associations;

- design programmes in response to identified problems in the informal economy;
- encourage informal economy operators to form associations; and
- encourage the national unions to review their constitutions and develop policies appropriate for the informal economy.

This was done in different ways. In some unions, workers were recruited into existing structures whilst in others associations of informal workers were affiliated. All unions had to change their own constitutions to make this possible. The following services are provided by the trade unions to the informal economy workers and members:

- negotiate with metropolitan authority on behalf of the informal economy operators in terms of payment of tax and location of their business;
- ensure that informal economy operators apply good health and safety standards, especially operators who may not know the side effects of chemicals that they use;
- provide educational programmes for simple management and bookkeeping skills;
- organise funding and credit to support informal sector activities; and
- make credit available for the purchasing of grains during the harvesting season and marketing during the lean season through a Commodity Inventory Loan Scheme, to eliminate dependency on middle persons and improve income for members. (Source: Boakye, 2004)

Different union models and new services for self-employed workers, Europe

Traditional unions in Europe are grappling with increasing numbers of workers who do not 'fit into the system' as it is currently organised. These range from professional workers to street vendors. In the Netherlands, the FNV (national federation of unions) set up a special union for self-employed workers. This was linked to the big, merged union for industry, agriculture, transport and commercial services. The self-employed workers' union provides members with services such as advice on company law, legal and tax matters, negotiating contracts and debt collection. A similar model was chosen by Dutch construction workers. The FNV has set up an advisory board to co-ordinate activities by various unions for self-employed workers.

In Austria, the largest union found that the majority of self-employed workers were in that position as a result of employers trying to avoid social insurance and taxation. They needed to be organised. To do so they needed new structures and orientation. The union set up work@flex, which offers services such as tax and social security advice, assistance with contracts, legal protection and insurance policies. It holds regular meeting for workers around Vienna and uses special new websites to help keep isolated members in touch with each other and the union.

The Catalunya regional organisation of the trade union confederation in Spain is organising the self-employed, including street vendors, those contracted to companies, construction workers, etc. The intention is to bring these workers into the mainstream world of the union movement. In March 2001 the union set up an association of self-employed workers as the law did not allow them to form unions. Union statutes were changed so that the association could be incorporated into the structures and have full voting rights. Now the union is organising sector by sector, building more than one association. It provides education on collective bargaining techniques and about worker rights. It gives advice on tax and contract issues. It discusses and negotiates with many groups, such as business and public authorities. In the major transport industries in Catalunya, a single agreement has been reached for all types of transport workers.

In Germany, self-employed workers are organised directly into the ver.di union, rather than a separate union or association. Members can belong for their whole life, whatever their profession or employment status. Ver.di has a help-line open to all self-employed workers. This is supported by government funds. (Source FNV, 2003)

Hat seller, Tanzania
INTERNATIONAL LABOUR ORGANIZATION/M. CROZET

Promoting collective bargaining

Street vendors lobby for secure space, Jamaica

In Negril, itinerant food vendors formed an association to lobby for a permanent and secure site from which they could pursue their trade. By reaching out to the Negril Chamber of Commerce, the office responsible for improving the quality of Jamaica's tourism, the association of food vendors forged a collaboration that attracted public and private financing to construct such a space. With all parties working together, the Negril Vendors' Plaza opened in 1994 and 56 vendors moved from the streets to the new facility. Jointly owned and operated by the vendors association and the Negril Chamber of Commerce (through a non-profit corporation), the plaza has yielded immediate benefits. Not only has it alleviated the area's heavy traffic congestion, it has also enabled vendors to operate in a hygienic and secure environment. The proven entrepreneurial and organising talents of the association's leadership will support the vendors in continuing to have a voice in decisions regarding their welfare and the quality of their operations. In fact, the association's founder has since been invited to serve on the Negril Chamber of Commerce, becoming the first street vendor in Jamaica to be so honoured. (Source: Cohen et al, 2000)

Trade union includes informal economy workers in existing statutory bargaining forum, Uganda

In 1999, the Uganda Public Employees Union (UPEU) was the second-largest affiliate of the National Organisation of Trade Unions (NOTU) of Uganda with 17,000 members. Prior to this, the membership of UPEA had dropped to a mere 700 in a few years as a result of job losses in the public sector through economic liberalisation and privatisation programmes. UPEA and other affiliates of NOTU were faced with total collapse unless they could adapt to the changes that were taking place around them. The obvious path was to start organising workers in the growing informal economy, and NOTU took a policy decision that each of its affiliates should identify workers in the informal economy in its own sector and make the necessary adjustments to equip them to expand their organisation into the informal economy. UPEU re-defined the meaning of 'public employees' to mean anybody working to serve the public. This was a radical shift from the previously very constrained definition of public employees as civil servants employed by the government.

UPEU went further and amended their constitution to introduce seven different categories of union membership. The seventh category consists of "self-employedworkers and/or informal sector workers rendering service to the public" such as street and market vendors. These workers would be recruited through their associations, who would collect and pay subscriptions to the union at the same flat-rate membership amount per member. There is an Assistant General Secretary in charge of the Informal Sector, who would lead negotiations in the Joint Negotiating Committee (a statutory bargaining forum for all members of UPEU) on matters concerning the informal sector membership, who automatically have the right to be represented in collective bargaining at this forum once they are members of the union. (Source: Horn, 2003)

Building international alliances

During the 1980s, various trade unions, membership-based organisations and NGOs working with home-based workers and street vendors in both the global North and South began to establish linkages. In the mid-1990s, at two separate meetings in Europe, these organisations came together to form two international alliances of workers, especially women, in the informal economy: one of home-based workers called HomeNet; the other of street vendors called StreetNet (see Box 26).

At the first HomeNet meeting in 1994, the founding members planned a global campaign for an international convention that would recognise and protect home-based workers. The culmination of that campaign was the June 1996 decision at the annual International Labour Conference in favour of an international convention on homework (see Appendix 1). Since the adoption of this convention, HomeNet has established national and regional branches that organise homeworkers and lobby for national policies to support them, including ratification of the Homework Convention. The regional branches of HomeNet in South-East Asia and South Asia are particularly active.

Box 26 International Alliance of Street Trader and Hawker Organisations

At the first international meeting on street vendors, held in Bellagio, Italy in 1995, a group of activists from 11 countries adopted an International Declaration that set forth a plan to promote local and national policies to support and protect the rights of street vendors (see Appendix 4). For the next several years, they organised regional meetings of street vendors in Asia, Africa and Latin America and provided support to newly-emerging local and national associations of street vendors in several countries. StreetNet International was formally established in November 2002 and held its first International Congress in March 2004, attended by 58 delegates from 15 organisations, at which an International Council was elected for a three-year term.

Membership-based organisations (unions, co-operatives or associations) directly organising street vendors, market vendors and/or hawkers among their members, are entitled to affiliate to StreetNet. The aims of StreetNet are: to promote the exchange of information and ideas on critical issues facing street vendors and practical organising and advocacy strategies; to promote local, national and international solidarity between organisations of street vendors, market vendors and hawkers; and to stimulate the development of national alliances of such organisations. Its four main objectives are to:

- expand and strengthen street vendor networks at the international, regional and national levels;
- build an information base on street vendors in different parts of the world;
- document and disseminate information on effective organising strategies for promoting and protecting the rights of street vendors; and
- build a solid institutional base from which to advance StreetNet's work.

> **Box 26** (continued)
>
> To date, over 15 street vendor organisations – with a combined total membership of over 275,000 members – have affiliated with StreetNet.
>
> Source: www.streetnet.org.za

StreetNet and HomeNet are part of a wider global movement that has come together over the past decade or so to promote organising in the informal economy. The constituent elements of this wider movement include:

- local unions: SEWA, SEWU and SIBTTA (see above);
- national unions: Ghana Trade Union Congress, General Agricultural Workers' Union (GAWU) of Ghana, Nigerian Labour Congress and Uganda Public Employees Union (UPEU);
- a global research policy network: Women in Informal Employment: Globalizing and Organizing (WIEGO) is a research and policy think-tank for the organisations of informal workers; and
- regional and international associations: the International Federation of Workers' Education Associations (IFWEA), at its congress in 2000, decided to provide workers' education to informal workers; the Committee for Asian Women (CAW), since 2001, has been working on the informal economy and organised a regional workshop in Asia with other allies (WIEGO and HomeNet South-East Asia); and the International Restructuring Education Network Europe (IRENE) has organised several workshops on workers in the informal economy in Europe, in co-operation with trade union organisations and other allies (WIEGO and IFWEA).

This movement was instrumental in securing the Conclusions to the General Discussion on Decent Work and the Informal Economy at the International Labour Conference in 2002. It did so by writing technical papers on the informal economy for the International Labour Office, organising regional workshops of organisations working in the informal economy to draft a common platform of demands and convening a coalition of delegates and observers at the conference.

MAINSTREAMING INFORMAL EMPLOYMENT AND GENDER IN POVERTY REDUCTION

To strengthen the voice of informal workers in the policy process, their contributions to the economy and the nature of their work need to be visible to policy-makers.

> ### Box 27 Building the Network of Organisations of Informal Workers
>
> In December 2003, the Ghana Trade Union Congress, HomeNet Thailand, the Nigeria Labour Congress, the Self Employed Women's Association (SEWA) and StreetNet International organised an international conference in Ahmedabad, India on 'Organising in the Informal Economy'. The conference was attended by 60 participants (28 from Asia, 16 from Africa, five from North and Latin America, two from Europe and nine from international organisations). They elected an International Co-ordinating Committee and drafted a follow-up plan of action in support of organising efforts in the informal economy worldwide. In June 2004, during the International Labour Conference in Geneva, Switzerland, the International Co-ordination Committee organised a workshop on 'Organising Workers in the Informal Economy'. More than 50 persons attended the workshop, mostly from trade unions who are working in the informal economy or interested in doing so. To continue to build the emerging network of organisations of informal workers, the International Co-ordinating Committee plans to hold three regional workshops followed by an international meeting in December 2005.

Supporting Strategy – Collecting Statistics on the Informal Economy

To strengthen the voice of informal workers in the policy process, their contributions to the economy and the nature of their work need to be visible to policy-makers. What is needed is improved labour statistics and other information on informal labour markets. In recognition of the fact that statistics are of vital importance in the economic planning process, the ILO Statistics Bureau, together with the International Expert Group on Informal Sector Statistics (the Delhi Group), has been working actively with central statistical offices and informed data users in various countries, including the global research policy network WIEGO, to develop improved methods for the collection and compilation of data on the full range of workers in the informal economy, including the self-employed in informal enterprises and a whole range of informal wage workers. New data and statistics are already becoming available and being utilised by selected governments around the world.

Conclusion

These examples illustrate how international agencies; national, state and local government; the private sector; and civil society can support the informal economy. It is important to note that most of these initiatives require advocacy and/or monitoring by civil society – notably by organisations of informal workers – to ensure that they are properly designed and implemented. In sum, these examples suggest a key pathway to poverty reduction and gender equity through supporting informal enterprises, improving informal jobs, providing protection to informal workers and recognising organisations of informal workers.

Notes

1. Improving skills and technologies is covered separately in the next section.
2. As noted earlier, 'unorganised worker' is the term used in India for workers in informal employment and does not imply that such workers are not organised into unions or other organisations.

5. Informal Employment and Gender: A Strategic Policy Approach

Broad-based growth needs to be employment-intensive in order to effectively reduce poverty.

It is now widely acknowledged that market-oriented reforms need to be accompanied by: (a) a set of *complementary* policies to ensure reforms lead to poverty reduction; and (b) a set of *compensatory* policies to offset the costs of adjustment. It is also widely acknowledged that *broad-based growth*, not growth per se, leads to poverty reduction: what is needed is growth that increases the security and voice of the poor as well as their ability to seize new opportunities (World Bank, 2000).[1] But it is less widely acknowledged that broad-based growth needs, more specifically, to be *employment-intensive* in order to effectively reduce poverty. Among the inter-governmental organisations, only the International Labour Organization (ILO) has actively promoted this notion and the related notion that what is really needed is more 'decent work' opportunities (ILO, 2004a).

This is partly because mainstream policy economists do not view employment creation as an explicit objective of economic and social policies, but rather as a hoped-for result – a residual outcome – of sound macroeconomic policies. For instance, under a discussion on the investment climate and small firms, a recent publication of the World Bank states that "(e)mployment in the small and medium-sized firms in towns and rural areas will be central to raising the living standards of the rural poor" (World Bank, 2002:15). Yet the authors do not recommend employment creation as either a goal or a key area of action in their agenda for building an inclusive world economy.[2] Many poverty specialists do not see the need for an explicit focus on employment either. Most notably, employment was not included among the major goals – or even targets – of the Millennium Development Goals (MDGs).

This Handbook has made the case that, in order to effectively reduce poverty, it is important to support the working poor in the informal economy and, in so doing, to take into account the gender segmentation of the informal economy.

Clearly, there is no single policy prescription for this. Instead, what is needed is a strategic policy approach that can be used to formulate *context-specific responses* by governments and other key actors. In this concluding chapter, we present a strategic policy framework for policy-makers who want to take up this challenge. The framework has five component parts:

- informed and comprehensive *policy perspective*;
- specific and overarching *policy goals*;
- key substantive *policy areas*;
- a *stakeholder analysis* of the roles of different key actors; and
- guidelines for an equitable and effective *policy process*.

Policy Perspective

Alternative policy perspectives

Historically, policy-makers have taken differing policy stances on the informal economy: some observers view informal workers as a nuisance to be eliminated or strictly regulated; others see them as a vulnerable group to be assisted through social policies; still others see them as dynamic entrepreneurs to be freed from cumbersome government regulations. Another, more recent, perspective is that the informal workforce is comprised of unprotected producers and workers who need to be covered by labour legislation and social protection. Subscribing to one or another of these perspectives, policy-makers have tended to over-react to the informal economy, trying to discourage it altogether, to treat it as a social problem or to promote it as a solution to economic stagnation or employment creation.

Reflecting these differences in perspective, mainstream economists have tended to subscribe to one or other of the following positions in answer to the question: should governments intervene in the operation of the informal economy?

(a) that the informal economy is comprised largely of poor people engaged in survival activities that should be the target of social policies, not economic policies.

MAINSTREAMING INFORMAL EMPLOYMENT AND GENDER IN POVERTY REDUCTION

Today ... there is growing recognition that the informal economy is here to stay and that an appropriate policy response to it is needed.

(b) that markets operate efficiently, that government interventions lead to inefficiencies and distortions and that the informal economy will, in any case, decline with economic growth.

(c) that the informal economy is beyond the reach of government because the dynamic entrepreneurs avoid regulation and taxation while the poorest workers are not easy to target (World Bank, 1995:2002).

Today, however, there is growing recognition that the informal economy is here to stay and that an appropriate policy response to it is needed. Given the size and significance of the informal economy, a comprehensive and informed approach is called for. Before developing such an approach, governments and policy-makers might stop to consider what their own perspective on the informal economy has been and how this has affected their policy-making in the past. This is because most governments and policy-makers have an implicit perspective on the informal economy whether or not they have formulated an explicit policy in response to it.

Informed and comprehensive policy perspective

An informed policy approach to the informal economy should be premised on the understanding that the informal economy:

- is diverse, including:
  - survival activities and dynamic enterprises;
  - unprotected workers as well as risk-taking entrepreneurs;
- contributes to both economic growth and poverty reduction;
- needs to be the target of both economic and social policies;
- is caused variously by jobless growth, economic crises, global competition, corporate business strategies, changes in investment patterns, lack of unemployment insurance and safety nets, cutbacks in social spending, increased costs of living, retrenchment of formal workers and privatisation of public enterprises – not just by decisions taken by informal workers;
- is affected by all policies, both general and targeted; and

- is affected in different ways by policies than formal enterprises and formal workers are.

A *comprehensive* policy approach needs to take into account the different dimensions of the informal economy:

- its component segments and their specific needs and constraints:
  - the self-employed and their enterprises/economic activities;
  - informal wage workers and their employers;
  - disguised wage workers, such as homeworkers, and their employers;
  - women and men within each of these categories;
- the informal workforce as a whole and its common needs and constraints; and
- organisations of informal workers and their lack of recognition and voice.

Most importantly, for the purposes of poverty reduction, an informed and comprehensive policy approach to gender segmentation in the informal economy needs to take as its point of departure the basic premise that addressing informality is an essential pathway to reducing poverty (as detailed in Box 28).

An informed and comprehensive policy approach to gender segmentation in the informal economy needs to take as its point of departure the basic premise that addressing informality is an essential pathway to reducing poverty.

Box 28 Addressing Informality, Reducing Poverty

- There are some 550 million working poor earning less than $1 a day (ILO, 2004a);
- The vast majority of the working poor earn their living in the informal economy;
- Poverty alleviation programmes will not work unless they address the root causes of the low level and insecurity of incomes in the informal economy;
- The root causes of low and insecure incomes in the informal economy include the lack of productive resources and opportunities, the lack of worker rights, the lack of social protection and the lack of organisation and representation.

Policy Goals

Specific goals

In Chapter 4, we proposed a set of strategies, with promising examples, to address the 'downside' effects (detailed in Chapter 3) of economic reforms on the working poor, especially women, in the informal economy. These strategies translate into a set of specific goals that, taken together, represent a comprehensive policy strategy:

- to promote labour-intensive growth;
- to protect informal workers against possible loss of jobs or markets and to enhance their ability to cope with such losses;
- to improve the quality of jobs of informal wage workers by promoting secure contracts, benefits and legal protection;
- to increase market access and competitiveness of the self-employed;
- to regulate 'job flight' and provide protection to migrant workers; and
- to minimise the risks associated with informal employment and to provide social protection to informal workers.

Most critically and fundamentally, an informed and comprehensive approach to the informal economy needs to take into account the different roles, responsibilities, needs and constraints of men and women in it. If the gender segmentation of the informal economy – and of the wider economic processes that affect it – is ignored, the desired outcomes will not be realised. And the benefits that are realised will not affect women and men equally.

Overarching goals

Most of these specific goals are incorporated in the four pillars of the Decent Work agenda of the ILO. Reflecting the Decent Work agenda, the *overarching* policy goals of an informed and comprehensive policy approach toward gender segmentation in the informal economy should be to:

> *Most critically and fundamentally, an informed and comprehensive approach to the informal economy needs to take into account the different roles, responsibilities, needs and constraints of men and women in it.*

- ***promote opportunities:*** to increase the assets, skills, productivity and competitiveness of the informal workforce – both self-employed and wage workers (both women and men) – through a mix of service provision (micro-finance, training, improved technologies and other business development services) as well as policy interventions (workforce development, incentive packages);

- ***secure rights:*** to secure the rights of (a) informal wage workers through extending the scope of existing legislation, promoting collective bargaining agreements and/or enforcing labour standards; and (b) the self-employed though enabling equal access to credit and other resources and through equitable policies for formal and informal enterprise development;

- ***protect informal workers:*** to provide insurance coverage for illness, maternity, disability, old age and death and for property through extending existing schemes and/or developing alternative schemes; and to provide safety nets to 'cushion' informal workers during economic crises or business downturns;

- ***build and recognise the 'voice' of informal workers:*** to promote the organisation of informal workers, especially women's organisations and/or women as leaders in gender-integrated organisations, and their representation in relevant policy-making or rule-setting institutions or in collective bargaining agreements.

To promote the opportunities, rights, protection and voice of women in the informal economy, the special problems and constraints of women workers need to be assessed in policy design and the participation of women workers in the planning process needs to be promoted.

Substantive Policy Areas

As noted above, a basic premise of an informed and comprehensive policy approach to gender segmentation in the informal economy is that most (if not all) policies – both general and targeted, both economic and social – have an impact on

MAINSTREAMING INFORMAL EMPLOYMENT AND GENDER IN POVERTY REDUCTION

Rag picker, India
MARTHA CHEN

informal enterprises and the informal workforce. In what follows, we focus on four key policy areas that are of particular relevance and concern to the informal economy:

- macroeconomic policies;
- regulatory environment;
- labour policies; and
- social protection policies.

In addition, we make recommendations on why and how *labour statistics* – specifically statistics on the informal economy – need to be improved.

An important first step in promoting supportive policies is to assess the impact of existing policies, specifically to identify existing biases or constraints that work against the interests of the informal workforce. In most countries, as we noted in Chapter 3, existing macroeconomic policies are strongly biased in favour of capital (over labour), large formal businesses (over small informal businesses), formal workers (over informal workers) and, within each of these categories, men (over women). Assessments of these policy biases are needed to inform an appropriate policy response (see Box 29 for a framework for assessing policy biases against informal enterprises and informal wage workers).

In brief, macroeconomic policies need to be more sensitive to the informal economy and its gender segmentation and more balanced in terms of both gender and class. To correct for these biases requires an understanding of how they operate. Such an understanding can be gained through surveys and other assessments of: (a) the gender segmentation of informal markets and associated transaction costs and asymmetries of information, property rights and bargaining power; and (b) gender and class biases in existing policies, laws and regulations (Williams, 2003).[3]

Macroeconomic policies

As outlined in Chapter 3, macroeconomic policies help determine employment and poverty outcomes through various channels, including influencing:

- *aggregate demand for labour* by shaping investment and production decisions;
- *aggregate demand for domestic products* by setting the price for competing imports (or imported raw materials), by setting the price at which exports can be sold and by determining the scale and pattern of government procurement;
- *price of inputs and outputs* in capital and product markets by, respectively, setting exchange rates and interest rates and determining tariff rates and price controls; and

> ### Box 29 A Framework for Assessing Policy Biases Affecting Informal Enterprises and Informal Workers (Women and Men)
>
> Policy biases against informal enterprises may emerge at several levels as follows:
>
> 1. Generic constraints and disadvantages faced by *all sizes of enterprises* – due to general problems in the external environment, reflected variously in the economic system and policies, the political system and governance, the social cultural environment and market structure and competition;
>
> 2. Specific constraints and disadvantages faced by *all smaller enterprises* – due to biases in favour of larger businesses in private sector development strategies or in economic policies;
>
> 3. Specific constraints and disadvantages faced by *informal micro-enterprises or own account operations* – due to biases in favour of small and medium enterprises (SMEs) in SME development strategies or in SME policies and regulations;
>
> 4. Specific constraints and disadvantages faced by *women-run micro-enterprises and own account operations* – due to biases in favour of men in various private sector/SME strategies or in economic policies and regulations and to gender norms that restrict women's mobility and access to resources.
>
> Similarly, policy biases against informal wage workers can take various forms:
>
> 5. Generic constraints and disadvantages faced by *labour* – due to systemic biases in favour of the owners of capital in the wider environment, the structure of labour markets and the system of production;
>
> 6. Specific constraints and disadvantages faced by *informal wage workers* – due to the nature of the employment relationship;

INFORMAL EMPLOYMENT AND GENDER: A STRATEGIC APPROACH

> **Box 29** (continued)
>
> 7. Specific constraints and disadvantages faced by *female informal wage workers* – due to gender segmentation within the informal economy and to gender norms that assign to women the responsibility for unpaid housework and care work and that constrain their physical mobility.
>
> At each of these levels, it is important to determine whether the policy biases are due to a poor understanding of gender segmentation in the informal economy; its lack of visibility in official statistics; exclusion of informal producers and workers, especially women, from rule-setting or policy-making institutions; and/or to the weak bargaining power of informal producers and workers.

- *incentives and subsidies* to businesses through trade and industry policies, tax and expenditure policies, labour legislation and industrial relations regulations.

A fundamental goal of the policy approach we propose here would be to shift the structure of aggregate demand, the prices of inputs and outputs and the set of incentives and subsidies in favour of informal workers, ensuring that women benefit to the same extent as men. For instance, policy-makers need to redress the imbalance in policies that favour large enterprises over small and micro-enterprises in tax breaks, subsidies and other incentives; in licensing procedures for importing and exporting; and in technical assistance for innovation and upgrading. And policy-makers need to redress the imbalance in policies that favour formal workers over informal producers and workers in statutory benefits, such as unemployment insurance, pension funds or safety nets.

Taxes

Revenue is an area with substantial impact on those working in the informal economy. However, most analysis of the impact of government budgets looks exclusively at public spending, to the neglect of the differential impact of revenue generation (direct, indirect and corporate taxes) on workers in the infor-

A fundamental goal of the policy approach we propose here would be to shift the structure of aggregate demand, the prices of inputs and outputs and the set of incentives and subsidies in favour of informal workers, ensuring that women benefit to the same extent as men.

mal economy. In most countries, tax policies place a heavier burden on the informal than the formal economy. In South Africa, for example, all non-standard employment is taxed at 25 per cent, a rate often higher than that paid by equivalent standard employees. Also, many countries lower corporate income tax rates for those who export; if informal enterprises do not export directly, as is often the case, they cannot benefit from these lower rates.

Macroeconomic policy also needs to consider the working poor in the informal economy as *consumers*, not just as workers. Poor informal sector workers tend to spend a higher percentage of their income than other workers and are, therefore, badly affected by certain regressive tax policies. For instance, they spend a higher percentage of their incomes on food than other workers and are particularly affected by flat value-added tax rates on basic food stuff. Also, user fees for social services such as health care and education hit the poorest workers (especially women) hardest. While business organisations regularly lobby vocally for lower taxes, those advocating for workers in informal employment have not yet tackled the taxation issue. Progressive tax policy that would benefit the working poor in the informal economy would include lowering taxes on: (a) the goods and services whose consumption constitutes a high fraction of the spending of low income groups; and (b) the size and type of businesses in which the poor are likely to be engaged.

Expenditures

To increase the competitiveness of their economies, governments provide incentives – in the form of tax breaks, subsidies and services – to businesses. These incentives are unlikely to reach micro-enterprises, much less own account operations. For example, few micro-entrepreneurs or own account operators are invited to participate in export-promotion fairs. At their most negative, export-promotion policies can shift production away from small production units (often owned by women) to larger mechanised units (often owned by men) as happened, for example, in the coir industry in Sri Lanka.

Macroeconomic policies can help to address the disadvantages of the informal workers that derive from their lack of access to training and credit. But policy-makers need to recognise that the formal institutions dealing with training and credit tend to stigmatise those who work in the informal economy and to be unfriendly to the poor, especially women. Similar attitudes prevail in the private sector. Also, formal training and credit programmes often do not reach the smallest enterprises: own account operations and family businesses that do not hire workers. Given these concerns, where there are NGOs to provide micro-finance and business development services, the most appropriate role for government is to finance and regulate these organisations rather than provide the services directly. See Box 30 for a set of recommendations on how to ensure that fiscal policies do not disadvantage those who work in the informal economy.

> *... where there are NGOs to provide micro-finance and business development services, the most appropriate role for government is to finance and regulate these organisations rather than provide the services directly.*

Box 30 Fiscal Policies and the Informal Economy

(a) Expenditures

Expenditures on skills development and enterprise development services:

- Budget allocations for vocational skills training and non-formal education should be targeted to help informal wage workers, particularly those working as casual or contract labourers and homeworkers. Most skills-development programmes target formal wage workers.

- Budget allocations for business development services should be targeted to micro-enterprises, particularly those with five or fewer paid workers and those run by women. Most such programmes target SMEs to the neglect of the vast majority of informal entrepreneurs.

Social expenditures:

- Government spending on social services and social protection should be targeted to workers in the informal economy, who represent the majority of workers in most developing countries and are often the most disadvantaged workers in developed countries. Most statutory social security schemes exclude informal workers, yet informal workers often have limited capacity to subscribe to privatised schemes.

Box 30 (continued)

Government procurement:
- Government policies on the procurement of goods and services and related bidding procedures should be modified to ensure that micro-enterprises can compete on an equal – if not stronger – footing with larger enterprises. Most government procurement policies are biased in favour of large, registered enterprises.

(b) Revenue

Value-added taxes:
- Value-added taxes affect those who work in the informal economy as both consumers and producers. Because they operate in highly competitive and price-sensitive markets, informal producers and traders often find it difficult to 'pass on' the value-added tax to their customers. Moreover, a flat rate value-added tax – especially on basic foodstuffs – can prove regressive for informal consumers. This is because low-income households spend a larger proportion of their income on food – and earn a higher proportion of their income in the informal economy – than higher-income households.

Indirect taxes:
- Informal producers and workers are often subject to indirect taxes. Most notably, street vendors often pay more in transaction costs (bribes, fees to shopkeepers to use toilets and store goods, etc) than they would have paid in direct taxes. Cost-benefit analyses should take into account the indirect taxes paid by the informal workforce and whether they receive any benefits in return.

Corporate taxes:
- As part of export-promotion incentive packages, many countries lower the corporate income tax rate. Few micro-entrepreneurs and no self-employed producers pay corporate income taxes. They would, however, benefit from lower personal income tax rates.

In sum, as part of an informed and comprehensive approach to the informal economy, policy-makers need to determine whether the informal economy shares in benefits from government expenditure and procurement policies. New methods for assessing government budgets – called social audits or people's budgets – can be used to assess the differential impacts of policies on the formal and informal economy (see Box 31). However, collection of budget data is made difficult because allocations affecting those who work in the informal economy may be the responsibility of many different government departments (such as labour, housing, small enterprise development and public health) at different levels of government (national, state and local).

At present, in South Africa, a budget analysis from the perspective of the informal economy is being carried out. This analysis considers the policy direction and budget allocations of all national government departments as well as all the departments in one province – KwaZulu-Natal – and the city of Durban/eThekwini. The focus is on the 2003/2004 budget. Given that multi-year budgeting is being introduced, reference is made to broader trends over time. The research is informed by an analysis of the most recent statistics on the informal economy in South Africa. The researchers are assessing both targeted and mainstream expenditures but are also concentrating on the implications of revenue collection policy and processes. Attention is being paid to how state institutions are structured and where the responsibility for those working in the informal economy is housed. Further, the involvement of those working in the informal economy in budget formulation processes is being assessed.

Preliminary findings indicate that national government targeted expenditure on the informal economy is inadequate. For example small business support strategies are not designed for micro and survivalist enterprises. However, South Africa, in comparison to other developing countries, has a better developed social security net. State grants, like the old age pension and the child support grant, are likely to support informal activities. National government policy thus falls into the trap of dealing with the informal economy as a welfare rather than an economic issue. There are however promising policy developments both within the province of KwaZulu-Natal and the

... as part of an informed and comprehensive approach to the informal economy, policy-makers need to determine whether the informal economy shares in benefits from government expenditure and procurement policies.

city of Durban/eThekwini (Budlender, Skinner, and Valodia forthcoming).

> **Box 31 Government Budgets and the Informal Economy**
>
> New tools are available to assess the differential impact of policies on the formal and informal economy (and women and men within them). These include social audits or people-centred budgets that can be used to assess the impact of government budgets on the informal economy, bringing to light the meagre resources that this area frequently receives or the policy biases that frequently operate against it. Such tools were first used in Australia in 1985, with a government-initiated gender budget analysis that analysed the whole government budget from the point of view of women.[4]
>
> In order to develop policy toward the informal economy, governments would need to know how much and what kinds of assistance the economy receives. Social audits allow governments to know:
>
> - which structures deal with the informal economy;
> - what kinds of goods and services various levels of government give to informal economy units and workers (as compared to formal economy units and workers);
> - whether budget allocations support social and economic goals; and
> - how budgets calibrate with plans and needs.
>
> Further action in developing policy can proceed through consultations with the concerned workers to find out what their needs are and whether they are being met.

Regulatory environment

As discussed in Chapter 3, there are several contradictory perspectives on regulation and the informal economy. One perspective, popularised by Hernando do Soto, is that excessive regulation of entrepreneurial activities drives informality as entrepreneurs seek to avoid the costs and time involved in registering their businesses. Another perspective, shared by observers who focus on informal jobs rather than enterprises, is that deregulation of labour markets allows employers to reduce labour costs and increase their 'flexibility' by recruiting workers under informal employment relationships. A third perspective notes that the regulatory environment often overlooks – or turns a blind eye to – specific categories of informal activities such as street trade. The first school of thought advocates deregulation of commercial activities, the second advocates re-regulation of employment relations while the third recommends regulation of heretofore unregulated activities. As noted earlier, part of the confusion stems from that fact that the different observers are talking about different types of regulation: of commercial activities, of labour markets, of property or of urban space. The essential issue is not to make a choice between regulation and deregulation, but rather to formulate *appropriate regulations* through a process in which those to be regulated have a voice.

Consider, for example, the case of the urban regulatory environment. Estimates suggest that, by the year 2010, more than half of the population in most developing countries will be urban (UN-HABITAT, 2004). And current trends suggest that the informal economy will continue to account for a major share of the urban workforce: it now accounts for anywhere from 40 to 60 per cent of urban employment in developing countries where data are available (ILO, 2002b). Street trade – which comprises roughly one third of the urban informal economy today – will remain a major policy challenge: the key policy questions are how to manage street trade and how to support street traders. Vendors seek the right to vend without harassment and to have regular selling spaces in places that customers frequent, storage facilities and basic infrastructure such as water, shelter and toilets. Policy regarding street vendors deals with zoning and space (places to vend, relocation), licenses and registration (licenses or ID cards to afford freedom from harassment and protection from extortion from various sources), infrastructure and services.

Urban informal economy policies should also address the situation of other categories of the urban informal workforce, including home-based workers, garbage and paper pickers,

> *The essential issue is not to make a choice between regulation and deregulation, but rather to formulate appropriate regulations through a process in which those to be regulated have a voice.*

construction day labourers and informal transport workers. All urban informal workers share some common concerns, including the right of access to social services (health, education and childcare), establishment of law and order so as to be able to work without disruptions and fear of violence and establishment of a negotiation framework and local appeals mechanism.

Negative attitudes towards the informal economy often impede rational policy analysis. Most informal economy entrepreneurs operating in urban areas are thought to be unregulated or avoiding regulation. Many cannot get licenses through no fault of their own. Street vendors have to bear many costs – both legitimate (permits, licenses, site payments, storage and water and toilet fees) as well as illegitimate (middleman's fees, bribes and extortion). Many so-called 'illegal' operators would be happy for a chance to get licenses and leave behind their current situation based on extortion and fear. Many street vendors, when asked, clamour for the right to pay the relevant authority whatever revenue is required because this would afford them recognition and legal status. However, they expect some services and other benefits for the payments they make and clear and transparent agreements about rights and responsibilities.

In order to realise the economic and social contributions of the urban informal economy and at the same time protect the rights of all citizens, urban policies and regulations could adopt the following principles:

- regulate, but do not prohibit, street trade;

- decriminalise violations of street vending laws and regulations and move to a system of administrative, rather than criminal, control;

- regard license fees as taxes entitling street vendors to infrastructure for the improvement of their work environment (lighting, toilets, shelter, storage space and water) – which both they and the public want; and

- ensure the participation of street vendors and other stakeholders in developing appropriate regulation (Durban Metropolitan Council, 2001).

Recent efforts have been made in India, Kenya and South

Africa to frame appropriate regulations for street vendors. The policy process in eThekwini/Durban, South Africa, and the policy process in India leading to the National Policy on Street Trade (ratified by the Government of India in January 2004) are particularly promising examples of negotiated reforms involving all stakeholders, including street vendors themselves (see Chapter 4).

Labour policies

By definition, informal wage workers are not covered by labour legislation. In the past, they were also not organised by trade unions. Today, informal workers and labour advocates around the world are demanding workers' rights for all workers, including informal workers. Some of the impetus behind this demand relates to concerns about informalisation and the negative consequences for the working poor of economic liberalisation and restructuring (outlined in Chapter 3).

International labour standards

During the last century, through the ILO, a system of international *labour standards and labour conventions* was developed. Workers' rights include core labour standards around which there is widespread international agreement and other basic rights. The long-standing commitment of the ILO to protecting the rights of all workers, irrespective of where they work, was reinforced in 1998 when the International Labour Conference unanimously adopted a Declaration on Fundamental Principles and Rights at Work that applies to all those who work, regardless of their employment relationship. The core rights encompassed in this Declaration include: freedom of association and the right to collective bargaining; elimination of all forms of forced or compulsory labour; elimination of discrimination in respect of employment and occupation; and the effective abolition of child labour. At a minimum, these core rights, which in principle apply to all workers, need in practice to be extended and enforced for informal workers.

Other areas of basic rights include safe and healthy working conditions, reasonable working hours, severance notice and pay, paid sick leave and vacations and retirement compensation. Some of these are incorporated in existing international

Today, informal workers and labour advocates around the world are demanding workers' rights for all workers, including informal workers.

MAINSTREAMING INFORMAL EMPLOYMENT AND GENDER IN POVERTY REDUCTION

In consultation with organisations of workers in the informal economy, national governments need to review how existing labour legislation can be extended to protect the rights of workers in the informal economy and whether additional labour legislation needs to be introduced to adequately protect their rights.

standards and conventions and should, in principle, apply to informal workers. Most ILO standards apply to all workers or, if targeted at workers in the formal economy, have explicit provisions for extension to other categories of workers. One ILO Convention – the 1996 Home Work Convention – focuses on a specific category of worker in the informal economy: homeworkers or industrial outworkers, mainly women, who work from their homes (see Appendix 1). And two ILO Conventions – one on rural workers, the other on indigenous and tribal peoples – focus on groups who are often in the informal economy. Most recently, the ILO has explicitly incorporated the informal economy in its policy framework called 'Decent Work' (ILO, 2002a).

National labour legislation

International labour standards need to be ratified and enforced by individual countries. In consultation with organisations of workers in the informal economy, national governments need to review how existing labour legislation can be extended to protect the rights of workers in the informal economy and whether additional labour legislation needs to be introduced to adequately protect their rights. The Government of India recently undertook such a review (see Box 32).

Some countries have adopted progressive labour legislation that addresses the insecurity and disadvantages of specific categories of informal or non-standard wage workers, as below (see Chapter 4 for other promising examples):

Homeworkers: A law in Ontario, Canada, mandates that homeworkers should be paid a 10 per cent premium on the minimum wage to compensate for the costs of production they have to bear by working at home.

Temporary workers: A law in France mandates that workers in what is called non-standard or temporary employment must receive the same wages as those doing the same work in regular employment, plus a premium at the end of their contract period because of the precarious nature of their work. French workers in this category are also covered by collective bargaining agreements and receive a number of benefits.

Sweatshop garment workers: A 1999 labour law in California, USA, imposes a wage guarantee, provides an expedited process for recovering unpaid wages and allows garment workers to bring court action against manufacturers who subcontract to unregistered contractors.

> ### Box 32 Review of National Labour Legislation in India
>
> The National Commission on Labour in India, set up in 1999, decided to recognise informal workers and to formulate umbrella legislation for the sector. Touring the country and holding hearings with both worker and employer organisations, the Commission focused on the country's changing economic environment, with particular regard to globalisation of the economy and liberalisation of trade and industry. It examined ways in which labour protection and welfare measures could apply in a flexible labour market. The Commission was also charged with improving the effectiveness of social security, occupational health and safety measures and minimum wages, with attention to safeguarding women and handicapped workers.
>
> The study group on Women Workers and Child Labour, one of five study groups set up under the Commission, has recommended broadening the definition of worker to accommodate more categories of informal workers, promoting equal pay for men and women workers, extending maternity coverage to many informal workers and mandating the provision of childcare facilities in small and medium-scale industries. The concrete and comprehensive ideas of this study group regarding how to extend national labour legislation to cover informal women workers are presented in Appendix 2. The umbrella legislation for the unorganised sector (informal economy) proposed by the Commission has not yet been adopted (see Appendix 3).

Other approaches to promoting labour standards

In addition to the ratification and enforcement of existing international labour standards by countries and the enforcement of national labour legislation, various global approaches to promoting labour standards have been tried or proposed, though none as yet predominates.

Current initiatives:

- adoption by companies of *verifiable codes of conduct*, either firm-specific codes developed by individual firms or industry-wide codes developed (often) by joint initiatives involving consumer groups as well as corporate representatives. Some of these involve monitoring by independent monitors; and

- *transnational organising of workers* in specific industries to advocate for and demand their rights.

Proposed initiatives:

- building *regional consensus on minimum standards of work* and, perhaps, regional inspectorates and courts to monitor and enforce them; and

- building global versions of national systems based on ILO core labour standards by establishing *universal minimum standards of work* and international inspectorates and courts to monitor and enforce them (ILO, 2003).

Social protection policies

Although they face a common set of core risks with those who work in the formal economy and usually face greater costs and risks associated with work, informal economy workers seldom receive social benefits from either their employer or their government.

With the growth in the informal economy, there is a concomitant growth in the number of workers without benefits. Most of those who work in the informal economy are without unemployment insurance, health insurance and retirement or disability benefits. At the same time, their incomes are lower, on average, than those of formal workers. In the past, governments ignored the social protection needs of informal workers, assuming that family and community support did the job. However, informal insurance mechanisms are seldom adequate and never secure. At the same time, those who work in the informal economy probably face more hazards than other workers. If workers demand better security and protection, employers frequently respond by replacing them. Both social arguments (for basic human rights) and economic arguments (increased productivity of workers in a secure setting) can be used to make the case for providing these benefits. Basic insurance, pensions and safety nets are needed to provide work-based security for workers who have been left out of social security schemes.

Social insurance for the informal economy may be most easily realised through schemes where workers contribute. Even very poor workers are willing and able to save, but they should not have to bear all the responsibility for protecting against risk and social provision. There are active roles for the state, the private sector, trade unions and other civil society organisations in providing social protection for informal economy workers. The state can be involved by making financial contributions, managing the scheme or delivering the benefits. Employers – including lead firms in sub-contracting chains – can be involved in making financial contributions. When individual employers are unwilling to contribute, the total output of specific industries can be taxed (see description of welfare funds in India in Chapter 4). The private insurance industry or the government may be willing to negotiate with organised groups of informal workers (such as domestic or migrant workers) about shared contributions to insurance funds. Financing can be a combination of subscriber fees, employer contributions, taxes on entire industries, grants and government subsidies.

Throughout the world, but particularly in developing countries, there is a range of promising approaches to providing social protection for informal workers. These include:

- ***mutual insurance schemes***: e.g. mutual health insurance schemes in West Africa;

- ***means-tested government-funded targeted pensions***: e.g. old-age pensions for agricultural workers with below-poverty incomes introduced by the state of Kerala in India;

- ***universal health insurance or pension schemes***: e.g. the national pension system in Japan that provides health insurance and pension insurance for more than 90 per cent of its people, including informal workers (Japan was a middle income country in the early 1960s when it introduced this system); and

There are active roles for the state, the private sector, trade unions and other civil society organisations in providing social protection for informal economy workers.

Greater priority needs to be given to the collection of data on informal employment, which is a relatively new topic in labour statistics.

- ***extension of existing statutory schemes:*** e.g. extension of Portugal's statutory social security system to cover home-based embroiderers in Madeira for old age, disability, maternity and sick days.

Whatever approach to promoting social protection for the informal workforce is adopted, the approach should adhere to certain basic principles, namely to promote:

- incremental schemes, providing a core set of provisions that can be expanded over time;

- participatory processes, involving the beneficiaries in design, implementation and monitoring of the scheme;

- equitable financing, possibly from several sources, including government subsidies and employer contributions; and

- decentralised, flexible and user-responsive mechanisms.

Labour statistics

To ensure that appropriate policies are put in place, the informal workforce needs to be visible to policy-makers. Also, the informed and comprehensive policy approach to gender segmentation in the informal economy proposed here needs to be evidence based. Yet, as this Handbook has highlighted, there are currently limited data on the informal economy and fewer still on the links between informal employment and poverty. Greater priority needs to be given to the collection of data on informal employment, which is a relatively new topic in labour statistics.

In 1993, in response to the data collection efforts that were taking place in countries, the International Conference of Labour Statisticians (ICLS) adopted an international statistical definition of employment in the informal sector to bring about greater harmony and comparability in data being collected. In subsequent years more countries have collected these data (ILO 2000c). In 2003, as described in Chapter 2, the ICLS expanded the definition to include informal employment outside of the informal sector. However, while much progress has been made, the collection of data on informal employment broadly defined is not yet part of the regular data collection and tabulation efforts of any national statistical office.

In 2002, the 90th Session of the International Labour Conference recommended that member states should: "collect, analyse and disseminate consistent, disaggregated statistics on the size, composition and contribution of the informal economy that will help enable identification of specific groups of workers and economic units and their problems in the informal economy" (ILC, 2003b). This Handbook – with its focus on the wages, conditions of work and general economic well-being of workers in informal employment – has looked mainly at the latter part of this recommendation. It has outlined the kinds of data and research that have helped to focus the debate on the contribution of the informal economy to economic growth and the linkages between informal employment arrangements, gender and poverty. Hopefully, it has shown the usefulness and importance of these data, which in turn will justify devoting greater efforts and resources to this topic by national, regional and international agencies.

What follows is a list of what needs to be done to improve statistics on the informal economy and its relationship to poverty:

- Additional countries need to collect statistics on the informal economy, and countries that already do so need to improve the quality of statistics they already collect. In many cases this will require technical assistance from the ILO and additional funding from international donor agencies.

    – Statistics on the size and composition of the informal economy need to be improved and their availability increased.

    – Statistics on the earnings and working conditions of those who work in informal employment, classified by employment status, also need to be improved and their availability increased.

    – Data need to be developed on the contribution of the informal sector and informal employment more broadly to GDP.

    – Data need to be developed on informal enterprises,

MAINSTREAMING INFORMAL EMPLOYMENT AND GENDER IN POVERTY REDUCTION

Research needs to be undertaken using existing national data to analyse the linkages between informal employment, gender and poverty, and the results should be published in user-oriented publications.

specifically on the conditions that lead to success and failure.

- Research needs to be undertaken using existing national data to analyse the linkages between informal employment, gender and poverty, and the results should be published in user-oriented publications. For example, a major source of data for this book was the analysis and publications prepared by researchers and statisticians in India, Mexico and South Africa. Such research will provide not only needed data analysis but also support for new data collection activities. This is because the resources required to undertake national surveys are enormous and need to be justified in terms of the usage of data.

- Labour statisticians, labour lawyers and researchers working on labour issues need to collaborate on the development of an overarching framework that allows the classification, comparison and analysis of the full set of employment statuses/work arrangements that exist in both developed and developing countries. This will contribute to improved understanding of the changing nature of work as well as the links between employment and poverty.

Other policy areas

Functional areas of policy

Other functional areas of policies that have particular relevance for informal enterprises and the informal workforce include:

- **micro-finance and enterprise development services** to increase the productivity of their enterprises;

- **infrastructure and services** to improve their housing and living environment and **social policies** to improve their health and education;

- **property rights** to give them the ability to transform their assets into capital assets; and

- **intellectual property rights** to protect their traditional knowledge and their rights to natural resources.

Small farmer, Jamaica
FOOD AND AGRICULTURE ORGANIZATION/F. MATTIOLI

Sectoral policies

Most sector-specific policies also have effects on the informal economy. Seen from the perspective of the working poor in the informal economy, especially women, these include the following key sectors and concerns:

- ***agriculture:*** food security and sustainable livelihoods;
- ***forestry:*** sustainable and equitable access to non-timber forest products, wood fuel, pastures and other common property resources;
- ***fishery:*** sustainable and equitable management of water resources and sustainable and equitable allocation of fishing rights;
- ***manufacturing:*** balance of efficiency and equity concerns in choice of sector of production, technology, site of production and employment relations; and
- ***construction:*** balance of efficiency and equity concerns in choice of technology and employment relations.

In addition to governments, a range of other actors can and should intervene to promote a strategic response to gender segmentation in the informal economy.

Key Actors

In addition to governments, a range of other actors can and should intervene to promote a strategic response to gender segmentation in the informal economy. These include inter-governmental organisations, employers and companies, the private insurance industry, consumers and the public, trade unions and workers' organisations, NGOs, community-based organisations, individuals and families. What follows is a suggestive – but by no means exhaustive – list of what these different actors might do to promote the opportunities, rights, protection and/or voice of informal producers and workers, especially women. Examples of good practice by these various actors, sometimes in collaboration, are provided in Chapter 4.

Inter-governmental organisations

Inter-governmental organisations, such as the Commonwealth Secretariat, can promote and encourage the mainstreaming of informal labour market analysis, from a gender perspective, into national and international poverty reduction strategies through policy-oriented interventions of various kinds, such as:

- supporting additional policy-oriented research and documentation of the linkages between market-oriented reforms, informal employment, gender and poverty;

- promoting and encouraging the collection of improved statistics on the informal economy, and enhancing the availability of sex-disaggregated statistics on the informal economy and related income and expenditure data; and

- promoting policy dialogues or briefings to facilitate the integration of an understanding of gender segmentation in the informal economy in trade and other economic policies at the national, regional and international levels.

Employers or corporations

In response to mounting pressures from consumer groups and others, the corporate sector has begun to adopt 'voluntary' codes of conduct to self-regulate their treatment of labour. These codes of conduct and related monitoring efforts need to be extended to cover working conditions outside of factories or workshops, especially homework.

In addition to adopting voluntary codes of conduct, socially responsible business associations could establish and promote systematic competition between firms based on their performance in the treatment of workers, making outstanding social performance a marketable commodity or brand standard – an approach that has been called Ratcheting Labour Standards (RLS) (Sabel et al, 2000).

Industries or economic sectors

The informal workforce – both the self-employed and informal wage workers – contributes to growth in different industries. How can they share in the benefits of growth in the specific industries or trades in which they operate? One mechanism is to tax the aggregate output of designated industries to finance benefits for the informal workforce in those industries. For an example of how this can work, see the discussion of welfare funds in India in Chapter 4.

Private insurance industry

One dimension of welfare reforms over the past decade in many countries, particularly in Latin America, has been the privatisation of social insurance, whereby social insurance funds to cover pensions, health insurance and other contingencies have been consolidated and replaced, wholly or partially, by individual savings plans (Barrientos, 2001). A related dimension of economic reforms over the past decade in several countries has been the privatisation of the insurance industry, which was previously under government control. In some countries, such as India, the privatisation of insurance has led to the loss of government-mandated coverage for informal workers (Jhabvala et al, 2001).

The net result is a worldwide crisis in insurance, with particularly dire consequences for the working poor in the informal economy. If poverty is to be reduced, the privatisation of insurance needs to be fundamentally re-assessed. Most of the working poor are unable to save (and contribute) enough to subscribe to private insurance schemes to protect themselves against even common core contingencies.

Consumers and the public

The collective action of consumer groups, student groups, church groups and others in Fair Trade campaigns has con-

If poverty is to be reduced, the privatisation of insurance needs to be fundamentally re-assessed. Most of the working poor are unable to save (and contribute) enough to subscribe to private insurance schemes to protect themselves against even common core contingencies.

> *Everywhere, around the world, the informal workforce is excluded from or under-represented in the processes and institutions that make policies. To gain representation and voice, workers in the informal economy need to be organised.*

tributed significantly to building awareness and putting pressure on the corporate sector regarding the rights of workers in the global economy. From the perspective of the informal economy, these campaigns need to be encouraged but also expanded to include a more systematic focus on homeworkers and to include the very small producers who are affected by the behaviour of TNCs. Also, more systematic links need to be developed between the organisations of informal workers in the South and the Fair Trade movement in the North to ensure that campaigns truly represent the interests of the working poor.

Formal trade unions

Formal trade unions have traditionally organised around the conflict of interest between formal wage workers and employers. As such, they have found it very difficult to deal with informal workers, whose employment status is uncertain. Given the recent expansion of employment in the informal sector and the decline in union membership, however, some formal trade unions have begun to consider and debate whether or not to intervene. A few have begun to organise informal workers and/or to collaborate with organisations of informal workers (see Chapter 4 for promising examples). However, many issues have yet to be resolved. Some of the serious strategic questions include: Should informal workers be organised in separate unions or organisations? Should trade unions get involved with the self-employed? What services can trade unions offer self-employed producers and traders? Can or should the rights won for formal workers be extended to informal workers? Many trade unions, particularly in developing countries, have limited funds and personnel. Should they stretch their resources to cover a new group of workers when they can barely serve their existing membership?

Organisations of informal workers

People in informal work represent the largest concentration of needs without voice, the majority of the world economy. (ILO, 2002a)

Everywhere, around the world, the informal workforce is excluded from or under-represented in the processes and institutions that make policies. To gain representation and voice, workers in the informal economy need to be organised. Although they were rarely organised in the past, there are a growing number of organisations of informal workers, including village or neighbourhood associations, credit groups, trade unions, co-operatives and emerging labour organisations. Yet many remain small, weak and isolated and most are not recognised as legitimate worker organisations by formal trade unions in their respective countries or by the international trade union movement.

Over the past decade, however, some of these organisations, notably those working with women in the informal economy, have begun forming alliances at the national, regional and global levels. During the 1990s, inspired by the Self Employed Women's Association (SEWA) in India, three international alliances were established: one of home-based worker organisations (called HomeNet); another of street vendor organisations (called StreetNet); and a third of researchers, activists and policy-makers working on the informal economy (called Women in Informal Employment: Globalizing and Organizing or WIEGO) (see Chapter 4). More recently, at an international meeting in December 2003, an international network of trade unions and other membership-based organisations, and NGOs organising in the informal economy has been formed. In mutually reinforcing ways, these global alliances seek to increase the visibility and voice of those who work in the informal economy and to promote supportive policies for the informal workforce worldwide. Together, these alliances – and their member organisations – constitute a growing international movement of the informal workforce with a particular, but not exclusive, focus on women.

Non-governmental organisations
Large numbers of NGOs around the world provide services to, advocate on behalf of and/or organise the working poor in the informal economy. However, more of these NGOs need to organise the working poor – including women – around their work identities (i.e. as small-scale producers, traders or wage workers) and, in so doing, to find ways to work more closely with trade unions, especially those organising informal workers.

Individuals, families and communities

In the absence of formal systems of social protection, the working poor rely on informal systems of social protection (e.g. support from friends and relatives, social or kinship networks and rotating savings-and-credit societies) as well as their own resources (e.g. use of savings, sale of assets or sending children to work). However, the benefits from such informal sources are seldom adequate and often uncertain, especially during widespread or prolonged crises, and the associated costs and risks are often quite high. Furthermore, women worldwide do a disproportionate amount of this unpaid 'community work'.

Policy Process

Clearly, there is no universal policy prescription for the informal economy. However, the following guiding principles should be seen as essential aspects of a positive policy process:

- It should be *participatory and inclusive* and allow for policies to be developed through consultation with informal workers, and through consensus of relevant government departments, the organisations of informal workers and other appropriate social actors. In order to have a voice, those who work in the informal economy must be organised and their efforts to organise into trade unions and co-operatives at every level should be encouraged and supported.

- It should be *context-specific* based on the reality of different categories of informal workers in specific locales and industries. It should recognise and support both the self-employed and paid workers in the informal economy. The lack of recognition and understanding of these two components of the informal economy often hinders the development of appropriate policy. Further, taking into account local and national circumstances is critical to developing appropriate policy.

- It should be *gender sensitive*, taking into account the roles and responsibilities of women and men in the informal economy. In most regions of the world, a larger share of the female than of the male workforce is in the informal economy and, within the informal economy, women tend to be concentrated in lower-return segments than men (see Chapter 2). As a result, even within the informal economy, there is a significant gender gap in earnings and in the benefits and protection afforded by work. Understanding relations between men and women, their different positions in the economy and their access to and control of resources is crucial to understanding the informal economy, where a gendered approach is a pro-poor approach. Supporting women's work will, in effect, lead to support for poor households and poor children.

- It should be based on an informed understanding of the *economic* contribution of informal workers and serve to *mainstream* the concerns of the informal workforce in those institutions that deal with economic planning and development. In the past, the management or regulation of informal activities has often been relegated to social policy departments or, in urban areas, to those departments (such as the police or traffic) that deal with law and order issues. Locating governance of the informal economy in traffic, health, policy or social departments ignores its economic aspects. Institutions that govern the informal economy should be those dealing with economic planning and development.

The framework, guidelines and successful examples presented in this Handbook are intended to help develop an informed and comprehensive policy approach. Of course, formulating appropriate policies is never an easy task. However, with the involvement of the organisations that represent informal workers, particularly women, it is likely to succeed. The way ahead has to be one of negotiated solutions, and these negotiations have to be about rights and responsibilities. While the inclusion of the voice of all stakeholders in making policy is essential to its success, the input of informal workers and their organisations, based on recognition of their right to organise, is crucial.

Notes

1 This growing consensus is reflected in several recent reports by various inter-governmental organisations, including: *A Fair Globalization: Creating Opportunities for All* (WCSDG, 2004); and *Globalization, Growth and Poverty: Building an Inclusive World Economy* (World Bank, 2001).

2 In this World Bank report on trade and poverty, the six recommended areas of action for building an inclusive world economy are: a 'development round' of trade negotiations; improved investment climate in developing countries (including control of corruption, well-functioning bureaucracies and regulations, contract enforcement and protection of property rights); good delivery of education and health services; good provision of social protection tailored to the more dynamic labour market in an open economy; greater volume of foreign aid; and debt relief (World Bank, 2002).

3 *Gender Mainstreaming in the Multilateral Trading System* by Mariama Williams, another handbook in this series, looks at the linkages between trade and investment policy and gender equality objectives and priorities, as well as presenting recommendations on the key issues.

4 Gender-responsive budgets have now been carried out in around 40 countries, nearly half of them in the Commonwealth. The Commonwealth Secretariat has produced a number of publications about these experiences, including a guide for practitioners called *Engendering Budgets* (in the Gender Mainstreaming Series). See *www.thecommonwealth.org/gender*.

References

African Centre for Gender and Development/WIEGO (2002). 'Report of African Regional Workshop on Food Processing and Minor Forest Product Global Value Chains'. Kampala, Uganda, December.

Amadeo, Edward (1998). *A globalização e sua dimensão trabalhista*. Brasilia: Ministerio do Trabalho.

Appleton, Helen, Maria E. Fernandez, Catherine L.M. Hill and Consuelo Quiroz (1995). 'Claiming and Using Indigenous Knowledge'. In Gender Working Group, UN Commission on Science and Technology for Development. *Missing Links: Gender Equity in Science and Technology Development*. New York: UNIFEM.

Asemoah, Kofi (2004). Personal communication.

Baden, Sally (1998). 'Gender Issues in Agricultural Liberalisation'. Topic paper prepared for Directorate General for Development (DGVIII) of the European Commission. *Bridge (Development-Gender)* Report, Number 41. Brighton: Institute of Development Studies (IDS). Available online at: *http://www.ids.ac.uk/bridge/Reports/re41c.pdf*

Bajaj, Manjul (2000). 'Invisible Workers, Visible Contributions: A study of home-based women workers in Five Sectors Across South Asia'. Background Paper for Regional Policy Seminar, Nepal.

Barndt, W. (1999). 'Virtual Civil Society?', *Foreign Policy*, 117 (Winter): 22.

Barrientos, Armando and Stephanie Ware Barrientos (2002). 'Extending Social Protection to Informal Workers in the Horticulture Global Value Chain'. *SP Discussion Paper*, No 0216, Washington, D.C.: World Bank.

Barrientos, Stephanie, A. Kritzinger and H. Rossouw (2004). 'National Labour Regulations in an International Context: Women Workers in Export Horticulture in South Africa'. In Carr, M. (ed). *Chains of Fortune: Linking Local Women Producers and Workers with Global Markets*. London: Commonwealth Secretariat.

Barrientos, Stephanie Ware, Sharon McClenaghan and L. Orton (1999). 'Gender and Codes of Conduct: A Case Study from Horticulture in South Africa'. Research Report to the UK Department for International Development (DFID). London: Christian Aid.

Barrientos, Stephanie Ware, C. Dolan and A. Tallontire (2001). *Gender and Ethical Trade: A Mapping of the Issues in African Horticulture*. Report No 2624, Natural Resources Institute, July.

Bhagwati, Jagdish N. (2004). *In Defense of Globalization*. New York: Oxford University Press.

Bhattacharya, D. and M. Rahman (1999). 'Female Employment Under Export Propelled Industrialization: Prospects for Internalizing Global Opportunities in the Apparel Sector in Bangladesh'. Occasional Paper No. 10, Geneva: United Nations Research Institute for Social Development.

Boakye, Edna Opoku (2004). 'Organizing in the Informal Economy in Ghana', *International Union Rights*, 11(2).

Bravo, Rosa (2003). 'The Millennium Goals and Gender Equity: The Case of Peru'. ECLAC Women and Development Unit/UNIFEM Andean Region.

Budlender, Debbie (2004). Personal communication.

—— and Guy Hewitt (2002). *Gender Budgets Make More Cents*. London: Commonwealth Secretariat.

—— (2003). *Engendering Budgets: A Practitioner's Guide to Understanding and Implementing Gender-responsive Budgets*. London: Commonwealth Secretariat.

Budlender, Debbie, Peter Buwembo and Nozipho Shabalala (2002). 'The informal economy: statistical data and research findings. Country case study: South Africa'. Background document prepared for *Women and Men in the Informal Economy: A Statistical Picture*. Geneva: International Labour Office.

Budlender, Debbie, Diane Elson, Guy Hewitt and Tanni Mukhopadhyay (2002). *Gender Budgets Make Cents*. London: Commonwealth Secretariat.

Budlender, Debbie, Caroline Skinner and Imraan Valodia (forthcoming). 'South African Informal Economy Budget Analysis'. *School of Development Studies Working Paper*, University of KwaZulu-Natal, Durban, South Africa.

Burns, M. and M. Blowfield (2000). *Approaches to Ethical Trade: Impact and Lessons Learned*. London: Ethical Trade and Natural Resources Programme, Natural Resources Institute.

Business Standard (2003). 'Unorganised Sector Closer to Safety Net'. *Business Standard*. 27 September. Available at *http://www.business-standard.com/search/storypage_new.php?leftnm=lmnu2&leftindx=2&lselect=0&autono=142286*

Cagatay, Nilüfur (2001). 'Trade, Gender and Poverty'. New York: Social Development Group, United Nations Development Programme.

——, Diane Elson and Caren Grown (1995). 'Introduction'. *World Development*, Special Issue on Gender, Adjustment and Macroeconomics, 23 (11), November.

Cambon, S. (2003). *Upgrading in the Cashew Nut Value Chain: The Case of Casamance, Senegal*. M. Phil Dissertation, University of Sussex.

Cardero, M.E. (2000). 'The Impact of NAFTA on Female Employment in Mexico'. In L. de Pauli (ed), *Women's Empowerment and Economic Justice: Reflecting on Experience in Latin America and the Caribbean*. New York: UNIFEM.

Carmody, Padraig (1998). 'Neoclassical practice and the collapse of industry in Zimbabwe: the cases of textiles, clothing, and footwear'. *Economic Geography*, 1 October.

Carr, Marilyn (1997). 'Gender and Technology: Is there a problem?' In *Technology and Development, Strategies for the Integration of Gender: Conference Reader*. Amsterdam: TOOL.

—— and Martha Chen (2004). 'Globalization, social exclusion and gender'. *International Labour Review*, 143 (1–2): 25–26.

—— and Jane Tate (2000). 'Globalization and Homebased Workers'. *Feminist Economics*, 6 (3): 123–142.

Castells, Manuel and Alejandro Portes (1989). 'World Underneath: The Origins, Dynamics, and Effects of the Informal Economy'. In Alejandro Portes, Manuel Castells and Lauren A. Benton (eds), *The Informal Economy: Studies in Advanced and Less Advanced Developed Countries*. Baltimore: Johns Hopkins University Press.

Chatterjee, Mirai and Jayshree Vyas (2000). 'Organising Insurance for Women Workers'. In Renana Jhabvala and R.K.A. Subrahmanya, *The Unorganised Sector: Work Security and Social Protection*. New Delhi: Sage Publications.

Charmes, Jacques and Jeemol Unni (2003). 'Measurement of Work'. In Martha Chen, Renana Jhabvala and Guy Standing (eds) (forthcoming), *Rethinking Informality and Work*.

Charmes, Jacques and Mustapha Lekehal (2003). 'Industrialisation and New Forms of Employment in Tunisia'. In Martha Chen, Renana Jhabvala and Guy Standing (eds) (forthcoming), *Rethinking Informality and Work*.

Chen, Martha and Ruby Ghuznani (1979). *Women in Food-for-Work*. Rome: United Nations World Food Programme.

Chen, Martha and Donald Snodgrass (2001). 'An Assessment of the Impact of SEWA Bank in India: Baseline Findings'. *AIMS Paper*. Washington, D.C.: Harvard Institute for International Development.

Chen, Martha Alter, Renana Jhabvala and Frances Lund (2002). 'Supporting Workers in the Informal Economy: A Policy Framework'. *Working Paper on the Informal Economy*, Number 2. Geneva: Employment Sector, International Labour Office.

Chen, Martha Alter, Jennefer Sebstad and Leslie O'Connell (1999).

'Counting the Invisible Workforce: The Case of Homebased Workers'. *World Development*, 27 (3): 603–610.

Chenery, Hollis, Montek Ahluwalia, C.L.G. Bell, John Duloy and Richard Jolly (1974). *Redistribution with growth: policies to improve income distribution in developing countries in the context of economic growth – a joint study by the World Bank's Development research center and the Institute of Development Studies at the University of Sussex*. Washington D.C.: Oxford University Press.

Cohen, Monique, Mihir Bhatt and Pat Horn (2000). 'Women Street Vendors: The Road to Recognition'. *SEEDS*, 20. New York: Population Council.

Cornea, Giovanni Andrea, Richard Jolly and Frances Stewart (1987). *Adjustment with a Human Face – Volume 1: Protecting the Vulnerable and Promoting Growth*. London: Oxford University Press.

Cretney, J. and A. Tafuna'I (2004). 'Tradition, Trade and Technology: Virgin Coconut Oil in Samoa'. In Carr, M. (ed), *Chains of Fortune: Linking Local Women Producers and Workers with Global Markets*. London: Commonwealth Secretariat.

Dasgupta, Sukti and Smita Barbattini (2003). 'Own Account Work as Work Status: Learning from the PSS in Bangladesh and Tanzania'. In Martha Chen, Renana Jhabvala and Guy Standing (eds) (forthcoming). *Rethinking Informality and Work*.

Deaton, Angus and Jean Dreze (2002). 'Poverty and Inequality in India: A Re-Examination'. *Economic and Political Weekly*, 7 September.

Deshingkar, Priya, Usha Kulkarni, Laxman Rao and Sreenivas Rao (2003). 'Changing Food Systems in India: Resource-sharing and Marketing Arrangements for Vegetable Production in Andhra Pradesh'. *Development Policy Review*, 21 (5–6), London.

de Klerk, M. (date unknown). 'Deciduous Fruit Industry Study'. Commission of Inquiry into the Provision of Rural Financial Services, Cape Town.

Desai, Sonalde and Maitreyi Bordia Das (2004). 'Is Employment Driving India's Growth Surge?' *Economic and Political Weekly*, 39 (27), 3 July.

DFID (Department for International Development) (2003). *Labour Standards and Poverty Reduction*. Consultation Document, October. Available at: http://www.dfid.gov.uk/Pubs/files/labour_poverty_cons2.pdf

de Soto, Hernando (2000). *The Mystery of Capital: Why Capitalism Triumphs in the West and Fails Everywhere Else*. New York: Basic Books.

—— (1989). *The Other Path: The Economic Answer to Terrorism*. New York: HarperCollins.

Dickens, W.T. and L.F. Katz (1987). 'Inter-industry Wage Differences and Theories of Wage Determination'. *NBER Working Paper*, No. W2271.

Diller, J. (1999). 'A Social Conscience in the Global Market Place? Labour Dimensions of Codes of Conduct, Social Labelling and Investor Initiatives'. *International Labour Review*, 138 (2).

Dolan, Catherine and Meenu Tewari (2001). 'From What We Wear to What We Eat: Upgrading in Global Value Chains'. *IDS Bulletin*, 32 (3), July.

Dollar, David (1992). 'Outward-Oriented Developing Economies Really Do Grow More Rapidly: Evidence from 95 LDCs, 1976–1985'. *Economic Development and Cultural Change* (1993): 552–44.

—— and Aart Kraay (2002) 'Growth is Good for the Poor'. *Journal of Economic Growth* 7: 195–225.

Dubey, Amaresh, Shubhashis Gangopadhyay and Wilima Wadhwa (2001). 'Occupational Structure and Incidence of Poverty in Indian Towns of Different Sizes'. *Review of Development Economics*, 5 (1): 49–59.

Durban Metropolitan Council (2001). *Durban's Informal Economy Policy*. Available online at: *http://www.streetnet.org.za/espanol/policy-durban.htm*

Economist, The (2004). 'The parable of the cockle-pickers: Why did 19 Chinese cockle-pickers drown in Morecambe Bay?' *The Economist*, 12 February.

El Mahdi, Alia and Mona Amer (2003). 'The Workforce Development Research: Formal Versus Informal Labor Market Developments In Egypt During 1990–2003'. Report to the Global Policy Network, Cairo University, Cairo.

Elson, Diane and Nilüfur Cagatay (2000). 'The Social Context of Macroeconomic Policies'. *World Development*, 28 (7): 1347–1364.

Elson, Diane and Barbara Evers (1996). *Uganda: Gender Aware Country Economic Report*. Report to DAC/WID Task Force on Gender Guidelines for Programme Aid and Other Forms of Economic Policy Related Assistance, Funded by the Special Programme, Women in Development, DGIS, Ministry of Foreign Affairs, The Netherlands, October.

Elson, Diane and Ruth Pearson (1997). 'The Subordination of Women and the Internalization of Capital'. In Nalini Visnathan, Lynn Duggan, Laurie Nisonoff and Nan Wiegersma (eds), *The Women, Gender and Development Reader*. London: Zed Books.

Fleck, S. (2001). 'A Gender Perspective on *Maquila* Employment and Wages in Mexico'. In E. Katz and M. Correia (eds), *The Economics of*

Gender in Mexico: Work, Family, State and Market. Directions in Development Series. Washington, D.C.: World Bank.

FNV (2003). *From Marginal Work to Core Business: European trade unions organising in the informal economy*. Report of the FNV/IRENE workshop, Soesterberg, the Netherlands, 11–12 January.

Forstater, Maya, Jacqui MacDonald and Paula Raynard (2002). *Business and Poverty: Bridging the Gap*. Resource Centre for the Social Dimensions of Business Practice, International Business Leaders Forum, London.

Frankel, Jeffrey and David Romer (1999). 'Does Trade Cause Growth?' *American Economic Review*, 89(3), June: 379–399.

Funkhouser, Edward (1996). 'The Urban Informal Sector in Central America: Household Survey Evidence'. *World Development*, 24 (1): 1737–1751.

Galli, Rossana and David Kucera (2003). 'Informal Employment in Latin America: Movements over Business Cycle and the Effects of Worker Rights'. Geneva: International Institute for Labour Studies, ILO.

Gallin, Dan (2004). Personal communication.

Gammage, Sarah, Helene Jorgensen and Eugenia McGill, with Marceline White (2002). *Trade Impact Review*. New York: Women's Edge Coalition.

—— (1994). 'The organization of buyer-driven global commodity chains: How U.S. retailers shape overseas production networks'. In G. Gereffi and M. Korzeniewicz (eds), *Commodity chains and global capitalism*. Westport, CT: Praeger.

Ghana Statistical Service (2000). 'Ghana Living Standards Survey: Report of the Fourth Round (GLSS4)'. Table 4.4, p 30.

Ghiara, Ranjeeta (1999). 'Impact of Trade Liberalization on Female Wages in Mexico: An Econometric Analysis'. *Development Policy Review*, 17 (2): 171–190.

Ghosh, Jayati (1995). 'Trends in Female Employment in Developing Countries: Emerging Issues'. Background Paper for the *Human Development Report 1995*, New York: UNDP.

Gibbon, Peter (2001). 'Upgrading primary production: a global commodity chain approach'. *World Development*, 29 (2): 345–363.

Global Labour Institute (2003). *Note on Domestic Workers' Unions*. Geneva: Global Labour Institute.

Government of India (2004a). *Unorganised Sector Workers' Social Security Scheme*.

—— (2004b). *Report of the Study Group on Women Workers and Child Labour*. National Commission on Labour.

—— (2003). *Unorganised Sector Workers' Bill*.

Government of India (Ministry of Textiles) (2004). Ministry of Textiles homepage. Available online at: *http://texmin.nic.in/pb_0001_c1.htm*

Government of India (Ministry of Urban Development and Poverty Alleviation) (2004). *National Policy on Street Vendors*. Available online at: *http://urbanindia.nic.in/mud-final-site/policies/policyUSV.htm*

Government of India (Planning Commission) (2001). 'Report of the Special Group on Targeting 10 Million Employment Opportunities per year over the Tenth Five-Year Plan period (2002–2007)'.

Grown, Caren, Diane Elson and Nilüfur Cagatay (2000). 'Introduction to Special Issue on Growth, Trade, Finance and Gender Inequality'. *World Development*, 28 (7): 1145–1156.

Grunberg, Isabelle (1998). 'A Rejoinder'. In B. Debroy (ed), *Perspectives on Globalization and Employment*. United Nations Development Programme, Office of Development Studies.

Hafkin, Nancy and N. Taggart (2001). *Gender, Information Technology and Developing Countries*. Washington D.C.: Academy for Education Development.

Hart, Keith (1973). 'Informal Income Opportunities and Urban Employment in Ghana'. *The Journal of Modern African Studies*, 11 (1): 61–89.

Heeks, R. and R. Duncombe (2003). *Ethical Trade: Issues in the Regulation of Global Supply Chains*. Manchester: Institute for Development Policy and Management (IDPM).

—— and Robert Pollin (2002) 'Informalization, Economic Growth and the Challenge of Creating Viable Labor Standards in Developing Countries'. Paper prepared for the Rethinking Labor Market Informalization: Precarious Jobs, Poverty and Social Protection Conference, Cornell University.

Horn, Pat (2003). 'Voice Regulation in the Informal Economy and New Forms of Work'. In Martha Chen, Renana Jhabvala and Guy Standing (eds) (forthcoming). *Rethinking Informality and Work*.

Jennifer Hurley (ed) (2003). *Garment Industry Subcontracting and Workers Rights*. Manchester, UK: Women Working Worldwide.

Ihrig, Jane and Karine Moe (2000). 'The Dynamics of Informal Employment'. International Finance Discussion Papers, No. 664 (April). New York: Board of Governors of the Federal Reserve System. Available online at *http://www.federalreserve.gov/pubs/ifdp/2000/664/664.pdf*

IIED (International Institute for Environment and Development) (1997). 'Changing Consumption and Production Patterns: Unlocking Trade Opportunities'. New York: UN Department of Policy

Coordination and Sustainable Development.

Institute for Natural Resources (2003). 'Strategy and Business Plan for Development of the eThekwini Medicinal Plants Industry'. Report prepared for the Durban Unicity Council.

International Labour Office (2004a). *Global Employment Trends for Women*. Geneva: International Labour Office.

—— (2004b). 'Towards a Fair Deal for Migrant Workers in the Global Economy'. *Report VI, International Labour Conference, 92nd Session*. Geneva: International Labour Office.

—— (2003). 'Scope of the Employment Relationship'. *Report IV, International Labour Conference, 91st Session*. Geneva: International Labour Office.

—— (2002a). 'Decent Work and the Informal Economy'. *Report VI, International Labour Conference, 90th Session*. Geneva: International Labour Office.

—— (2002b). *Women and Men in the Informal Economy: A Statistical Picture*. Geneva: Employment Sector, International Labour Office.

—— (2002c). 'ILO Compendium of Official Statistics on Employment in the Informal Sector'. *STAT Working Paper* 2002, No 1, Geneva.

—— (2002d). 'Conclusions to the General Discussion on Decent Work and the Informal Economy'. International Labour Conference, 90th Session. Geneva: International Labour Office.

—— (2002e). 'Developing a conceptual framework for a typology of atypical forms of employment: Outline of a strategy'. Paper prepared for Joint UNECE-Eurostat-ILO Seminar on Measurement of the Quality of Employment, Geneva, 27–29 May.

—— (2002f). 'Poverty Reduction Strategy Papers (PRSPs): An Assessment of the ILO's Experience'. Background Paper for November 2002 meeting of the Governing Body of the ILO.

—— (2001). 'Reducing the Decent Work Deficit: A global challenge'. *89th Session, Report 1 (A)*. Geneva: International Labour Conference.

—— (1998). *Labour and Social Issues Relating to Export Processing Zones*. Geneva: Labour Law and Labour Relations Branch, ILO.

—— (1996). 'Minimum Wage Fixing in Mauritius'. In Focus Programme on Strengthening Social Dialogue. *Briefing Note No 6*. Geneva: ILO.

—— (1993). Report of the Fifteenth International Conference of Labour Statisticians, Geneva, 19–28 January. Doc. ICLS/15/D.6 (rev.1), Geneva.

—— (1972). *Employment, Incomes and Equality: A Strategy for Increasing Productive Employment in Kenya*. Geneva: International Labour Office.

Islam, Rizwanul (2004). 'The Nexus of Economic Growth, Employment and Poverty Reduction: An Empirical Analysis'. Geneva: Recovery and Reconstruction Department, International Labour Office.

Jhabvala, Renana (2004). Personal communication.

—— and Ravi Kanbur (2002). 'Globalization and Economic Reform as Seen from the Ground: SEWA's Experiences in India'. Paper presented to the Indian Economy Conference, Cornell University, 19–20 April.

Jhabvala, Renana and Jane Tate (1996). 'Out of the Shadows: Homebased Workers Organize for International Recognition'. *SEEDS*, 18. New York: Population Council.

Jiwa, F. (2002) 'Honey Care Africa's Tripartite Model: A New Approach to Solve an Old Problem in Kenya'. Mimeo. Nairobi: Honey Care.

Jocum, M. and F. Cachalia (2002). 'Training inner city garment operators in South Africa: challenges and lessons for the future'. Paper presented at the international conference on clothing and footwear in African industrialisation, Mombasa, Kenya, 5–6 July.

Joekes, Susan (1999). 'Gender, property rights and trade: constraints to Africa growth'. In Kenneth King and Simon McGrath (eds), *Enterprise in Africa: between poverty and growth*. Trowbridge: Cromwell Press.

—— (1995). 'Trade Related Employment for Women in Industry and Services in Developing Countries'. *Occasional Paper, No. 5*, UNRISD.

Kabeer, Naila (2003). *Gender Mainstreaming in Poverty Eradication and the Millennium Development Goals: A Handbook for Policy-Makers and Other Stakeholders*. London: Commonwealth Secretariat.

Kaihuzi, M. (1999). 'LDCs in a Globalizing World: A strategy for gender and balanced sustainable development'. In *Trade, Sustainable Development and Gender*. New York: UNCTAD.

Kanbur, Ravi (2001). 'Economic Policy, Distribution, and Poverty: The Nature of Disagreements'. *World Development*, 29 (6): 1083–1094.

Kanji, Nazneen, C. Vijfhuizen, C. Braga and Luis Artur (2004). 'Cashing in on Cashew Nuts: Women Producers and Factory Workers in Mozambique'. In Carr, M. (ed), *Chains of Fortune: Linking Local Women Producers and Workers with Global Markets*. London: Commonwealth Secretariat.

Kanji, Nazneen and Stephanie Ware Barrientos (2001). 'Trade Liberalization, Poverty and Livelihoods: Understanding the Linkages'. *IDS Working Paper*, Institute of Development Studies.

Kanji, Nazneen and S. Menon-Sen (2001). 'What Does Feminisation of Labour Mean for Sustainable Livelihoods?' London: IIED. Available online at *http://www.iied.org/pdf/wssd_13_gender_long.pdf*

Keller-Herzog, Angela (1996). *Globalisation and Gender. Development Perspectives and Interventions*. Discussion Paper, Canadian International Development Agency (CIDA).

Khan, Azizur Rahman (2001). 'Employment Policies For Poverty Reduction'. *Issues in Employment and Poverty, Discussion Paper Number 1*. Geneva: Recovery and Reconstruction Department, International Labour Office.

King, Kenneth (1996). *Jua Kali Kenya: Change and Development in an Informal Economy 1970–95*. Oxford: James Currey.

Kritzinger, A. H. Prozesky and J. Vorster (1995). 'Die Arbeidsopset in die Suid Afrikaanse Sagtevrugte-uitvoerbedryf, plaaswerkers'. Werkopset Deel III. Stellenbosch: University of Stellenbosch.

Kurien, Rachel (1998). 'Labour Markets in Developing Countries Are Quite Different From Those in Developed Countries'. In B. Debroy (ed), *Perspectives on Globalization and Employment*. United Nations Development Programme, Office of Development Studies.

Lampietti, Julian A. and Linda Stalker (2000). 'Consumption Expenditure and Female Poverty: A Review of the Evidence'. *Policy Research Report on Gender and Development, Working Paper Series*, 11. Washington D.C.: World Bank.

Lara, Edgar (2004). 'El Empleo Formal y No Formal en El Salvador, Un Estudio sobre El Desarrollo de la Fuerza Laboral'. Report to the Global Policy Network, Fundación Nacional para el Desarrollo, San Salvador.

Lee, Eddy (1998). *The Asian Financial Crisis: The Challenge for Social Policy*. Geneva: ILO.

—— (1997). 'Globalizing and Labor Standards: A Review of Issues'. *International Labor Review*, 136: 172–189.

Lewis, W. A. (1954). 'Economic Development with Unlimited Supplies of Labour'. *Manchester School*, 22 (May): 139–191.

Lindert, P. and J. Williamson (2001). 'Globalization and Inequality: A Long History'. Paper prepared for the World Bank Annual Bank Conference on Development Economics – Europe, Barcelona, 25–27 June.

Loayza, Norman V. (1996). 'The Economics of the Informal Sector: A Simple Model and Some Empirical Evidence from Latin America'. Paper Presented at the Carnegie-Rochester Conference on Public Policy, Pittsburgh, Pennsylvania, November.

Lund, Francie and Jillian Nicholson (eds) (2003). *Chains of*

Production, Ladders of Protection. Washington, D.C.: World Bank.

Lund, Francie and Smita Srinivas (2000). *Learning From Experience: A Gendered Approach to Social Protection for Workers in the Informal Economy*. Geneva: International Labour Office.

Lund, Francie and Jeemol Unni (2004). 'Reconceptualizing Security'. In Martha Chen, Renana Jhabvala and Guy Standing (eds) (forthcoming), *Rethinking Informality and Work*.

Madeley, John (2000). *Trade and Hunger: An Overview of Case Studies on the Impact of Trade Liberalization on Food Security*. Report of the Church of Sweden Aid, Forum Syd, the Swedish Society for Nature Conservation and the Programme of Global Studies. Stockholm: Forum Syd.

Mander, M. (1998). 'Marketing of Indigenous Medicinal Plants in South Africa, A Case Study of KwaZulu-Natal'. Rome: Food and Agricultural Organisation of the United Nations.

Martínez Franzoni, Juliana and Carmelo Mesa-Lago (2003). *La Reforma de la Seguridad Social en Costa Rica en Pensiones y Salud: Avences, Problemas Pendientes y Recomendaciones*. San Jose, Costa Rica: Fundación Freidrich Ebert, April.

Mayoux, Lynda (2001). 'Jobs, Gender and Small Enterprises: Getting the Policy Environment Right'. *SEED Working Paper No 15*. Geneva: International Labour Office.

McCormick, Dorothy and Winnie Mitullah (2004). Personal communication.

McCormick, Dorothy and Hubert Schmitz (2002). *Manual for Value Chain Research on Homeworkers in the Garment Industry*. Brighton: Institute of Development Studies, University of Sussex.

McCulloch, Neil, L. Alan Winters and Xavier Cierra (2001). *Trade Liberalization and Poverty: A Handbook*. London: Centre for Economic Policy Research.

Mehra, Rekha and Sarah Gammage (1999) 'Trends, Countertrends, and Gaps in Women's Employment'. *World Development*, 27 (3): 533–550.

Millennium Project Task Force on Education and Gender Equality (2004). 'Task Force 3 Interim Report on Gender Equality'. 1 February.

Millennium Project Task Force on Poverty (2004). 'Task Force 1 Interim Report on Poverty and Economic Development'. 10 February.

Mitter, Swasti (2003). 'Globalization and ICT: Employment Opportunities for Women'. Paper prepared for the Gender Advisory Board, UNCSTD.

Moser, Caroline N. (1978). 'Informal Sector or Petty Commodity Production: Dualism or Independence in Urban Development'. *World Development*, 6: 1041–1064.

Mgingqizana, N. (2002). 'Running a Drop-off Recycling Centre and Buy-Back Centre – What to Expect'. Conference Proceedings of the International Waste Congress and Exhibition of the Institute of Waste Management South Africa (IWMSA).

Nadvi, Khalid (2004). 'Globalisation and Poverty: How Can Global Value Chain Research Inform the Policy Debate?' *Institute of Development Studies Bulletin*, 35 (1): 20–30.

National Labour and Economic Development Institute (NALEDI) (2004). 'Global Poverty Network, Workforce Development Study'. A report to the Global Policy Network, Johannesburg, South Africa.

Organisation for Economic Co-operation and Development (OECD) (2003). *Trends in International Migration: Continuous Reporting System on Migration – Annual Report*, 2003 edition. Paris: OECD.

Owusu, F.X. (2003). 'Ghana: Where the Strong Help the Weaker'. In FNV, *From Marginal Work to Core Business: European trade unions organising in the informal economy*. Report of the FNV/IRENE workshop, Soesterberg, the Netherlands, 11–12 January.

Oxfam International (2004). *Trading Away Our Rights: Women Working in Global Supply Chains*. Oxford: Oxfam International.

—— (2002a). *Mugged: Poverty in your Coffee Cup*. Oxford: Oxfam International.

—— (2002b). *Rigged Rules and Double Standards: Trade, Globalization and the Fight Against Poverty*. Oxford: Oxfam International.

Pela, Mokgadi and Thabiso Mochika (2004). 'Seta Learnership Targets "Will be Met"'. *Business Report*, 26 April. Available online at: http://www.busrep.co.za/index.php?fSectionId=561&fArticleId=415094

Perret, Bernard (1998). 'After the Fordist Bargain, Then What?' In B. Debroy (ed), *Perspectives on Globalization and Employment*. United Nations Development Programme, Office of Development Studies.

Piore, Michael and Charles Sabel (1984). *The Second Industrial Divide*. New York, Basic Books.

Portes, Alejandro, Manuel Castells and Lauren A. Benton (eds) (1989). *The Informal Economy: Studies in Advanced and Less Developed Countries*. Baltimore: John Hopkins University Press.

Quisumbing, Agnes R., Lawrence Haddad and Christine Peña (2001). 'Are Women Overrepresented Among the Poor? An Analysis of Poverty in Ten Developing Countries'. *FCN Discussion Paper* 115, International Food Policy Research Institute.

Ravallion, Martin (2001). 'Measuring Aggregate Welfare in Developing Countries: How Well Do National Accounts and Surveys Agree?' *Working Papers – Poverty, Income Distributions, Safety Nets, Microcredit*. Washington, D.C.: World Bank.

Redfern, A. and P. Snedker (2002). 'Creating Market Opportunities for Small Enterprises: Experiences of the Fair Trade Movement'. *SEED Working Paper No 30*. Geneva: International Labour Office.

Republic of Kenya (1997). 'National Development Plan 1997–2001'. Nairobi: Office of the Vice-President and Ministry of Planning and National Development.

Rodríguez, Francisco and Dani Rodrik (2000). 'Trade Policy and Economic Growth: A Skeptic's Guide to the Cross-National Evidence'. In Ben Bernake and Kenneth S. Rogoff (eds), *Macroeconomics Annual 2000*. Cambridge, MA: MIT Press for NBER.

Rodrik, Dani (1997). *Has Globalization Gone too Far?* Washington, D.C.: Institute for International Economics.

Sabel, Charles, Dara O'Rourke and Archon Fung (2000). *Ratcheting Labor Standards: Regulation for Continuous Improvement in the Global Workplace*. Social Protection Discussion Paper No 0011. Available online at: *wbln0018.worldbank.org/HDNet/hddocs.nsf/0/649bcebfe08d3b27852568fd00477ef1/$FILE/0011.pdf*

Sachs, Jeffrey D. and Andrew Warner (1995). 'Economic reform and the process of global integration'. *Brookings Papers on Economic Activity*, 1–118.

Sastry, N.S. (2004). 'Statistical Studies Relating to Informal Economy in India'. Discussion Paper presented at the Seventh Meeting of the Expert Group on Informal Sector Statistics, New Delhi, India, 2–4 February.

Scheckenberg, K. (2003). *Appropriate Ownership Models for Natural Product-based Small and Medium Enterprises in Namibia*. London: MTI.

Seager, Joni (2003). *The Penguin Atlas of Women in the World*. New York: Penguin Books.

Seguino, Stephanie (2000a). 'Gender Inequality and Economic Growth: A Cross-Country Analysis'. *World Development*, 28 (7): 1211–1230.

—— (2000b). 'The Effects of Structural Change and Economic Liberalisation on Gender Wage Differentials in South Korea and Taiwan'. *Cambridge Journal of Economics*, 24: 437–459.

—— (1997). 'Gender Wage Inequality and Export-Led Growth in South Korea'. *Journal of Development Studies*, 34 (2): 102–132.

—— and Caren Grown (2002). 'Feminist-Kaleckian Macroeconomic

Policy for Developing Countries'. Under review, *World Development*.

Self Employed Women's Union (SEWU) website: *http://www.sewu.pit.za*

Sethuraman, S.V. (1976). 'The Urban Informal Sector: Concept, Measurement and Policy'. *International Labour Review*, 114 (1): 69–81.

Shramshakti (1988). *Report of the National Commission on Self-Employed Women and Women in the Informal Sector*. New Delhi: Ministry of Women and Child Welfare, Government of India.

Shiva, Vandana (2000). *Stolen Harvest*. Cambridge, MA: South End Press.

Singh, Ajit (1998). 'Global Unemployment, Growth and Labour Market Rigidities: A Commentary'. In B. Debroy (ed), *Perspectives on Globalization and Employment*. United Nations Development Programme, Office of Development Studies.

Sinha, Shalini (2004). 'Laws for Informal Economy in India'. Unpublished manuscript for WIEGO.

Smith, S. et al (2003). 'Preliminary Report for Multi-Stakeholders Workshop,' 26 June, IDS, University of Sussex, UK.

Somavia, Juan (2004). Remarks of ILO Director General, ECOSOC High-Level Segment, 'Resource Mobilisation and Enabling Environment for Poverty Eradication in the Context of Brussels Programme of Action (LDCs)', United Nations, 28 June.

Srikajon, Daonoi (2004). 'The Informal Garment Workers in Thailand: The Case of Banthi Homeworkers Group'. Mimeo. Bangkok: HomeNet Thailand, May.

Standing, Guy (1999). *Global Labour Flexibility: Seeking Distributive Justice*. New York: St Martin's Press.

—— (1989). 'Global Feminization Through Flexible Labor'. Geneva: World Employment Programme, ILO.

Stiglitz, Joseph (2003a). 'Special Contribution: Poverty, Globalization and Growth: Perspectives on Some of the Statistical Links'. *Human Development Report 2003*. New York: Oxford University Press.

—— (2003b). *Globalization and Its Discontents*. New York: WW Norton.

StreetNet (2003). 'Annual Report 2003'. Durban: StreetNet International.

Subrahmanya, R.K.A. (2000). 'Welfare Funds: An Indian Model for Workers in the Unorganised Sector'. In Renana Jhabvala and R.K.A. Subrahmanya, *The Unorganised Sector: Work Security and Social Protection*. New Delhi: Sage Publications.

Tang, Stephanie. Personal communication.

Technoserve (2002). *Business Solutions to Rural Poverty: Technoserve Annual Report 2002*. Available online at *http://www.technoserve.org/TNS2002AR.pdf*

Textile, Clothing and Footwear Union of Australia (TCFUA) (1995). *The Hidden Cost of Fashion: Report on the National Outwork Information Campaign*. Carlton, Victoria: TCFUA.

Thai Development Newsletter (1998). 'Impacts of Economic Meltdown in the Villages'. *Thai Development Newsletter*. No 34: January–June.

Tiffen, P., J. MacDonald, H. Maamah and F. Osei-Opare (2004). 'From Tree Minders to Global Players: Cocoa Farmers in Ghana'. In Carr, M. (ed), *Chains of Fortune: Linking Local Women Producers and Workers with Global Markets*. London: Commonwealth Secretariat.

Tokman, Victor (1978). "An Exploration into the Nature of the Informal-Formal Sector Relationship". *World Development*, 6 (9/10): 1065–1075.

—— (ed) (1992). *Beyond Regulation: The Informal Economy in Latin America*. Boulder, CO: Lynne Rienner Publishers.

United Nations (2000). *The World's Women: Trends and Statistics*. New York: United Nations.

—— (1995). *The World's Women 1995: Trends and Statistics*. New York: United Nations.

—— (1991). *World's Women 1970–1990: Trends and Statistics*. New York: United Nations.

UNCTAD (United Nations Conference on Trade and Development) (2001). Expert Meeting on Mainstreaming Gender in order to Promote Opportunities: Note by the UNCTAD Secretariat, Geneva.

—— (2000). *The Least Developed Countries Report, 2000: Aid, Private Capital Flows and External Debt: The Challenge of Financing Development in the LDCs*. New York: United Nations.

UNDAW (United Nations Division for the Advancement of Women) (1999). *World Survey on the Role of Women in Development: Globalization, Gender and Work*. New York: United Nations.

UNDP (United Nations Development Programme) (1996). *Human Development Report*. New York and Oxford: Oxford University Press.

—— (1990). *Human Development Report*. New York and Oxford: Oxford University Press.

UN-HABITAT (2004). Global Trends Website. Available online at: *www.unhabitat.org/habrdd/global.html*

UNICEF (United Nations Children's Fund) (1994). *Analyse de la Situation des Femmes et des Enfants en Haiti (Periode 1980–1993)*.

Port-au-Prince: UNICEF.

UNIFEM (United Nations Development Fund for Women) (2000). *NAFTA's Impact on the Female Work Force in Mexico*. Polanco, Mexico City: United Nations.

United Nations Millennium Development Declaration (2000). Available online at: *http://www.un.org/millennium/declaration/ares552e.htm*

United Nations Millennium Project (2004). 'Task Force 3 Interim Report on Gender Equality', February. Accessed at *www.unmillenniumproject.org*

Unni, Jeemol (2002). 'Size and Contribution of Informal Employment in India'. Background document prepared for *Women and Men in the Informal Economy: A Statistical Picture*. Geneva: International Labour Office.

—— and Uma Rani (2003a). 'Social protection for Informal Workers: Insecurities, intruments and institutional mechanisms'. *Development and Change*, 34(1): 127–161

—— (2003b). 'Gender, Informality and Poverty'. *Seminar*, 531 (November).

—— (2002). 'Insecurities of Informal Workers in Gujarat, India'. *SES Papers*, 30. Geneva: International Labour Office.

Vasudeva-Dutta, Puja (2004). 'Trade Liberalization and the Industry Wage Structure in India'. Paper presented at the Third GEP Postgraduate Conference, University of Nottingham, 31 March.

White, Howard and Edward Anderson (2001). 'Growth versus Distribution: Does the pattern of growth matter?' *Development Policy Review* 19(3), 267–89.

White, M. (2001). 'GATS and Women'. Foreign Policy in *Focus* 6 (2).

Whitehead, J.A. (2001). 'Trade, Trade Liberalization and Rural Poverty in Low-Income Africa: A Gendered Account'. Background paper prepared for the Least Developed Countries Report 2002, UNCTAD, Geneva.

Williams, Mariama (2003). *Gender Mainstreaming in the Multilateral Trading System: A Handbook for Policy-Makers and Other Stakeholders*. London: Commonwealth Secretariat.

Winters, L. Alan (2000). 'Trade Liberalization and Poverty'. *PRUS Working Paper No 7*, Poverty Research Unit at Sussex, University of Sussex.

——, Neil McCulloch and Andrew McKay (2004). 'Trade Liberalization and Poverty: The Evidence So Far'. *Journal of Economic Literature*, XLII (March): 72–115.

WIEGO (2002). *Addressing Informality, Reducing Poverty: A Policy*

Response to the Informal Economy. Cambridge, MA: WIEGO.

World Bank (2002). *Globalization, Growth and Poverty: Building an Inclusive World Economy*. Washington, D.C.: World Bank.

—— (2000). *World Development Report 2000/2001: Attacking Poverty*. Washington, D.C.: World Bank.

—— (1995a). *World Development Report: Workers in an Integrating World*. New York: Oxford University Press.

—— (1995b). 'Mauritius: Sustaining the Competitive Edge'. Findings, Africa Region, No 37, April.

—— (1990). *World Development Report, 1990*. Washington, D.C.: World Bank.

World Commission on the Social Dimensions of Globalization (2004). *A Fair Globalization: Creating Opportunities for All*. Geneva: International Labour Office.

Appendices

Appendix 1 ILO Convention on Home Work, 1996[1]

Date of coming into force: 22 April 2000

The General Conference of the International Labour Organization,

Having been convened at Geneva by the Governing Body of the International Labour Office, and having met in its Eighty-third Session on 4 June 1996, and

Recalling that many international labour Conventions and Recommendations laying down standards of general application concerning working conditions are applicable to homeworkers, and

Noting that the particular conditions characterising home work make it desirable to improve the application of those Conventions and Recommendations to homeworkers, and to supplement them by standards which take into account the special characteristics of home work, and

Having decided upon the adoption of certain proposals with regard to home work, which is the fourth item on the agenda of the session, and

Having determined that these proposals shall take the form of an international Convention;

adopts, this twentieth day of June of the year one thousand nine hundred and ninety-six, the following Convention, which may be cited as the Home Work Convention, 1996:

Article 1

For the purposes of this Convention:
a. the term *home work* means work carried out by a person, to be referred to as a homeworker,
   i. in his or her home or in other premises of his or her choice, other than the workplace of the employer;
   ii. for remuneration;
   iii. which results in a product or service as specified by the

employer, irrespective of who provides the equipment, materials or other inputs used, unless this person has the degree of autonomy and of economic independence necessary to be considered an independent worker under national laws, regulations or court decisions;
b. persons with employee status do not become homeworkers within the meaning of this Convention simply by occasionally performing their work as employees at home, rather than at their usual workplaces;
c. the term *employer* means a person, natural or legal, who, either directly or through an intermediary, whether or not intermediaries are provided for in national legislation, gives out home work in pursuance of his or her business activity.

Article 2

This Convention applies to all persons carrying out home work within the meaning of Article 1.

Article 3

Each Member which has ratified this Convention shall adopt, implement and periodically review a national policy on home work aimed at improving the situation of homeworkers, in consultation with the most representative organisations of employers and workers and, where they exist, with organisations concerned with homeworkers and those of employers of homeworkers.

Article 4

1. The national policy on home work shall promote, as far as possible, equality of treatment between homeworkers and other wage earners, taking into account the special characteristics of home work and, where appropriate, conditions applicable to the same or a similar type of work carried out in an enterprise.
2. Equality of treatment shall be promoted, in particular, in relation to:
   a. the homeworkers' right to establish or join organisations of their own choosing and to participate in the activities of such organisations;

b. protection against discrimination in employment and occupation;
c. protection in the field of occupational safety and health;
d. remuneration;
e. statutory social security protection;
f. access to training;
g. minimum age for admission to employment or work; and
h. maternity protection.

Article 5

The national policy on home work shall be implemented by means of laws and regulations, collective agreements, arbitration awards or in any other appropriate manner consistent with national practice.

Article 6

Appropriate measures shall be taken so that labour statistics include, to the extent possible, home work.

Article 7

National laws and regulations on safety and health at work shall apply to home work, taking account of its special characteristics, and shall establish conditions under which certain types of work and the use of certain substances may be prohibited in home work for reasons of safety and health.

Article 8

Where the use of intermediaries in home work is permitted, the respective responsibilities of employers and intermediaries shall be determined by laws and regulations or by court decisions, in accordance with national practice.

Article 9

1. A system of inspection consistent with national law and practice shall ensure compliance with the laws and regulations applicable to home work.

2. Adequate remedies, including penalties where appropriate, in case of violation of these laws and regulations shall be provided for and effectively applied.

Article 10

This Convention does not affect more favourable provisions applicable to homeworkers under other international labour Conventions.

Article 11

The formal ratifications of this Convention shall be communicated to the Director-General of the International Labour Office for registration.

Article 12

1. This Convention shall be binding only upon those Members of the International Labour Organization whose ratifications have been registered with the Director-General of the International Labour Office.
2. It shall come into force 12 months after the date on which the ratifications of two Members have been registered with the Director-General.
3. Thereafter, this Convention shall come into force for any Member 12 months after the date on which its ratification has been registered.

Article 13

1. A Member which has ratified this Convention may denounce it after the expiration of ten years from the date on which the Convention first comes into force, by an act communicated to the Director-General of the International Labour Office for registration. Such denunciation shall not take effect until one year after the date on which it is registered.
2. Each Member which has ratified this Convention and which does not, within the year following the expiration of the period of ten years mentioned in the preceding paragraph, exercise the right of denunciation provided for in this Article, will be bound for another period of ten years

and, thereafter, may denounce this Convention at the expiration of each period of ten years under the terms provided for in this Article.

Article 14

1. The Director-General of the International Labour Office shall notify all Members of the International Labour Organization of the registration of all ratifications and denunciations communicated by the Members of the Organization.
2. When notifying the Members of the Organization of the registration of the second ratification, the Director-General shall draw the attention of the Members of the Organization to the date upon which the Convention shall come into force.

Article 15

The Director-General of the International Labour Office shall communicate to the Secretary-General of the United Nations, for registration in accordance with article 102 of the Charter of the United Nations, full particulars of all ratifications and acts of denunciation registered by the Director-General in accordance with the provisions of the preceding Articles.

Article 16

At such times as it may consider necessary, the Governing Body of the International Labour Office shall present to the General Conference a report on the working of this Convention and shall examine the desirability of placing on the agenda of the Conference the question of its revision in whole or in part.

Article 17

1. Should the Conference adopt a new Convention revising this Convention in whole or in part, then, unless the new Convention otherwise provides –
    a. the ratification by a Member of the new revising Convention shall *ipso jure* involve the immediate denunciation of this Convention, notwithstanding the

provisions of Article 13 above, if and when the new revising Convention shall have come into force;

b. as from the date when the new revising Convention comes into force, this Convention shall cease to be open to ratification by the Members.

2. This Convention shall in any case remain in force in its actual form and content for those Members which have ratified it but have not ratified the revising Convention.

Article 18

The English and French versions of the text of this Convention are equally authoritative.

Note

1 The Convention can be found online at *www.ilo.org/public/english/employment/skills*

Appendix 2 Recommendations to Extend National Labour Legislation to Informal Women Workers in India

A. General Acts

1. Minimum Wages Act
- broaden definition of worker to accommodate more categories of informal workers
- include piece rates not just time rates under minimum wage
- set a common national minimum wage
- authorise designated local civil society organisations in each state to hear and review complaints from workers

2. Unprotected Manual Workers (Regulation of Employment and Welfare) Act, 1979 (Tamil Nadu)
- Enact similar acts in other states
- Expand coverage to include informal workers in the trades and industries covered by the Act
- Set up Boards in the various trades and industries to administer benefits
- Empower civil society organisations to identify informal workers, especially women, in the designated trades and industries

3. Inter-State Migrant Workers Act
- Extend coverage to cover workers who have migrated on their own – not only those who were recruited through a contractor

B. Equal Remuneration Act, 1975

The Equal Remuneration Act should be amended to promote equal remuneration between all workers – men and women, formal and informal, as follows:
- Extend application of Act to cover unequal remuneration not just within units/establishments but across units/establishments by occupational group, industry or sector, or region
- Replace clause "same work or work of a similar nature" by clause "work of equal value"
- Provide guidelines and mandate training for labour inspec-

tors – e.g., to help them to identify discriminatory practices pertaining to the ERA
- Authorise greater role and more power to civil society organisations in the implementation of the provisions of the Act – e.g. a role in the setting of wages or the power to inspect

C. Sector-Specific Acts

1. Bidi and Cigar Workers (Conditions of Employment) Act, 1996
- Include those who work under "sale-purchase" system in definition of "employee"
- Fix a National Minimum Wage for bidi rolling to be adopted by all states

2. Building and Other Construction Workers (Regulation of Employment and Conditions of Service), 1996
- Extend the coverage of the Act to building projects involving costs below current minimum rupee value
- Extend the coverage of this Act to contractors and construction projects involving less than 10 workers
- Stipulate worker's record of number of days worked will be registered, to meet the stipulated "90 days of construction work" requirement, unless challenged and proven otherwise by the employer
- Extract levy from the contractor's construction budget at the time that they submit it to the necessary authority (e.g. Municipal Corporation) for approval

D. Women-Specific Measures

1. Maternity Benefit Act – coverage needs to be expanded:
- Expand sphere of this Act to cover:
  - Shops and establishments employing fewer than 10 employees
  - Informal workers who complete 180 days of work in a year
- Increase amount prescribed as medical bonus
- Increase authorised leave period from six weeks to eight weeks
- Authorise 15 days of paternity leave

- Extend maternity and paternity leave to employees who adopt a child of one year of age or less

2. Industrial Disputes Act
- Include prohibitions against all forms of sexual harassment as per 1992 Order of the Supreme Court (W.P. CRL Nos: 666–70), including: physical contact and advances; demand or request for sexual favours; sexually-coloured remarks; showing of pornography; and other unwelcome physical, verbal or non-verbal conduct of a sexual nature
- Give proportionate representation to female employees in the Worker Committee
- Include scope for convening Private Conciliation Boards to facilitate speedy disposal of grievances filed by female employees
- Mandate separate Labour court to hear and decide the cases of female workers

3. Workmen's Compensation Act, 1923
- Increase amount of compensation for women workers because of their dual work burden at home
- Empower Workmen's Compensation Commissioner to pass interim relief orders during the hearing of such cases
- Provide coverage for all female workers under medical insurance schemes

4. Factories Act, 1948 (and other Acts – with child care provisions)
- Mandate provision of crèches in all factories employing more than 10 workers (either men or women)

5. Employees State Insurance Act 1948 – cash benefit to insure women for pregnancy-
- Extend coverage to units of 10 workers and to workers who earn less than Rs. 3,000 p.m.

E. Advisory, Worker and Tripartite Committees or Boards (mandated under most of these Acts)

- Empower and expand the activities of these institutions to review and regularise irregular tactics by employers, such as

shifting from sub-contract to sale-purchase arrangements to avoid employer-status
- Set time frames for such reviews and for revising standards, such as Minimum Wage
- Include at least one woman from all sides (employer, formal employees, informal workers, and government)
- Include representatives of trade unions of informal women workers and formal women workers
- Mandate appropriate levels of contribution from employers, employees, and state governments to help the Committees/Boards oversee implementation of benefits and services mandated under the various Acts.

Appendix 3 Draft Umbrella Legislation on Informal Sector Workers, India

Second National Commission on Labour: Proposed Umbrella Legislation for Unorganised Sector Workers – Unorganised Sector Workers (Employment and Welfare) Bill

Introduction

The Umbrella legislation for unorganised sector workers' employment and welfare should be seen as an enabling legislation that will lead to the growth of the economy, improve the quality of employment, provide a decent life to the workers and integrate them with the growing opportunities in the country.

The proposed Umbrella legislation has to be seen in a holistic way. The unorganised sector is in no way a homogeneous, independent and exclusive sector. It is dependent and linked to the organised sector and the rest of the country.

The proposed Umbrella legislation is different from earlier labour laws as they defined 'industries' and those working in the 'industries' were 'workers', hence covered by protective labour legislation. In the proposed Umbrella legislation, the basic approach of the legislation is recognition and protection for all types of workers regardless of industry, occupation, work status and personal characteristics. Unorganised sector workers are economically engaged all over the economy of India – in fields, in homes, on streets, underground, in small workshops, in forests, on coasts, on hills, everywhere.

A worker in the unorganised sector is an apprentice, casual or contract worker, home worker, service provider or self-employedperson (who is economically dependent) engaged in any industry/agriculture/service directly or indirectly through a contractor to do any manual, unskilled, skilled, technical, operational, teaching, sales promotion, clerical, supervisory, administrative or managerial work for hire or reward, whether the terms of employment are expressed or implied or none.

It needs to be recognised that the Umbrella legislation cannot be effective without integrating it into other existing laws, policies and schemes that basically control the economies of these sectors.

The essence of the proposed Umbrella legislation is removal of poverty of the working population of India through improving their productivity and quality of work, enhancing income earning abilities and increasing their bargaining power.

A better quality of employment should mainly aim at: (i) an income above poverty level, (ii) some insurance against sickness, old age and redundancy and (iii) some prospects of career advancement.

The following are the obligations of the Government, employment providers and the society towards the country's working population: (i) minimum wage/income, (ii) social security like health and old age insurance, (iii) welfare like childcare and (iv) prospects for skill/technical advancement. Similarly, the working population has the following obligations towards the nation: (i) minimum age limit i.e. no child workers, (ii) receptive to develop skill and better technology and (iii) belong to workers' organisations.

Statement of objects and reasons

The unorganised sector is a vast and significant segment of the Indian economy in terms of its economic worth through its economic contribution and the growing number of workers the sector engages. Workers in the unorganised sector constitute a vast majority of the workforce in India, who have remained outside the purview of the present labour laws. Also these laws have proved inadequate to ensure work security and social security workers in the unorganised sector or to safeguard their constitutional rights.

In order to ensure, under an Umbrella legislation, economic and social security to all unorganised sector workers and to mould them into a productive and secure workforce, an Act on Unorganised Sector Workers Employment and Welfare is proposed.

Contents

Part I
1. Short Title, Extent and Commencement
2. Objectives of the Act
3. Interpretations

Part II
- 4. Unorganised Sector Workers' Board
- 5. Functioning of the Board through Worker Facilitation Centres
- 6. Functions of the Board
- 7. Functions of the Board towards the Self-Employed

Part III
- 8. Registration
- 9. Identity Card
- 10. Funds
- 11. Investment of Funds
- 12. Ceiling on Administrative Costs

Part IV
- 13. Workers' Organisations

Part V
- 14. Minimum Wage/Return
- 15. Allowances
- 16 Social Security
- 17. Health and Safety
- 18. Holidays etc.
- 19. General Provisions

Part VI
- 20. Education, Training and Skill Development

Part VII
- 21. Registers and Records
- 22. Grievance Redressal
- 23. Framing of Rules and Schemes

The Bill

An Act to consolidate and amend laws relating to the regulation of employment and welfare of workers in the unorganised sector in India, to provide protection and social security to the workers and to confer upon certain Courts jurisdiction in matters concerning them.

Part I

1. **Short title, Extent and Commencement**
   1. This Act will be called the 'Unorganised Sector Workers (Employment and Welfare) Act'
   2. It extends to the whole of India
   3. It shall come into force on the date on when it receives the assent of the President of India.

2. **Objectives of the Act**
   The objectives of the Act are:
   1. To obtain recognition of all workers in the unorganised sector,
   2. To ensure a minimum level of economic security,
   3. To ensure minimum levels of opportunities for women and children by progressive emanation of labour,
   4. To ensure equal opportunities of work, for men and women workers,
   5. To encourage formation of membership-based organisations of workers,
   6. To ensure representation of the workers through their organisations in local and national economic decision-making processes.

3. **Interpretations**
   1. 'Worker' refers to an unorganised sector worker registered with the Unorganised Sector Workers Board through WFCs. An unorganised sector worker includes a person who is working in an unorganised sector workplace or is self-employed, including a home-based worker or a person who works under no clear employment contract. It also includes workers who are not covered by the ESI Act and PF Act. In case of any doubt, the decision of the Board or State Board shall be final. Worker invariably means an adult worker (male and female) with a minimum age of 16 years and maximum age of 65 years.
   2. 'Local bodies' mean Panchayats in rural areas and the municipal and similar bodies in urban areas, or Panchayati Raj Institutions (PRIs) and local self-governments.

Part II

4. Unorganised Sector Workers' Board

1. 'Unorganised Sector Workers' Board' (in short referred as the 'Board') refers to the Central level Motherboard. It will be constituted by the Central Government for the effective implementation of the provisions of this Act and to co-ordinate functions under this Act at the national level.

2. 'State Board' means the State level Motherboard of the Board. The Board in consultation with the concerned State Government will constitute State Boards. The State Board will co-ordinate functioning at the State or Union territory level under the supervision of the Board.

3. 'State Welfare Board' refers to bodies working under the State Board. The Sate Boards in consultation with the State Government will constitute State Welfare Boards. Each of them is meant for studying and devising schemes for each class of workers. It will work for the respective labour sectors under the supervision of State Boards. Welfare Boards shall assist the State Board to formulate schemes/rules for the respective sector of workers in the State.

4. 'District Board' means the district level body of the Board. The State Board in consultation with the concerned District Panchayats will constitute District Boards. The District Board will function as co-ordained by the respective State Boards. It shall also discuss problems arising out of the functioning of WFCs and find solutions for the same.

5. 'Worker Facilitation Centres' (WFCs) are the local centres of activities of the Board co-ordinated by the respective District Boards. The District Board in consultation with local Panchayats will constitute them. WFCs will work in Panchayats and areas of worker concentration, including those in Autonomous Districts and Hill Councils.

6. The number of members in the Board, State Board, State Welfare Board and District Board shall not exceed

nine (including representatives of trade unions, women workers, NGOs, employment providers and Government/local bodies). WFCs can have more members if required and decided by them and sanctioned by the District Board. A member of eminence/expert who will work full time will be the Chairperson of the respective bodies. The term of office shall be for 3 years.

5. **Functioning of Board through Worker Facilitation Centres**
    1. Workers will be enrolled/registered by the WFC according to the norms fixed by the State Board. Funds collected and benefits will be provided by the WFCs. WFCs shall directly or through other means promote tripartite or multipartite bodies for conciliation and if disputes are not settled, undertake or promote arbitration to facilitate the speedy resolution of labour disputes. They may take the help of Labour Adalats or Labour Courts. WFCs shall act as the closest linkage of the Board with the workers. It shall meet as frequently as will be prescribed. It shall also register complaints against non-compliance with the provisions of the Act.

    2. The Board will implement the Act with the help of the Government, local bodies, welfare departments, trade unions, employer's organisations, non-governmental organisations, health department, and other social and charitable organisations.

    3. Local government shall assist WFCs on the enforcement of the provisions of the Act according to the norms fixed by the Board or State Board.

    4. The Board or its lower level bodies up to WFCs can either directly or through authorised agents inspect any work place to verify the implementation of the provisions of the Act. The labour machinery of the Central or State Government shall assist the Board in this respect.

6. **Functions of Board**
    1. The Board shall have statutory powers to take all steps to make the provisions of this law benefit the workers and the nation, particularly to ensure payment of

wages/return, delivery of social security and welfare measures, registration of workers, formation of workers' organisations and workers' education and training programmes.

2. The Board will have power to create comprehensive multi-tier structures at State, District and Panchayat level to reach at the grassroots and to make the structures effective. The Board, if found necessary, will create structures and bodies to serve the workers in specific employment sectors and sub-sectors.

3. The Board will effectively involve Panchayats, local/municipal bodies, education and training institutions, research institutions, banks, voluntary organisations and such other development agencies to reach the provisions of this law to the worker.

4. The Board will devise schemes and programmes for job security, social security and training of the workers.

5. The functioning of the Board will be democratic, participative and result-oriented.

6. The Board will serve as an active bridge between the workers and the Labour Ministry.

7. The Board will devise programmes for creating proper co-operation among unorganised sector workers, employers, local bodies and various organisations working in the unorganised sector.

7. **Functions of the Board in Relation to the Self-Employed**
   1. For workers who are not wage earners but are self employed, the Board will take measures suitable to the self-employed, to ensure they can earn fair incomes, receive benefits of social security, training and other development services.

   2. The Board will facilitate a support system that provides access to financial services, market infrastructure and infrastructure like power, roads, warehousing, workplace, information and skill development interlinked in a holistic way.

PART III

8. Registration

Every worker, whether or not self-employed in the area of the WFC, should be provided with the opportunity to register himself with the Board.

1. Registration will be compulsory. But membership in schemes will be voluntary.

2. Registration will be a one-time affair. But registration will be periodically renewed and updated.

3. Local public bodies, NICNET (National Informatics Centre) or trade unions or other recognised non-governmental organisations closer to the workers can be entrusted to do the registration process, as per the guidelines and supervision of the Board.

9. Identity Card

Each worker on registration will be given a registration number and a permanent identity card or work card on payment of a registration fee. It shall have the details of his person, name, address, work wages/income, social security entitlements and his photograph. The permanent registration number will be valid all over India. The registration of a worker will not change on his movement from one place to another within the country.

10. Funds

1. The Board will decide the system of raising funds in consultation with its lower boards for different classes of workers.

2. The Board will raise funds by way of contribution, cess, assistance, grant from Government through budget allocation or donations from employment providers, private sector, workers and other legally permitted sources. Board and State Boards shall plan management of funds efficiently.

3. The Fund shall be utilised for the discharge of the functions at various levels under the Act. The Board will create general or specific contributory funds and

will set Rules for fair delivery of the benefits of the Fund.

4. The Board will receive funds from the national budget, employers and workers to deliver social security services to the workers.

5. The Board may raise funds for the purpose of skill development of workers.

6. The Board will facilitate a decentralised delivery of the funds, using such places and means closest to the worker like post offices, banks etc.

7. Existing welfare funds and welfare fund Boards at the Central and State levels will be free to merge with the Board.

8. Board shall take steps to co-ordinate or merge the existing welfare funds and the welfare Boards so that they must be well co-ordinated, cutting down delays and red tapism who decide to merge with the Board or work to co-ordinate.

9. Board shall have powers to co-ordinate the welfare funds and welfare fund Boards that have not emerged, for the betterment of the respective labour sector in the unorganised sector.

11. Investment of Funds

Funds shall be best invested as decided by the Board only in safe securities of the Government.

12. Ceiling on Administrative Costs

The administrative cost of the Board functioning will not exceed 7 per cent of the total budget of the Board.

PART IV

13. Workers' organisations

1. Board will encourage the growth of (formation of) organisations in the unorganised sector. Workers will receive opportunities to represent their interests at all possible decision-making committees and forums at

local and national levels. For the purpose, formation of workers' own member-based organisations as trade unions, cooperatives, associations, federation, or similar democratically run workers' organisations will be encouraged by the Board.

2. The Board will encourage and facilitate the small self-employed workers to form their Associations or marketing co-operatives so as to build capacity to stand firm in the competitive market.

3. Workers' organisations will strive to create an efficient and productive workforce, and generate or improve their productive capacity and bargaining capacity.

4. Representative of the workers' organisations will be made part of implementation, planning and conflict resolution processes.

5. Workers' organisations will ensure participation of their members in training and education on on-going basis.

PART V

14. Minimum Wage/Return

1. The worker shall receive minimum economic returns or minimum wages for his work as prescribed by law.

2. The Board shall have the right to fix minimum wages of the occupations and avocations not covered under other laws, and where there is employer-employee relationship.

3. There shall be a national or regional minimum wage.

4. There shall be no gender discrimination in deciding wages or benefits.

5. The Board and its appointed machinery shall perform the implementation of minimum wage.

6. Non-payment of minimum wage/return shall be punishable.

15. Allowances

1. Workers are entitled to special allowance to special work. There shall be special payments for overtime work, underground work, high altitude work and works of specified risks.

2. Allowances like festival allowance, bonus and such other benefits shall be in addition to minimum wages fixed.

16. **Social Security**
    1. Workers will be covered by social protection measures included in social security especially those who are not covered by EST Act or P F Act.

    2. The worker shall be eligible to social security protection, namely, health and life insurance, old age, invalidity or dependent's insurance, loss of work insurance, group insurance, sickness, medical and employment injury benefits.

    3. The woman worker shall be eligible for maternity benefits and childcare/daycare facility while on work.

    4. Board through its machinery or schemes visualised for workers in all sectors will implement the social security services.

    5. Board shall frame schemes for amenities to workers including housing, drinking water, sanitation, savings and credit facilities.

    6. Local authorities will create and invest their resources to develop better living conditions for the workers by providing amenities like housing, safe drinking water, sanitation, etc.

    7. The Board shall take steps to provide Maternity Benefits Act, Workmen's Compensation Act, Gratuity law, ESI and PF Act to appropriate workers covered by this Act. Board may encourage alternate insurance for employment injury to absolve employer directly from the liability under Workmen's Compensation Act.

    8. The Board will create a gratuity insurance fund.

17. **Health and Safety**
    1. Work shall be permitted only in safe and healthy environment and working places.

18. **Working Hours, Holidays, etc.**
    1. Workers shall have sufficient rest, leisure, holidays, leave and optimal working hours.
    2. Maximum working hours per day shall be eight hours.
    3. Intervals for rest at least one hour shall be provided after four hours of work.
    4. The total number of hours of work, including overtime, shall not exceed ten hours in any day and spread over not more than ten and a half hours in any day.
    5. Worker shall be given one holiday in each week.

19. **General Provisions**
    1. The worker shall obtain recognition for his work irrespective of the absence of any written employment contract.
    2. The worker shall work diligently in the interest of the Nation.
    3. Child under the age of 14 years shall not work, and shall go to school.
    4. The worker shall be eligible to access the common natural resources to develop and increase his productivity through work.
    5. The worker's traditional right related to work and space will be maintained.
    6. Unorganised sector shall be protected from unfair labour practices.
    7. No employer shall dispense with the services of an employee employed continuously for a period of not less than six months, except for a reasonable cause.
    8. The existing laws wherever they apply shall continue

to apply. Nothing in this Act shall affect any better right or privilege that a worker is entitled to under any other law, contract, custom, usage, award, settlement or agreement.

PART VI

20. Education, Training and Skill Development

1. It will be workers' duty and right to undergo skill development and on job training, upgradation training, literacy and workers education sessions.

2. Such programmes will be organised by local government, employment providers and training institutes.

3. The Board will devise schemes and programmes for the purpose, considering the pace of change in technology.

4. The Board shall establish linkages with the education, training and research institutions right from local levels up to national level.

PART VII

21. Registers and records

Employer shall maintain
1. A service register

2. Master roll cum wage payment register and

3. Wage slips to be issued to the workers with the seal of the employer.

22. Grievance Redressal

1. The Board will encourage the parties to settle their issues and disputes relating to wages and conditions of work peacefully by tripartite or multi-partite negotiations. Bipartite negotiations shall be encouraged only where the workers are sufficiently organised.

2. Any aggrieved person, trade union, non-governmental organisation, local body, WFCs, officers and bodies under the Board or officers of the Central or State Government labour department can initiate a dispute or a complaint against violation of any of the provi-

sions of the Act. They shall have judicial remedy also.

3. The nearest court or Lok Adalat having jurisdiction over that area shall be empowered to hear complaints on the functioning of the machinery, appeals over arbitrations or try offences under this Act, in the absence of a regular and nearby Labour Court. State Government shall constitute the concerned Appellate Authority for the above matters. Court shall have power to pass interim orders to maintain peace at work place. The courts and arbitrators shall act according to principles of natural justice.

23. Framing of Rules and Schemes

1. Central Government may frame rules for the effective implementation of the above objectives, generally for all workers in the unorganised sector or for a specific group or area.

2. Board shall have power to make rules and schemes for effective implementation of the objects and provisions of the Act, which shall be placed before the concerned State legislature or Parliament.

Appendix 4 Bellagio Declaration of Street Vendors, 1995

Having regard to the fact:

- that in the fast growing urban sector there is a proliferation of poor hawkers and vendors including those who are children;
- that because of poverty, unemployment and forced migration and immigration, despite the useful service they render to society, they are looked upon as a hindrance to the planned development of cities both by the elite urbanites and the town planners alike;
- that hawkers and vendors are subjected to constant mental and physical torture by local officials and are harassed in many other ways which at times leads to riotous situations, loss of property rights or monetary loss;
- that there is hardly any public policy consistent with the needs of street vendors throughout the world.

We urge governments to form a National Policy for hawkers and vendors by making them a part of the broader structural policies aimed at improving their standards of living, by having regard to the following:

- give vendors legal status by issuing licenses, enacting laws and providing appropriate hawking zones in urban plans,
- provide legal access to the use of appropriate and available space in urban areas,
- protect and expand vendors' existing livelihood,
- make street vendors a special component of plans for urban development by treating them as an integral part of the urban distribution system,
- issue guidelines for supportive services at local levels,
- enforce regulations and promote self governance,
- set up appropriate, participatory, non-formal mechanisms with representation by street vendors and hawkers, NGOs, local authorities, the police and others,
- provide street vendors with meaningful access to credit and financial services,
- provide street vendors with relief measures in situations of disasters and natural calamities,

- take measures for promoting a better future for child vendors and persons with disabilities.

We further urge follow-up action by city governments:

- to recognise that vendors are an integral part of the urban environment and are not to be treated as criminals;
- to increase focus on the situation of special groups of vendors, such as children, people with disabilities, the elderly and others;
- to promote tripartite mechanisms, with a mandate to resolve disputes, at the city level to include representatives of consumers, municipal authorities and vendors;
- to recognise the impact of natural disasters, civil conflicts and wars on vendors and to appropriate relief measures within the national framework; and
- to engage in urban planning which takes into account the need of street vendors as producers and distributors of goods and services.